FAITH AND REASON

FAITH AND REASON

Vistas and Horizons

Edited by
NIGEL ZIMMERMANN
and SANDRA LYNCH

Foreword by
ANTHONY FISHER

☙PICKWICK *Publications* · Eugene, Oregon

FAITH AND REASON
Vistas and Horizons

Copyright © 2021 Wipf and Stock Publishers. All rights reserved. Except for brief quotations in critical publications or reviews, no part of this book may be reproduced in any manner without prior written permission from the publisher. Write: Permissions, Wipf and Stock Publishers, 199 W. 8th Ave., Suite 3, Eugene, OR 97401.

Pickwick Publications
An Imprint of Wipf and Stock Publishers
199 W. 8th Ave., Suite 3
Eugene, OR 97401

www.wipfandstock.com

PAPERBACK ISBN: 978-1-4982-0780-5
HARDCOVER ISBN: 978-1-4982-0782-9
EBOOK ISBN: 978-1-4982-0781-2

Cataloguing-in-Publication data:

Names: Zimmermann, Nigel, editor. | Lynch, Sandra, editor | Fisher, Anthony, O.P., foreword writer

Title: Faith and reason : vistas and horizons / edited by Nigel Zimmermann and Sandra Lynch, with a foreword by Archbishop Anthony Fisher.

Description: Eugene, OR : Pickwick Publications, 2021 | Includes bibliographical references and index.

Identifiers: ISBN 978-1-4982-0780-5 (paperback) | ISBN 978-1-4982-0782-9 (hardcover) | ISBN 978-1-4982-0781-2 (ebook)

Subjects: LCSH: Faith and reason. | Faith and reason—Christianity. | Catholic Church and philosophy. | Catholic Church—Doctrines. | Knowledge, Theory of (Religion).

Classification: LCC BT50 Z56 2021 (print) | LCC BT50 (ebook)

10/08/21

In memory of St John Paul II and his vision of faith and reason

"Faith and reason are like two wings on which the human spirit rises to the contemplation of truth."

(Pope John Paul II, *Fides et Ratio*, 14 September 1998)

CONTENTS

Contributors | IX

Foreword | XI
   MOST REV ANTHONY FISHER OP

Introduction | XIX
   —NIGEL ZIMMERMANN AND SANDRA LYNCH

1 MISSION IMPOSSIBLE?
   Education and Formation in a Pluralistic Society | 1
   —SANDRA LYNCH

2 SHOUTS AND WHISPERS
   What Kind of Martyr to Faith Should a Catholic Writer Be? | 20
   —RENÉE KÖHLER-RYAN

3 LOGOS AND LOVE
   Reason's Tentative Understanding of the Doctrine of the Trinity | 38
   —PAUL MORRISSEY

4 RECENT DEVELOPMENTS AS AN EXAMPLE OF DIALOGUE BETWEEN FAITH AND REASON | 49
   —SR MOIRA DEBONO RSM

5 FAITH AND REASON AND METAPHYSICS | 67
   —ANGUS BROOK

6 COMPASSION AS A RESOURCE FOR PLURALISTIC SOCIETIES | 84
   —ANNETTE PIERDZIWOL

7 WHAT HAPPENS WHEN FAITH INTERRUPTS REASON?
   Critiquing a Dominant Discourse from the Perspective of the Other | 106
   —DANIEL J. FLEMING

8 BELIEF, ACCEPTANCE, AND DIVINE HIDDENNESS | 120
—Emma Wood

9 THE EUCHARISTIC HORIZON OF REASON | 140
—Nigel Zimmermann

Bibliography | 155
Index | 165

CONTRIBUTORS

Angus Brook is a scholar in philosophy and has taught across most areas of philosophy, including history of philosophy, metaphysics, Thomas Aquinas, natural law, ethics, and political philosophy. His research interests are Aristotle, Aquinas, and metaphysics.

Sister Moira Debono, RSM is a former lecturer in the School of Philosophy & Theology at the University of Notre Dame-Australia. Having returned to her native US, she is director for evangelization in two parishes and an instructor for the permanent diaconate program in the Archdiocese of Seattle. She remains an adjunct lecturer with UNDA.

Most Rev Anthony Fisher OP is the Catholic Archbishop of Sydney. He holds a DPhil from the University of Oxford, has lectured at several universities, including the Australian Catholic University, the University of Notre Dame Australia, and the John-Paul II Institute in Melbourne, Australia, where he was the founding director. He currently serves as a member of a number of Vatican congregations, and since 2004 has been an ordinary member of the Pontifical Academy for Life.

Daniel J. Fleming is group manager—ethics and formation for St Vincent's Health Australia. He holds a PhD in theological ethics. Daniel is a fellow in the Law, Health and Justice Research Centre in the Faculty of Law at the University of Technology Sydney and an adjunct lecturer for the Institute of Ethics and Society at the University of Notre Dame Australia.

Renée Köhler-Ryan is professor of philosophy and Head of the School of Philosophy and Theology at the University of Notre Dame Australia.. Her most recent book is *Companions in the Between: Augustine, Desmond, and Their Communities of Love*. A monograph exploring an Augustinian theory of Catholic imagination.

Contributors

Sandra Lynch was the inaugural director of the Institute for Ethics and Society at the University of Notre Dame Australia (Sydney). Sandra is adjunct professor in moral philosophy in the School of Philosophy & Theology at UNDA as well as adjunct professor in the IMPACCT Research Centre, Faculty of Health, University of Technology Sydney.

Paul Morrissey is president of Campion College, Australia's first higher education institution dedicated to the liberal arts. He completed his licentiate in sacred theology at the Lateran University in Rome and his doctorate in sacred theology at the Catholic Institute in Sydney. Paul taught systematic and moral theology at the University of Notre Dame Australia for eight years, and has published widely in these and other areas.

Annette Pierdziwol is Associate Dean Research in the Faculty of Education, Philosophy and Theology, and Assistant Director of the Institute for Ethics and Society at the University of Notre Dame Australia. Her research explores how we can cultivate compassion, drawing on insights from moral philosophy and psychology. She has been a visiting scholar at the University of Chicago and a postdoctoral fellow at the University of Edinburgh.

Emma Wood received her PhD from Victoria University of Wellington in 2015. Since then, she has worked as a research associate at the University of Notre Dame Australia's Institute for Ethics and Society, and has overseen the philosophy and theology program at Presbyterian Ladies College, Sydney. Her research interests include metaethics, applied ethics, and philosophy of religion.

Nigel Zimmermann is an adjunct lecturer in theology in the Institute for Ethics & Society, University of Notre Dame Australia and senior fellow with the PM Glynn Institute at Australian Catholic University. He has been a Wingate Scholar and writes on theology, bioethics, and contemporary issues facing the Church.

FOREWORD

— Most Rev Anthony Fisher OP

In *Fides et Ratio* St John Paul II wrote that "the Church has no philosophy of her own, nor does she canonize any one particular philosophy in preference to others."[1] Even the praises of the councils and popes for the method and conclusions of St Thomas Aquinas[2] do *not* mean "to take a position on properly philosophical questions nor to demand adherence to particular [philosophical] theses."[3] Thus, when he speaks of the need for "a philosophy of *genuinely metaphysical* range,"[4] St John Paul II was clear that he was not referring to "a specific school or a particular historical current of thought,"[5] so much as affirming "the concept of the person as a free and intelligent subject, with the capacity to know God, truth and goodness" and likewise

---

1. John Paul II, *Fides et Ratio: Encyclical on the Relationship between Faith and Reason (FR)* (1998), 49.

2. Including: Leo XIII, *Æterni Patris* (1879); Benedict XV, *Fausto Appetente Die* (1921); Pius XI, *Studiorum Ducem* (1923); Pius XII, *Humani Generis* (1950), 42; Vatican Council II, *Optatam Totius* 15 & 16; *Gravissimum Educationis* 10; St Paul VI, *Lumen Ecclesiæ* (1975), 23; Sacred Congregation for Catholic Education, *Ratio Fundamentalis Institutionis Sacerdotalis* (1970), 86; John Paul II, *Address to the Participants in the Eighth International Thomistic Congress* (13 September 1980); FR 43–45, 49, 57–58, 74, 78, nn. 89, 93, 99; *Message to the Sixth National Meeting of University Professors* (4 October 2001); Benedict XVI, *General Audience*, 21 May 2008. Pope Leo XIII claimed that Thomas Aquinas took an invisible part in the deliberations and decrees of the Councils of Lyons (1274), Vienna (1311–13), Florence (1439) and Vatican I (1869–70) and that the Fathers of Trent (1545–63) "made it part of the order of conclave to lay upon the altar, together with sacred Scripture and the decrees of the supreme Pontiffs, the *Summa* of Thomas Aquinas, whence to seek counsel, reason, and inspiration." (*Æterni Patris* 22)

3. FR 78.

4. FR 83

5. FR 83.

to affirm that such persons can come to "a unified and organic vision of knowledge."[6]

Yet even as our age craves ultimate truth there is a crisis of confidence in our ability to know and articulate it, and an inclination to join Pilate in saying dismissively, "Truth: what's that?" (John 18:38). There is likewise a subconscious or conscious fear that the truth (or those who claim to speak for it) will be subversive, demanding, even totalitarian. Yet John Paul insisted that the Church serves people best when it offers them humble but clear testimony to the true and good—a *diakonia of the truth*—in recognition of our shared struggle to arrive at truth.[7] Truth liberates us: from falsehood, superstition and fear; from the mirages created by various interests like government, commerce, advertising, social media; from the illusions we invent about ourselves or our world. Truth dis-illusions, without making us cynical, exposing make-believe, releasing unnecessary anxiety, healing inauthenticity, that division of heart that is so corrupting. The individual and joint pursuit of truth is thus radically humanizing. The present volume explores some of the ways that this is so.

Another proposition we might take from *Fides et Ratio* is that, despite appearances, there can be no real conflict between truths of faith and truths of reason. Sometimes the two may seem to be in tension. St Paul considered this problem at length in his letters to the Corinthians and the Romans. He knew that we cannot reduce propositions of faith, let alone the whole of the Father's saving plan, to purely human logic; faith turns our human reasonings inside-out, it "upside-downs" our worldly wisdom. Yet Paul was unafraid to use the language of philosophy to describe God. John Paul comments: "The preaching of Christ crucified and risen is the reef upon which the link between faith and philosophy can break up, but it is also the reef beyond which the two can set forth upon the boundless ocean of truth. Here we see not only the border between reason and faith, but also the space where the two may meet."[8]

In Evelyn Waugh's novel *Brideshead Revisited*, Rex, a Protestant, wants to marry Julia, a Catholic, and so decides to become a Catholic himself.[9] He presumes this is a simple matter of signing a form and paying a membership fee, but is told he must first receive instruction. A Jesuit father, renowned for his triumphs with obdurate catechumens, is chosen. After the third meeting, Julia's mother inquires of Fr Mowbray how he finds her future son-in-law.

---

6. FR 4, 33, 82, 85.
7. FR 2.
8. FR 23.
9. Waugh, *Brideshead Revisited*, 220–23.

"He's the most difficult convert I have ever met."

"Oh dear, I thought he was going to make it so easy."

"That's exactly it. I can't get anywhere near him. He doesn't seem to have the least intellectual curiosity or natural piety. The first day I wanted to find out what sort of religious life he had till now, so I asked him what he meant by prayer. He said: '*I* don't mean anything. *You* tell *me.*' I tried to, in a few words, and he said: 'Right. So much for prayer. What's the next thing?' I gave him the catechism to take away. Yesterday I asked him whether Our Lord had more than one nature. He said: 'Just as many as you say, Father.' Then again I asked him: 'Supposing the Pope looked up and saw a cloud and said "It's going to rain," would that be bound to happen?' 'Oh, yes, Father.' 'But supposing it didn't?' He thought a moment and said, 'I suppose it would be sort of raining spiritually, only we were too sinful to see it.'"

As the story progresses Fr Mowbray decides to treat Rex as a semi-imbecile, as he accepted everything the priest told him but remembered very little of it. His instruction came to crisis point, however, when Julia's little sister Cordelia took Rex aside and told him that in addition to the catechism there were other, more arcane Catholic doctrines that were being kept from him. For example: you have to sleep with your feet pointing East because that's the direction of heaven, and if you die you can walk straight there; that one of the popes made one of his horses a cardinal; that there is a box in the church porch into which pound notes are placed with people's names on them to get them sent to hell; that there are sacred monkeys in the Vatican; and so on.

The story is an amusing one, but my point in quoting it here is that Rex thought that a good Catholic would accept on faith anything the priests told him, no matter how irrational. There is one realm of empirical reality, grasped by the senses and human reason; there is another of religious reality, known by faith and Church authority; and ne'er the twain shall meet! This view was indeed proposed by Berengar and some of the mediæval Averroists, as of some of the fathers of the "Enlightenment" such as Hume and Voltaire, but it has been repeatedly critiqued by the Church and is completely at odds with the position proposed in the encyclical. In the industrial age it has been commonplace—at least amongst the *cognoscenti*—to think of faith and reason as opposed. By the nineteenth century, the cases of the crusades, the inquisition, and the supposed persecution of Galileo were celebrated as examples of the irrationality of religion in general and the Catholic religion in particular. Despite lacking any credible historical basis, these examples are still trotted out with monotonous regularity by the "new atheists" (from whom we hear very little that is new). But *Fides et Ratio* insists that, far from being opponent readings of reality, faith and reason are two means to the same goal: ultimate truth, whether about God, creation, or ourselves.[10]

Now if faith and reason are means to the same end, if truth is a unity, something cannot be theologically true but empirically or philosophically false—Rex, the Averroists, and David Hume notwithstanding. It cannot be raining spiritually. Reasoning with the aid of faith (here given the shorthand "faith") and reasoning unassisted by faith (here "reason") each has "its own scope for action," its different starting points and methodologies, and there is "no reason for competition of any kind between reason and faith."[11]

Thus, theology and philosophy are complementary and feed each other. Theology needs philosophy because "what matters most is that the believer's reason use its powers of reflection in the search for truth" and "philosophy, pursued in keeping with its own rules, can only help to understand God's word better." Philosophy needs theology because reason can go astray and needs to be "stirred to explore paths which of itself it would not even have suspected it could take."[12]

What's more, the very act of religious belief is pregnant with philosophical issues; for example, the relationship between faith and experience, the credibility of revelation and act of faith, natural knowledge of God, the nature of religious language, the compatibility of faith and freedom, and so on.[13] Our present volume addresses some of these matters also.

If we need reason in order to understand our faith, we need philosophy in order to theologize within the Catholic tradition. Philosophy offers us a scaffold for building and tools for thinking with. The theologian must use and explain Christian concepts and terms, and thus must understand the philosophy behind them if he is to do so correctly. One of the principal complaints against Catholicism of the great Protestant theologian Karl Barth was that its theology was too philosophical, too dependent upon the role of human reason in matters of faith. To which the Catholic tradition as vocalized by John Paul responds: how else can we do systematic theology except by use of reason? We must use concepts, words, and propositions even to express the limitations of those concepts. We must use philosophical terms such as God, person, unity, relation, revelation, creation, identity,

---

10. *FR* Intro, 1, 34 etc.
11. *FR* 15–17.
12. *FR* 73.
13. *FR* 15ff, 76ff.

substance, conscience, freedom, responsibility, and norms, if we are to say anything at all about our faith.[14]

But why can't we just have a simple, unsophisticated faith like Rex? Religious fanaticism is on the rise around the world: the past two decades have seen so many monstrous examples of its deadly effects. This has fed the view that faith and reason are mortal enemies. Yet without an interchange between them, philosophical and theological fundamentalism cannot be successfully critiqued and reformed. Theologies that are not cognizant of their philosophical premises will simply drive those assumptions underground and "run the risk of doing philosophy unwittingly and locking themselves within thought-structures poorly adapted to the understanding of faith."[15] Much of Christian teaching and praxis is unintelligible without knowing some philosophical background: we might consider the Johannine Prologue, so rich in the poetry of faith but also in Neoplatonist and Hebrew philosophy regarding "word" or "reason," "light" and "darkness," "life," "God," "beginning," and more. Or we might consider the different readings of Marxist-inspired liberation theologians and capitalist-inspired liberal theologians of some biblical texts. Or the efforts of Aquinas to make sense of the real presence of Christ in the Eucharist with the help of the Aristotelian categories of substance and accidents. Or the reinterpretation of the Eucharist by the Wittgensteinians in terms of trans-signification. Or the phenomenological presuppositions in Schillebeeckx's writing on the resurrection. Or the theological aesthetic and aesthetic theology of Hans Urs von Balthasar. Once again, the present volume offers some entry points into such questions.

But to say Christianity does not canonize one particular philosophical system is not to deny that some philosophies are more or less *simpatico* with Christian faith, and more or less useful for understanding and applying it. Thus, part of the role of theological reflection and of the Church's *magisterium* is a kind of mental hygiene with respect to certain systems of thought, concepts, and language.[16] Some approaches obscure more than they clarify, and may even jeopardize intellectual/theological freedom, by arbitrarily precluding any movement from phenomena to foundations, "a step as necessary as it is urgent"[17] in the search for truth. Hence the synthetic but effective critique of the "isms" in John Paul II's *Veritatis Splendor* and *Fides et Ratio* and in subsequent works of Pope Benedict XVI and Pope

14. FR 65–68, 77.
15. FR 77.
16. FR 42 etc.
17. FR 83.

Francis—skepticism, deconstructionism and nihilism,[18] individualism and subjectivism,[19] agnosticism, indifferentism, relativism and undifferentiated pluralism,[20] totalitarianism,[21] rationalism, positivism and scientism,[22] anthropocentrism and historicism,[23] globalism and universalism,[24] materialism, hedonism and consumerism,[25] secularism and atheism,[26] dualism,[27] utilitarianism and pragmatism,[28] idealism, gnosticism, pantheism, fideism and fundamentalism,[29] populism and economic liberalism,[30] reductionism,[31] eclecticism and syncretism.[32] These critiques, while often rather summary in form, indicate a concern not to shackle thought with pre-constituted theses, but rather to free the field from every acritical attack upon the properly human capacity for truth. They also serve to highlight the dangers of various forms of cultural relativism creeping not just into academic theology but then into catechetics: programs relying almost entirely upon the personal experiences or questions of the students themselves; or reducing all reality and history to mythology and hermeneutics; or asserting that there can be no metanarratives (such as the gospel) by which other stories might

---

18. *FR* 5, 45, 46, 81, 90, 91; John Paul II, *Message to the Catholic University of the Sacred Heart* (5 May 2000), 5; Pope Benedict XVI, *Address at the University of Regensburg* (12 September 2006); *Spe Salvi: Encyclical on Hope (SS)* (2007) 42; Pope Francis, *Fratelli Tutti: Encyclical on Fraternity and Social Friendship (FT)* (2020) 13, 15, 30, 75, 197.

19. John Paul II, *Veritatis Splendor: Encyclical on Fundamental Questions of Moral Theology (VS)* (1993) 32, 34, 106; *FR* 5, 98; *SS* 13; Pope Francis, *Laudato 'Si: Encyclical on Care for our Common Home (LS)* (2015) 119, 162, 208, 210; *FT* 13, 43, 105, 152, 170, 209, 222, 275.

20. *VS* 1, 5, 46, 48, 84, 101, 106, 112, fn. 131; *FR* 5, 45, 50, 54, 69, 80, 82; cf. Pope Benedict XVI, *Homily at the Mass for the Election of the Pope* (18 April 2005); Pope Benedict XVI, *Address at the University of Regensburg* (12 September 2006); *Caritas in Veritate: Encyclical on Integral Human Development in Charity and Truth (CV)* (2009) 26, 55, 61; *LS* 25, 122, 123; *FT* 185, 206, 209.

21. *VS* 99–101; *FR* 46, 51, 54; *LS* 104; *CV* 53; *FT* 273.

22. *VS* 112; *FR* 14, 45, 46, 52–55, 88, 91, 94; *CV* 48; *SS* 5; *FT* 275.

23. *FR* 54, 87, 95; *LS* 68, 69, 115–122.

24. *FT* 99, 100.

25. *SS* 21; *LS* 34, 50, 184, 203, 209, 210, 215, 219, 232; *CV* 51; *FT* 35, 136, 222.

26. *VS* 39, 70, 88; *FR* 46, 54, 60, 80, 89; Benedict XVI, *Deus Caritas Est (DCE)* (2005) 37; *CV* 29, 56, 78; *SS* 42, 43.

27. *LS* 98.

28. *VS* 74, 75, 106, 112 etc.; *FR* 5, 47, 81, 82, 89, 97, 98; *LS* 215, 217; *FT* 187.

29. *FR* 37, 46, 52–55, 59, 80; *SS* 42; *CV* 3, 29, 48, 56; *FT* 184.

30. *FR* 155–68

31. *CV* 76; *LS* 92, 107, 112.

32. *FR* 86, 87; *CV* 26, 55; *FT* 245.

be assessed; or encouraging young people to challenge traditional doctrine and morals before they have the formation to understand what they are embracing, critiquing, or rejecting. Once more, our present volume speaks to some of these concerns. Some would say that the "isms" critiqued in *Fides et ratio* and elsewhere in the magisterium are caricatures or at best very imprecise labels. But the treatment of those ideas in a few sentences does not pretend to be exhaustive analysis. John Paul II sometimes painted in very broad strokes.

The important thing here is not to resist modern thought—so much of which is insightful and useful—but rather to resist uncritically adopting the tropes and slogans of the age or, indeed, the minute. The project of harmonizing faith and reason is not an intellectual restorationism: indeed thinkers like John Paul II, Benedict, and Francis have often drawn on very recent philosophers (e.g., phenomenologists and personalists), valorized certain aspects of contemporary philosophy (such as linguistics, the rediscovery of praxis, scientific discourse), demonstrated an unprecedented openness to Eastern thought, engaged with international conferences and organizations, and drawn upon contemporary arts and sciences. But the *magisterium* stands prophetically against the perennial temptation to "jump into bed with the zeitgeist" and for the need to sift the latest ideological fashions carefully and not ignore the treasures of more traditional wisdom.

Two decades ago I edited with Hayden Ramsay a volume of papers, similar to the present one and with the same name, responding to John Paul II's invitation to reconsider the interplay between faith and reason.[33] Twenty years later, Sandra Lynch and Nigel Zimmermann have picked up the torch, bringing together various reflective minds, and demonstrating yet again that rather than fixing limits and bringing inquiry to a close, *Fides et Ratio* opened a wide field for genuine philosophical and theological research. The present writers draw upon the rich Catholic tradition, especially Sts Thomas Aquinas and John Paul II, but also more recent writers (Catholic or not) such as O'Connor, MacIntrye, Nussbaum, Levinas, West, Cavanaugh, and Schellenberg. The authors consider the interplay of faith and reason in the Catholic intellectual tradition, regarding the objectives and methods of metaphysics, the epistemology of acceptance and belief, the doctrines of the Trinity, the *imago Dei* and the Eucharist, and the "interruption" of reason by faith or ethics. They also identify many practical implications for Catholic education and formation, in Christian social teaching and liturgical praxis, in the witness of writers and martyrs, and in the role of religion

---

33. Fisher and Ramsay, *Faith and Reason: Friends or Foes in the New Millennium* (2004).

in cultivating the compassion essential for a pluralistic society. That's quite a range of topics! You will enjoy considering them all.

INTRODUCTION

—Nigel Zimmermann and Sandra Lynch

The editors are immensely grateful for the support of the School of Philosophy and Theology and the Institute for Ethics & Society, both at the University of Notre Dame Australia, for providing resources and encouragement for the successful completion of this project.

Strictly speaking we do not live in an age of reason, nor an age of faith. Neither category adequately describes the ways of thinking and acting that are primarily on display in our own time, and perhaps it is too early to make such an attempt at categorization with any certainty. Some may argue that reason pervades Western culture by referring to our reliance on scientific methodology and the development of technology, but it does not take much investigation to uncover the superficiality of that assumption. In fact, argument on contemporary issues can sometimes only be categorized as opinion, given that commentary is either not accompanied by evidence or the nature of the evidence provided raises doubts and suspicions as to its veracity or credibility. The irrational name-calling and political tribalism that arises in wave after wave of outrage on social media illustrates this phenomenon. On the other hand, faith as a religious concept has been on a fast-tracked decline in the high-income countries of the West for decades. Norris and Inglehart use survey data to confirm this, although they report that between 1981–2007 the majority of countries they studied (thirty-three of the forty-nine countries studied, containing 60 percent of the world's population) showed increases in belief in God over that period. Levels of religiosity increased most markedly in former communist countries and developing countries (e.g., Eastern Europe, Africa, parts of Asia), and this led Norris and Inglehart to report that a resurgence of religiosity and religious fundamentalism appeared to be reversing the global trend toward secularization in developed countries.[1] In other words, religiosity, overall, is increasing across the globe.

While religious faith has not disappeared from the West, a rapid decline in levels of religiosity has occurred in parts of the Western world, with some significant exceptions. In some countries, it remains vibrant and strong, and has even experienced a resurgence in confidence in certain demographics, such as in India and in eighteen Muslim-majority countries.[2] Alan Cooperman, director of religion research at the Pew Research Centre, noted that research at the Pew Centre confirmed an increase in secularization in countries with aging populations and low fertility rates; while religious identification is growing in Central and Sub-Saharan Africa, South Asia (India and Pakistan) and some parts of both the Middle East and Latin America.[3] On the basis of Pew survey data, Cooperman predicts that the share of the world's population that does not identify with a religion will decrease, from 16 percent in 2010 to approximately 12–13 percent by 2050.[4] The decline in large portions of developed countries has not resulted in an overall decline under any statistical analysis.

Faith cannot be said to characterize contemporary Western societies in any pervasive, significant, or meaningful way, unless one were to propose that an objective reliance on materiality and its persistent promise of satiation is a kind of faith. But if so, any similarity to religious faith is limited and disingenuous, given that such a proposition is undermined by evidence that the acquisition of material objects, of material protection against dangers and of experiences can only offer a temporary form of satisfaction that is referred to in the literature as "purchase happiness."[5] By comparison, the object of faith is God himself, faith entailing belief that his promises will be fulfilled in our eternal happiness and fellowship with him.

In such an age, a book titled *Faith and Reason* might be assumed to be considering the question of their relationship and whether or how the manner of their relating in the modern academy can be justified. Questions of the trust placed in revelation through the Scriptures as the foundation of religious belief can be compared to belief in scientific claims and the nature of evidence required, so to allow us to explore the ways in which we come to understand the world and our place in it. Alternatively, from an opposing

---

1. Norris and Inglehart, *Sacred and Secular: Religion and Politics Worldwide*.
2. Inglehart, "Giving Up on God: The Global Decline of Religion."
3. Tamir, Connaughton, and Salazar, "The Global Divide."
4. Cooperman, "The Big 20: The Changing Religious Landscape in the Last 20 Years."
5. Lee, Hall, and Wood, "Experiential or Material Purchases?"

point of view, we might undertake the project of dismantling the relationship between faith and reason. This book undertakes neither of these tasks. It does not focus on exploring the first-order questions of the faith-reason debate because such territory has been successfully navigated in many interesting ways already.

A good and useful start would be John Haldane's book *Faithful Reason* (2004) and his beautifully argued follow-up on a related theme, *Reasonable Faith* (2010). A stimulating journey through history can be taken to explore these themes, whether it be the treatment of faith in relation to reason in the high medieval period or the presuppositions of contemporary thinkers in the secular and the post-secular phases of modernity and postmodernity. To understand this debate in the context of the change of epoch through which we are living, Samuel Gregg's *Reason, Faith, and the Struggle for Western Civilisation* (2019) offers a startling read. It would be hard to surpass the enlightening thought of Charles Taylor, and naïve to presume either too much or too little of ancient writers, whom we might surmise may have been quite bewildered by some philosophical writing in the twentieth and twenty-first centuries, were interaction between these various epochs possible. In addition, we would direct readers to a previous edited collection of the same title as the current collection, *Faith and Reason: Friends or Foes in the New Millennium?* (2004). This collection, edited by the Most Rev Anthony Fisher OP and Hayden Ramsay, fruitfully explores questions that return to the synthesis of reason achieved in the Middle Ages, as well as the drama of the separation between faith and reason that John Paul II addresses in *Fides et Ratio* and an intriguing question of the faith of reason.

Explaining the genesis of this book will help the reader understand its purpose. The book is the fruit of a work undertaken in the School of Philosophy and Theology at the University of Notre Dame Australia, the first Catholic university in the Land of the Southern Cross. Lecturers in the School conducted a symposium, organized by Sandra Lynch and Nigel Zimmermann, and it was commonly agreed by participants that the threads of research being spun on the theme of faith and reason belonged together in a published volume. Each writer wished to explore the implications of debates on faith and reason for their particular research topic. Some write with a continental accent, while others write in an analytic tradition; some are philosophers, while others are more intentionally theologians, and a number of the writers have expertise in ethics and bioethics. As editors, we wished to encourage each writer to use their differing intellectual interests to offer vistas of the landscape to which their research contributes. In this respect, the intent has been to allow that research to shine light on fruitful areas of the faith-reason dialogue in a constructive way that reflects the kinds of research that a flourishing and mature Catholic university would hope to stimulate.

In Australia, two Catholic universities exist, plus a number of seminaries and theological colleges or institutes, but in general it can be said that the intellectual enterprise of soaring on the "two wings" of faith and reason that enable the human spirit to rise to the contemplation of truth, as the opening paragraph of John Paul II's encyclical *Fides et Ratio* announces, is under-appreciated. The Church in Australia is still a relatively young church, with about two hundred years of history, and only one canonized saint (St Mary of the Cross MacKillop, a formidable educator of under-privileged children, who founded the Sisters of St Joseph of the Sacred Heart with Fr Julian Tenison-Woods SJ). Because of its youth, we cannot expect the Church's institutions and places of study to have the gravitas and presence of the older universities in places like Italy, England, and the USA, never mind the ones stripped of their Catholic identity through the Reformation. Nevertheless, there is a noticeable lack of informed intervention in debate by Christian scholars in Australia, whether or not they work in a faith setting. In a post-Christian context, as the intellectual landscape of the West might be described, a high degree of religious illiteracy now pervades the views of our media and political commentariat. Christian scholars undoubtedly have a particular responsibility to attempt to remedy this.

Despite her youthfulness, the Church in Australia has faced hardship, persecution, sectarianism, racism, political intrigue, and in recent years a dark shadow of scandal and abuse. While the Church has made a great contribution in education and other services such as health, welfare, and advocacy for the most vulnerable, the voices of Church leaders have not been greatly heeded or prominent in the intellectual life of the nation. While Australian public life has yielded examples of thoughtful and striking leadership, Christian voices of reason are occasional bright sparks rather than constant sources of light and warmth. A Catholic university is an appropriate context within which to foster the stirrings of a new culture, to develop the currents of religious fidelity and critical thought that can bring us towards an engagement with the world that is more grounded, better informed, hopeful, and loving. It is the kind of institution in which the atheist and the religious believer should be able to learn alongside one another, free from irrational mud-slinging and the threat of violence, a place in which informed disagreement can be explored through reasoned debate. With this sentiment in mind, the University of Notre Dame Australia was established in 1989 in the hope that being grounded in a commitment to both faith and reason, it might be a blessing to the nation. In 2008 Cardinal George Pell said, "God has blessed this University and we pray that it may continue." His

Eminence was a great supporter of Catholic education, and was pivotal to the growth of both Notre Dame and Australian Catholic University (ACU), protecting their freedom to pursue world-class research and make a success of the energetic coincidence of faith and reason. The intention was to protect such places as communities of learning in which faith and reason carry on a conversation that has been going for countless generations.

This book is offered in a two-millennia-plus tradition, not as a *defense* of faith and reason, but as a *fruit* of their valuable, challenging work.

When scholars explore the various vistas in the dialogue between faith and reason, our humble efforts can lead to a rich discovery and interrogation of new horizons. We hope this book is a means by which that dialogue continues as a participation in contemplation of truth.

1

MISSION IMPOSSIBLE?

Education and Formation in a Pluralistic Society

—Sandra Lynch

This chapter focuses on the mission of Catholic tertiary education in Australia and addresses some of the challenges faced by Catholic universities operating within a fundamentally pluralistic society, such as we have in Australia. It articulates the mission of Catholic education and explores theoretical concerns associated with the interplay of faith and reason, while also drawing attention to issues associated with experience and practice, and questions of value, virtue, and character. Its aim is to canvass possibilities for ensuring within universities whose members include both Catholics and non-Catholics that all members of the university community have some familiarity with the Catholic religious tradition, and its ways of knowing and communicating. Finally, the chapter uses the exploration of two particular challenges as a catalyst to discussion that suggests strategies for consensus building, identity sharing, and a communal appreciation of mission—a "mission possible"—for Catholic educationalists embedded within an overwhelmingly secular tertiary sector and society.

1. Mission and Consensus in Catholic Universities

Alasdair MacIntyre argues in *God, Philosophy, Universities* that "[p]art of the gift of Christian faith is to enable us to identify accurately where the line between faith and reason is to be drawn." He goes on to tell his readers that this is "something that cannot be done from the standpoint of reason, but only from that of faith."[1] MacIntyre outlines a turn to Thomistic philosophy to guide us in this enterprise, but he acknowledges that the turn to Aquinas is an intellectually demanding one. There are no "stock answers" to complex questions and what is required, he argues, is constructive engagement with secular thought.

John Courtney Murray's book *We Hold These Truths: Catholic Reflections on the American Proposition* also deals with the challenges of constructive engagement with secular thought in the context of a modern pluralistic society. Murray, an American Jesuit theologian and philosopher, explores the idea of a civic consensus—a consensus that he accepts did not exist in the twentieth-century America he inhabited. He argues that a civic consensus allows a people to acquire an identity and sense of purpose and notes the inability of American universities to create such a possibility. As he puts it, "the American university long since bade a quiet goodbye to the whole notion of an American consensus—one that implied that there are truths we hold in common and a natural law that makes known to all of us the structure of the moral universe...."[2]

However, he argues that the ethical and political principles drawn from the natural law tradition provide the basis for such consensus among Catholics, at least. His perspective on the question of consensus is relevant to those addressing the idea of institutional mission within Australian Catholic universities, not least because the members of staff and the students at these universities reflect the pluralism of contemporary culture. For example, the basis of consensus-building at the University of Notre Dame Australia can be found in the University's Statutes, which state (not unexpectedly) that fidelity as a Catholic university is to be measured by commitment to the principles of the apostolic constitution on Catholic universities, *Ex Corde Ecclesiae* ("From the Heart of the Church"), issued by St. John Paul II and promulgated in 1990.

But we must nonetheless recognize the diversity of beliefs on the campuses of Catholic universities in relation to religion and to the philosophical presuppositions of religion. Not all the staff and students of Catholic universities share or even appreciate the need for—and worth of—a common language with which to address questions of mission, identity, purpose, and formation. Murray and MacIntyre are useful in regard to addressing such questions in that they draw attention to different aspects of the challenges we face. This chapter focuses on two challenges in particular.

---

1. MacIntyre, *God, Philosophy, Universities*, 152.
2. Murray, *We Hold These Truths*, 40.

The first of these is that of engaging with those keen to explore how we might approach drawing the distinction or what MacIntyre refers to as the line between faith and reason and determining how the content of the curriculum or programs offered within the University might be influenced by Catholic intellectual and moral tradition. Here the question of the relationship between educational practices and formation arises. The second of the challenges addressed here is that of engaging with secular culture so that we begin a dialogue or sustain current dialogue with all members of the University community and particularly with those who have no faith commitments at all. The question of the possibility of authentically and consistently implementing our mission arises in relation to this challenge.

In addressing the first challenge, it is necessary to be clear about what we take the nature and purpose of university education in general to be, as well as to state what we take to be the nature and purpose of Catholic university education.

2. The Nature and Purpose of University Education

Professor Margaret Gardner AO, president and vice-chancellor of Monash University (2014–present) and chair of Universities Australia, in an address to the National Press Club of Australia in February 2019, stated that a great university education imparts not only foundational knowledge and skills particular to a chosen discipline or profession, but a broader and more profound set of skills for life. She referred to the skills necessary to being able to analyze, decipher, and interpret—to the employment of logic, reasoning, curiosity, and creativity. Professor Gardner argued that in addition to imparting these skills, university education contributed to a broader and more profound set of skills for life and consequently that it was crucial to the health of democracies and nations. Her address included reference to the views of Nobel Laureate and Professor of Economics, Joseph Stiglitz, who argued (also in a speech to the Australian National Press Club in November, 2018) that the growth in the wealth of nations over the last 250 years was largely due to advances in two fields: (1) in science and technology and (2) in social organization, by which he meant the rule of law and the development of democracies characterized by sophisticated systems of checks and balances. Stiglitz warned that such development requires "systems of truth telling, of ascertaining, of discovering what the truth is, verifying the truth."[3] Gardner connected Stiglitz's points about the importance of truth-telling institutions (in the independent media, the judiciary, and universities) with

3. Stiglitz, "Progressive Reform in a Populist Era."

recent research indicating that Australians reported high levels of trust in university experts.

This emphasis on truth and the implication that universities must go beyond providing vocational or professional education is reminiscent of St. John Henry Newman's views that universities should teach universal knowledge, presenting the widest and most philosophical systems of intellectual education and focussing on the truth of their principles. Newman recommends a liberal education for what it can achieve in relation to the cultivation of the mind by developing: "the force, the steadiness, the comprehensiveness and the versatility of intellect, the command over our own powers, the instinctive, just estimate of things as they pass before us, which sometimes indeed is a natural gift, but commonly is not gained without much effort and the exercise of years."[4]

3. The Nature and Purpose of Catholic University Education

However, Newman's focus on truth is nuanced, going beyond the discovery and verification of truth by rational means and any attempt to guarantee the development of a particular type of citizen: one with "a clear, conscious view of his (sic) own opinions and judgments, [and] a truth in developing them."[5] Rather, he holds the conviction that truth is an ally of the Catholic university and that knowledge and reason are sure ministers to faith. Universities aim at the cultivation and enlargement of the mind of the "natural human being." They are valuable institutions within which we are able to investigate and question beliefs, expand on prior knowledge, and make sense of what some take to be a paradoxical commitment to the role of both faith and reason. But the distinctive feature of a Catholic university is its approach to truth and the relationship it takes to exist between philosophy and theology. Arriving at the truth for Newman implies faith.

Commentators on Newman, such as Frank Turner,[6] point out that there is some tension in his understanding of the education of the natural human being and the Christian. The world of knowledge within the liberal arts pertains to the natural human being and that person's participation in society. The university must teach this knowledge, but the Catholic university understands such learning as appropriate only to life on earth and not to the ultimate good of a human soul in eternity. Consequently, the Catholic

---

4. Newman, *Idea of a University*, 7.
5. Newman, *Idea of a University*, 126.
6. Turner, "Reading the Idea."

university is a place for teaching universal knowledge and this must include theology—a discipline that Newman regards as a science.[7]

Turner notes that Newman repeatedly oscillates between addressing issues that refer to the natural human being and issues that refer to the good of a student's soul. Newman argues that if we must assign a practical end to a University course, then:

> [I]t is that of training good members of society. Its art is the art of social life, and its end is fitness for the world. . . . It is the education which gives a man a clear, conscious view of his own opinions and judgments, a truth in developing them, an eloquence in expressing them, and a force in urging them. It teaches him to see things as they are, to go right to the point, to disentangle a skein of thought, to detect what is sophistical, and to discard what is irrelevant. . . . It shows him how to accommodate himself to others, how to throw himself into their state of mind, how to bring before them his own, how to influence them, how to come to an understanding with them, how to bear with them.[8]

But while urging such a maximally expansive view of the knowledge to be taught in a university, Newman nonetheless warns that that knowledge "must not displace in the human imagination the necessity for receiving religious truth through the Church."[9] So, from the perspective of the secularist or agnostic employed in a Catholic university, we can appreciate the possibility of a perceived tension—if not, complete disagreement—between conceptions of truth, between conceptions or understandings of persons as natural human beings and as members of God's kingdom, and between understandings of reason and faith.

In discussing the movement from theology's starting point ("the word of God revealed in history") toward a more perfect understanding of that revelation, MacIntyre notes that theologians are drawn into conversation with philosophers pursuing the search for truth through philosophical inquiry; and he draws attention to the fact that "both theologians and philosophers become aware of possibilities and problems to which otherwise they might have been oblivious."[10] MacIntyre goes on to argue that despite disagreement within the Catholic philosophical tradition, there is underlying agreement on two matters. Firstly, there is agreement on a set of

---

7. Turner, "Reading the Idea."
8. Newman, *Idea of a University*, 125.
9. Newman, xvi..
10. MacIntyre, *God, Philosophy, Universities*, p.169.

meaningful existential questions to be answered by the Catholic philosophical enterprise—as St. John Paul II set them out in *Fides et Ratio* ("Who am I? Where have I come from and where am I going? Why is there evil? What is there after this life?");[11] and secondly, there is a recognition that relativism, positivism, and idealism fail to provide adequate or truthful answers to those questions.

By comparison, and in relation to the topic of this chapter, in agreeing to join a Catholic university community in Australia, staff members must come to an underlying agreement—a consensus—about their responsibility to explore and develop some understanding of the Catholic intellectual and moral tradition; and in particular, they must be willing to address those questions that can be a source of tension or disagreement among members of the community: How is truth understood within the Catholic intellectual and moral tradition? How is the human person understood within that tradition? What is the distinction and the relationship between faith and reason held to be within that tradition?

MacIntyre's advice to those engaging in the Catholic philosophical enterprise as theologians and philosophers is also relevant to staff members engaging in the enterprise of exploring and clarifying the mission of the Catholic university. As MacIntyre puts it, "the summons to participate in the Catholic philosophical enterprise is a summons to situate oneself in an ongoing set of conflicts, conflicts that we inherited from an extended history."[12]

This summons, if applied to Catholic university communities, suggests that university leaders have a responsibility to try to ensure the development of a communal appreciation of mission and a sense of shared identity. This can be done through their processes of staff induction, their professional development training and staff discussions that aim to provide staff members with sufficient knowledge and skill to be able to critically engage with students in exploring the Catholic tradition and enterprise, and in addressing pertinent conflicts. Successfully achieving this will require offering staff the opportunity to experience and practice addressing disagreement and conflicts, and scripting and rehearsing how they might respond to students' questions. The overall goal of these activities is to ensure that staff members are able to carry out their particular roles in a way that supports—or at the very least does not undermine—the mission of the university.

---

11. John Paul II, *Fides et Ratio*, Sec.1
12. MacIntyre, *God, Philosophy, Universities*, 169.

4. Mission, Integrity, and Responsibility

There is room here for debate and for recognition of the value of academic freedom, but there is definite and undeniable tension between the idea of the Church's authority and the authority of revelation on the one hand and the autonomy of philosophical thought on the other. In *God, Philosophy, Universities*, MacIntyre argues that it is the philosopher's job to come to conclusions about the questions raised within the Catholic philosophical enterprise and to reflect on those conclusions. It is up to philosophers to determine how they respond to encyclicals such as *Fides et Ratio*, on MacIntyre's view. However, if they find that their conclusions are incompatible with the tenets of the faith and with the Catholic philosophical enterprise—and he notes that this enterprise is one that can be seriously at odds with the dominant culture of secularized modernity—then, MacIntyre argues, it is up to those who exercise the teaching authority of the Church to "point out" the discrepancy.[13] Equally, we could argue that it is a matter of integrity for philosophers that they engage with any tension or conflict that arises between their conclusions on an issue and the Church's teaching on that issue. These are complex issues, but they are ones that apply beyond schools of philosophy.

It is surely a matter of personal and professional integrity for all staff members, whether they teach or provide support to students within a Catholic university, to reflect on their own positions with regard to the Catholic philosophical enterprise, as MacIntyre suggests. Doing so raises questions of the cultivation of character and action in accord with conscience for individual staff members. Where a staff member's views differ from the Catholic faith and the Catholic philosophical enterprise, the demands of integrity oblige them to explore that divide, to the best of their ability. Such exploration presumes coming to an understanding of the Church's teaching on particular issues—including contentious social issues, such as attitudes toward abortion or voluntary euthanasia. Staff members have a responsibility to try to come to an understanding of why the Church holds the views that it holds and to establish the precise nature of their own disagreement, rather than to dismiss or avoid debate on these issues.

At the same time, the university has a responsibility to provide staff with the time necessary to allow them to undertake this kind of exploration. If the university requires staff members to commit to supporting the mission of the university within their contracts of employment, then it must act to ensure that it has processes in place to assist its staff in coming to an

---

13. MacIntyre, *God, Philosophy, Universities*, 170.

understanding of that mission. That assistance must include exploration of those issues mentioned above that are socially and politically contentious; issues that may arise in relation to curriculum content or within relevant public and social debate; and issues that are at odds with dominant attitudes in contemporary secularized society, since it is these that are likely to a source of ethical conflict for some staff members or students. Staff members should be given the opportunity to articulate their own formational needs, while also being encouraged to adopt strategies, concepts, and language that might be effectively employed with students and colleagues. Without training to assist staff in engaging with contemporary and secularized views, whether these are in conflict or harmony with the teaching of the Church, staff may not be sufficiently prepared or confident to facilitate critical discussion. This might apply particularly to staff members who themselves have no faith commitments.

Without such discussion in the classroom and in the broader university community, the possibility of authentically and consistently implementing the mission of the Catholic university is likely to be undermined.

As implied above, staff members who find themselves entirely at odds with the teachings of the Church or who disagree with the Church on particular issues have a responsibility to determine how they will approach and deal with that disagreement, especially if discussion of the issues on which they disagree with Church teaching arises within the context of their teaching or student engagement. Clearly, staff members in a variety of schools and departments at Catholic tertiary institutions deal with issues on which there are passionately opposing views within contemporary society. Consequently, we must ask how the university is to approach both the possibility and the reality that staff members disagree with Church teaching, given that it is committed to the uniqueness of its enterprise as a Catholic institution. How can staff members be encouraged to understand and appreciate that uniqueness and how does it manifest in practice, notwithstanding the reality of disagreement on contentious issues?

A set of beliefs and commitments ought to make a difference to the way in which we operate in the world if we are to operate with integrity. If we ask ourselves why we should practice the virtues of honesty or humility, it is because those virtues manifest in action that reflects particular commitments—commitments to the value of truth and to a recognition that each of us is one person among many, and that what talents we have are God-given.

This chapter suggests that in facing the challenges of tension or conflict between conceptions of truth, conceptions of persons, and understandings of faith and reason—tensions that affect our beliefs and commitments—we would be wise to build on the fledgling multi-dimensional approach that many universities already adopt. Doing so will require a sustained and well-targeted program of training and activity that engages with and appeals to staff members. Such programs and activities should be underpinned by a resolute commitment from the university to support the team of people already engaged in attempting to ensure that the Catholic philosophical enterprise is well-understood within the broad university community. Members of the teaching staff, given their responsibility for presenting the Church's tradition to students, should be the initial focus of support activities. Such support, which is both professionally developmental and formative for staff, requires financial and organizational commitments to be made by university leaders and to be demonstrated in a variety of ways. This might involve encouraging collaboration between staff in particular disciplines (e.g. in nursing or medical schools) and appropriate industry partners (e.g. Catholic healthcare providers) on optimal approaches to strengthening identity and implementing mission. It might also include developing innovative attempts at engagement such as online strategies that articulate mission and address conceptual and practical issues in ways that might appeal to individual students and staff members.

Within the university, compulsory core curriculum programs for students can be and have been adapted to be offered to staff members to engage them in discussion about the central topics and issues treated within those programs. Staff can also be offered the opportunity to undertake more intensive study toward a degree focused on the Catholic liberal arts tradition, which includes exploration of Catholic thought and focuses on the integration of reason and faith, the concepts of the human person and the nature of the good life. Within the Catholic enterprise, a theological framework unifies and guides philosophical exploration of conceptual and practical issues. But professional development training in the broad university setting should also recognize that the questions central to the Catholic philosophical enterprise, as identified above by St. John Paul II (in *Fides et Ratio*), are ones that he and many others recognize as fundamental and pervasive for all human beings and within all cultures.[14]

Finally, given *Ex Corde Ecclesiae*'s emphasis on the integration of knowledge as a process that is always incomplete and made increasingly difficult by the compartmentalization of knowledge within particular academic disciplines, Catholic universities must keep dialogue open within particular disciplinary curricula and with a range of academic staff.[15] They must also ensure that they appeal to those staff members unlikely to enrol

---

14. John Paul II, *Fides et Ratio*, Sec. 1.
15. John Paul II, *Ex Corde Ecclesiae*, Sec. 16.

in a course of study, to assist them to engage to some degree in the Catholic philosophical enterprise, so as to come to a better understanding of the Catholic intellectual and moral tradition. It would be wise to engage with staff in as many ways as possible: through discussions at staff meetings, professional development sessions for staff in particular discipline areas as well as for staff as a whole, through chaplaincy activities and in less formal settings. While these strategies are ones currently employed in Catholic universities in Australia to some extent, universities could fruitfully review, revise, extend, and better co-ordinate their efforts. The collaboration of philosophers, theologians, chaplaincy and talented teachers is crucial to the planning and implementation of activities in this regard; the mentoring of inexperienced staff is also crucial to ensuring the success of innovative strategies designed to raise the level of understanding of the Catholic intellectual and moral tradition among staff members.

5. A Practical illustration: The Interplay of Faith and Reason

This section turns to consider the second of the challenges noted in first section of the chapter: that of engaging with secular culture to begin a dialogue or sustain current dialogue on central philosophical issues with all members of the university community, particularly those who have no faith commitments. So how might one practically approach addressing with staff the philosophical issue central to this chapter: the question of articulating the relationship or line between faith and reason? At the outset it is important to recognize one feature of the context within which staff formation is undertaken today. In commenting on Pope John Paul II's encyclical *Fides et Ratio*, Alfred Freddoso draws attention to this feature, noting that the epistemological assumptions about reason that are common in the modern academy undermine the capacity of staff to understand and articulate the vision of intellectual inquiry that is integral to the Catholic intellectual tradition.[16]

Given that Pope John Paul II's emphasis on the essential complementarity of faith and reason is at odds with much modern secular thought, in approaching debate on reason and its relationship to faith, we must address conceptions of reason and understandings of reason's relationship to truth; in doing so, we must recognize the nuances of a commitment to reason and the paradox that some religious fundamentalists find in any commitment to reason in the context of religious belief.

---

16. Freddoso, "Editor's Note."

Rational argument and analysis is a form of activity that is often associated with a scientific view of the world within which we abstract from experience to develop concepts that mediate our experience and contribute to our understanding of ourselves—we observe behavior and make inferences about what is typical of human beings in particular settings. We form beliefs that reflect our understanding of ourselves as material beings. But rationality in the context of the scientific worldview can be seen to compete with natural reasoning or more practical rationality. Natural or practical rationality takes account of the interaction between reason, imagination, and emotion in coming to an understanding of self, of others, of particular concepts (e.g. love, friendship, responsibility, or freedom); as well as in understanding the contexts within which those concepts become meaningful to us.

At the same time, we also have an awareness of ourselves that transcends the limitations of our particularity as human beings. That awareness suggests the possibility of a different kind of knowledge and self-understanding, which can emerge from reflection, contemplative prayer and engagement with God's revelation to us; this knowledge complements faith and recognizes it as the source of certain truth. Our understanding of ourselves and of reality is thus multi-faceted and requires engagement with and exploration of a variety of sometimes contradictory propositions about the nature and purpose of our lives. But it is precisely this kind of engagement and exploration that the Catholic university should aim to encourage. We must make clear that our search for truth requires differentiating different modes of truth: those dependent upon empirical evidence and appropriate to everyday life and scientific inquiry; those that offer comprehensive visions and answers to our questions about ourselves and about the meaning and purpose of life; and those provided via revelation. Neither of the last two modes of truth can be designated or dismissed as irrational, in the sense that they cannot be subject to rational evaluation, but it is the nature of that evaluation that is to be discussed.

Encouraging exploration of philosophical and theological issues associated with the search for truth is likely to be difficult in relation to students and staff members who find themselves at odds with the Catholic tradition. Newman provides us with a novel way of approaching the central issue of the relationship between faith and reason, one that is likely to stimulate curiosity and elicit discussion about truth in matters of religion. He claims that while all belief in God requires faith, all disbelief in God also requires faith. As MacIntyre puts it, paraphrasing Newman, the point is that both "believers and unbelievers alike must commit themselves in a way and to a degree that cannot be justified by rational argument or evidence."[17]

Consequently, interrogating the way in which we understand reason and its relationship to other forms of knowledge would seem to be a basic and useful approach to opening discussion about the Catholic intellectual tradition. There are also serious and rigorous philosophical defenses of the existence and impact of transcendent dimensions of experience on understandings of the nature and purpose of human existence. Thus, it is surely the university's duty to ensure that staff members—appropriate to their positions—have some familiarity with those defenses, and that they have the opportunity to consider common conceptions of scientific and practical or natural reasoning in relation to notions of transcendent experience.[18]

Responding to that duty to create opportunities for reflection and debate takes the idea of intellectual formation within the Catholic tradition seriously. It also opens a pathway for considering how the content of the curriculum or the programs offered within the university might be influenced by that tradition. Such consideration will differ within different disciplines, but staff must be sufficiently competent and confident to address the questions that arise in class and to encourage dialogue on those questions within the classroom. Facilitating such dialogue requires particular knowledge, skills, and attitudes so that the Church's tradition is brought to life.

The argument here is that it is imperative that staff in a Catholic university understand, if not appreciate, the nature of the Catholic philosophical enterprise and the complementary relationship between philosophy and theology, reason and faith. This requires engaging staff in interrogating philosophical tendencies to emphasize the limits of human reasoning, as demonstrated by relativism and skepticism; but also in interrogating tendencies to overestimate the power of human reason, recognizing that this can be as problematic as a reliance on faith at the expense of reason. Again, as MacIntyre puts it, the goal of the Catholic philosophical enterprise is a search for an *adequate* understanding of the realities that St. John Paul II argues all religions explore in answer to fundamental existential questions.[19]

---

17. MacIntyre, *God, Philosophy, Universities*, 142.

18. For example, see Maritain and McInerny, *Degrees of Knowledge*, Vol. 7; and Stein, *Knowledge and Faith*.

19. MacIntyre, *God, Philosophy, Universities*, 165; John Paul II; *Fides et Ratio*.

6. Underlying and Guiding Principles

Underlying the approach taken in this chapter to articulating, communicating, and authentically implementing the mission of a Catholic university are a set of guiding principles inspired by the Catholic intellectual and moral tradition and Catholic social teaching. These principles are integral to and hence must underpin the institutional culture of Catholic universities. They focus on expectations about the character of human persons, about building social and educational capacity within institutions and about contributing to the common good.

The first of these principles emphasizes the importance of encouraging an attitude of self-reflexivity and the development of self-awareness in policymakers, administrators and other staff members. The Compendium of the Social Doctrine of the Church states that "[s]ocial institutions do not of themselves guarantee, as if automatically, the common good; the internal 'renewal of the Christian spirit' *must precede* the commitment to improve society."[20] The involvement of the whole person in this enterprise is emphasized. "The formation of a culture capable of enriching men and women requires . . . the involvement of the whole person, who, in the cultural sphere expresses his creativity, his intelligence, his knowledge of the world and of human persons; someone moreover who puts to good use his capacity for self-control, personal sacrifice, solidarity and readiness to promote the common good."[21]

Professional development strategies can be used to stimulate consideration of our own practice; of how well we understand and respond to the intersection between the principles of Catholic social teaching, its values and its corresponding virtues; and of how well we do this, particularly in the workplace when we might face conflict or pressure. The questions to address here include consideration of what it means to be genuinely present to those with whom we deal, how best to exercise authority, and how to integrate the duty to act responsibly with care for self and others.

The second principle draws attention to the importance of collaboration between philosophers, theologians, and the university chaplaincy in offering formational training to students and staff. While it is the duty of theologians and philosophers to explore the different aspects of truth,[22] the social doctrine of the Church expresses both theoretical and practical knowledge that supports those involved in formational training, so as to

---

20. Pontifical Council for Justice and Peace, *Social Doctrine*, Sec. 552.
21. Pontifical Council for Justice and Peace, *Social Doctrine*, Sec. 556.
22. John Paul II, *Fides et Ratio*, Sec.6.

help staff "to become capable of meeting their daily activities effectively ... and to develop in them a sense of duty that is at the service of the common good."[23] Questions as to what precisely is entailed in meeting one's daily activities effectively as a student, staff member and as a formational trainer must be carefully explored with reference to the Catholic intellectual and moral tradition. To some extent, an integrated approach to formation and professional development activities should be adopted, so that at the very least those involved in such activities understand one another's approaches, can reinforce one another's efforts and do not inadvertently undermine one another.

The third principle also has a formational focus and requires a commitment to effective induction processes. These processes should be well-planned, regularly reviewed, and included among the suite of integrated strategies designed to enhance formation. Employment selection processes can be used as a vehicle to draw attention to the university's goals and concerns with regard to formation and can thereby make some contribution to ensuring the authenticity of the mission of a Catholic university.

The fourth and final principle focuses on value of finding and building on what consensus we can establish, rather than unnecessarily and gratuitously emphasizing differences. An "awareness that all are brothers and sisters in Christ"[24] can help us to avoid alienating others; and to recognize that alienating members of our own university community who disagree with particular teachings of the Church is unlikely to be productive in overcoming the challenges Catholic universities face in effectively implementing their mission. Revising existing avenues for formation and making the principles of the Catholic intellectual and moral tradition explicit, rather than allowing them to remain implicit, is one way to begin building consensus. For example, existing service-learning programs and applied ethics programs can be revised in ways that help articulate and clarify the mission of the university.[25] This can be achieved by making explicit how those programs respond to the imperatives of Catholic social teaching. We can explain how service-learning programs are consistent with the social doctrine of the Church, and develop applied ethics programs that have at their

---

23. Pontifical Council for Justice and Peace, *Social Doctrine*, Sec. 531.

24. Pontifical Council for Justice and Peace, *Social Doctrine*, Sec. 535.

25. For example, the *Giving Voice to Values* curriculum provides such opportunities (Mary Gentile, 2010). While its curriculum argues for the recognition of a minimal consensus within civil society that provides the basis for the resolution of ethical conflicts within the workplace, the curriculum can also be used to draw attention to the principles of Catholic Social Teaching and to the practice of the virtues that are central to the Catholic moral tradition.

heart the principle and the issue of the common good. We can make explicit the value of the intention to be "*at the service of the human being at every level*"; the recognition that "*the human person cannot find fulfillment in himself, that is, apart from the fact that he exists 'with' others and 'for' others*";[26] and the contention that no one is exempt from cooperating in attaining and developing the common good (according to his/her possibilities). The *Compendium of the Social Doctrine of the Church* invites us to develop responses "inspired by moral values that permit people . . . to bring about a world of fairness and solidarity"; to be resourceful in "promoting the well-being of all men and all peoples" and to prevent "their exclusion and exploitation."[27] Staff within professional disciplines who are familiar with these imperatives can embed them within the curriculum content of ethics programs, given that they are consistent with, albeit more explicit than, codes of conduct for many professions.

The emphasis in the *Compendium of the Social Doctrine of the Church* on the preferential option for the poor pushes us toward the exercise of Christian charity toward the poor, the marginalized, and those whose living (and we might add, working) conditions interfere with their proper growth. We are encouraged to imitate the life of Christ and to recognize that the principle of Christian charity must apply to our social responsibilities and to our manner of living, including the way in which we practice professionally. The principle of subsidiarity stipulates that "[i]t is impossible to promote the dignity of the person without showing concern for the family, groups, associations, local territorial realities"; in short, without showing concern for the realm of civil society.[28]

Explicitly focussing on the notion of the common good and the maintenance and development of civil society in service-learning programs and applied ethics programs also provides an opportunity to explain how the teaching of ethics in a Catholic university is unique or distinctive. That teaching should be guided by the Church's social doctrine which explains "*the principles that must guide the building of a society worthy of man*" and indicates "*fundamental values.*"[29] Principles such as the common good and solidarity foster specific aspects of moral goodness; social values, such as truth, freedom, justice, and love are expressions of appreciation of that

---

26. Pontifical Council for Justice and Peace, *Social Doctrine*, Secs. 165 and 167.
27. Pontifical Council for Justice and Peace, *Social Doctrine*, Sec. 174.
28. Pontifical Council for Justice and Peace, *Social Doctrine*, Sec. 185.
29. Pontifical Council for Justice and Peace, *Social Doctrine*, Sec. 197.

goodness and they require "the personal exercise of virtue" corresponding to those values.[30]

Informed by both faith and reason, these conceptions of the human person and of the good life provide us with a comprehensive vision as to the meaning and purpose of life and which is given expression in the Christian practice of virtue.

Inserting the social doctrine of the Church into the teaching of ethics within the professional schools of the university provides many opportunities to bring together a focus on the way in which the personal and professional dimensions of the lives of staff members and students intersect. As the *Compendium* states, "putting them [social values] into practice is the sure and necessary way of obtaining personal perfection and a more human social existence."[31] Bringing together the personal and the professional dimensions of a disciplinary practice, such as nursing, medicine, education, or law, offers a different and more consolidated understanding of the nature and value of the practice in which students and/or staff are engaged. It assists students in appreciating precisely what the university envisages for its students and how they might best act to achieve the goals of their profession in a manner consistent with the university's mission and with their own conception of what they hope to become as persons and professionals. A focus on understanding fundamental values and developing the dispositions and habits of mind (that is, the virtues) that correspond to those values are likely to ensure that the goals of a practice are achieved, while also simultaneously helping to cement an identity and sense of purpose among staff and students in a Catholic university.

To take an example, the Australian Nursing and Midwifery Board's Code of Conduct for Nurses refers under Principle 4 to the expectation that "nurses embody integrity, honesty, respect and compassion."[32] The Code stipulates many examples of professional behaviors that manifest what it refers to as those four values. However, we might argue that to embody honesty or integrity is to display a virtue rather than a value, given that an honest person or a person of integrity could be described as putting into practice a commitment to the value of truth. The confusion evident in the "Code of Conduct for Nurses" in relation to the terms "value" and "virtue" is clarified by reference to the philosophical literature and to the Church's social doctrine. A virtue is an excellent and reliable trait of character, one

---

30. Pontifical Council for Justice and Peace, *Social Doctrine*, Sec. 197.

31. Pontifical Council for Justice and Peace, *Social Doctrine*, Sec. 197.

32. Australian Health Practitioner Regulation Agency, "Code of Conduct for Nurses."

strongly entrenched in the person who possesses the trait. As Rosalind Hursthouse describes honest people when discussing the virtue of honesty,

> [They] tend to avoid the dishonest deeds and do the honest ones in a certain manner—readily, eagerly, unhesitatingly, scrupulously, as appropriate. They hasten to correct a false impression their words have led you into which would be to their advantage; they own up immediately without waiting to see if they are going to be found out; they give voice to the truth everyone else fears to utter . . . .[33]

Hursthouse's explanation indicates that the person possessing a virtue or excellent character trait acts on that virtue for its own sake and not for the sake of any potential gain; but importantly she recognizes the value to which the virtue corresponds when she states that the honest person voices the truth.

Carefully defining what we mean by possessing a virtue in the context of discussing best practice and the virtues of the nurse helps to clarify the relationship between values and virtues, a relationship that is clearly articulated within the Catholic tradition. It also supports the exercise of the virtues by explaining why the enculturation of the virtues is important; it is required by our commitment to fundamental social values and principles that guide *"the building of a society worthy of man,"*[34] as noted above. The God-centred understanding of the human person and of the good life that is central to the Catholic tradition and underpinned by a commitment to social values, such as love and justice, is one that recognizes service to others and sacrifice as part of what it is to be fully human; it provides us with a comprehensive vision of the meaning and purpose of life, which is given expression in the Christian life of virtue and hence it can be fruitfully applied to investigations of responsible best practice in nursing and in professions generally.

Conclusion

This chapter is premised on the conviction that ensuring the authenticity of the unique mission of the Catholic university, given the predominantly secularized nature of modern culture in countries like Australia, is challenging but possible and imperative. Universities must develop pathways that invite and encourage staff to develop or expand their knowledge of

33. Hursthouse, *Virtue Ethics*, 11.
34. Pontifical Council for Justice and Peace, *Social Doctrine*, Sec. 197.

the Catholic intellectual and moral tradition, if they are to understand how the mission of the Catholic university differs from the mission of secular institutions. This understanding must then be translated into a capacity to articulate that mission with integrity and in a way that is appropriate to the role that particular staff members serve within the university.

Articulating and clarifying the nature and purpose of tertiary education within the Catholic tradition in Australia, the roles and responsibilities of staff, as well the intersection between supporting the mission of the university and serving in their roles with integrity are important topics to be addressed with staff members. Universities must spend time in carefully crafting professional development and formational opportunities for staff and extending existing initiatives to engage staff in discussion on the topic of the authenticity of mission. Doing so effectively requires developing a variety of strategies so as to deal with both philosophical and theological debate on relevant issues and with topical issues relevant to practice within particular professions. It requires encouraging debate in a variety of formats, including: specifically designed training for staff, formal and informal staff discussions, opportunities for study in programs in Catholic thought and the Catholic liberal arts tradition offered by the university, and outreach activities that engage the broader community in debate on topics relevant to mission. These strategies aim to build consensus, particularly among staff, as to the way in which the Catholic intellectual and moral tradition must be reflected in the university's mission. They will encourage and help staff—particularly those who are not Catholics or are not well aware of the Catholic tradition—to more effectively focus on and engage with students in ways that help authenticate the university's mission.

The employment of these strategies must be underpinned and guided by principles and attitudes that are core to Catholic social teaching and to the Catholic understanding of the human person and of the good life. Thus given that "[t]he witness of a Christian life has an extraordinary formative value,"[35] university staff must be encouraged to consciously model the behaviors and respond to the imperatives of the social doctrine of the Church so as to develop the kind of culture that the university's mission articulates.

Finally, it is important to recognize that Catholic university administrators would no doubt notice that among the challenges that have received only cursory attention in this chapter is the question of the costs of implementing what is suggested. Investments of time in planning, collaboration, and delivery, as well as funds to resource planned initiatives will be required. But given that the integrity of the Catholic university's enterprise

---

35. Pontifical Council for Justice and Peace, *Social Doctrine*, Sec. 530.

is dependent on grappling with concerns about ensuring the authenticity of the university's mission and developing the relationship between educational practices and formation, such investment is essential.

2

SHOUTS AND WHISPERS

What Kind of Martyr to Faith Should a Catholic Writer Be?

—Renée Köhler-Ryan

1. How Can Reason become a Martyr to Faith? On Seeing "Parker's Back"

In 1964, assured of imminent death, Flannery O'Connor penned the last edits to her short story "Parker's Back." Throughout her career as a Catholic fiction writer she had confronted what she perceived to be the growing faithlessness of her era, and had always chosen to fight back against this with strong writing and even violent imagery. As she had written years earlier to a friend: ". . . more than ever now it seems that the kingdom of heaven has to be taken by violence, or not at all. You have to push as hard as the age that pushes against you."[1] Now, she chose a stark image with which to end her final piece of fiction. In "Parker's Back," the protagonist feels compelled, after a moment of religious conversion in the face of his own death, to have the figure of a Byzantine Christ tattooed on his back. Responding to a command he feels, but does not entirely understand, he still tries to reason out what he is doing.

Part of Parker's motivation is that he thinks that this tattoo will finally impress his self-proclaimed God-fearing wife. Parker is tattooed everywhere anyone could ever see, except on his back. Every new tattoo has represented his longing both for a sense of wholeness, but also for recognition,

---

1. O'Connor, *Habit of Being*, 229.

particularly from his wife, that his skin is beautiful. Instead, without fail Sarah Ruth has raged about his "vanity of vanities"[2] and refused to look. Denying him this, she has also neglected to recognize or return his love for her. Parker simply cannot apprehend that Sarah Ruth is an iconoclast—someone who thinks that God's image should never be rendered. To him, God is not a "pure spirit," though this is something that he has not theorized. This is why fellow Catholic writer and critic Caroline Gordon Tate declared that O'Connor "succeeded where great Flaubert failed: in dramatizing that particular heresy which denies our Lord corporeal substance."[3] Paul Elie comments that by this Tate meant "that Sarah Ruth represents all those heretics who separate body and spirit, human and divine, denying the Word become flesh and walked the earth."[4] This particular form of heresy denies that there can ever be images of God in the world; it also denies the worth of sensible beauty, and with this the importance of perception.

Parker represents someone who has a Christian sensibility, rooted in the beauty of creation and incarnation; but this faith is not reasoned out. His love of images, from a very young age, has prodded him to make subtle but sure motions toward becoming Christian, so that he simply cannot understand those who do not see beauty, and who cannot recognize that the face of Christ is that of God. This chapter proposes that Parker exemplifies the Catholic understanding of the relationship between faith and reason, such that the believer might in some moments of work and trial let faith navigate the way. Thus, the believer performs an action that is *like* that of the martyr, which is a point that Thomas Aquinas makes. Two senses of martyrdom are at play here. In the first, one good thing is given up for the sake of another higher good: a martyr gives up his life on earth for what he believes to be even more valuable; and hence he gains eternal life at the same time. In another, a martyr is a "witness" to what she believes. She need not die to proclaim her belief, but she can demonstrate what it looks like to make her reason submit to what she believes, while she does not yet fully understand, or see. Both O'Connor and Parker are martyrs in this latter sense.

2. Thomas Aquinas and the Ways of Martyrdom

There is a strong connection between Thomas Aquinas and Flannery O'Connor. O'Connor says in her letters that for a time in her life she would

---

2. O'Connor, "Parker's Back," *Everything that Rises Must Converge*, 429.

3. As quoted in: Elie, *The Life You Save May Be Your Own*, 363. For O'Connor's comment on this see O'Connor, *Habit of Being*, 594.

4. Elie, *Life You Save*, 363.

read from Thomas's *Summa Theologica* every night; she also possessed and read at least parts of *De Veritate*.[5] Furthermore, O'Connor claims to have "cut her teeth" on Maritain's Thomistic understanding of the artwork, wherein the main claim is that a Catholic artist possesses a certain perspective on reality, through which she expresses everything in her work.[6] Maritain's theory proposes that the artist can write about whatever she wants. This will constitute her articulation of what it means to see with the eyes of faith, and to communicate that faith in words that illuminate reason and imagination. Furthermore, the more the artist internalizes and at the same time expresses an integrated relationship between faith and reason, the more she can embody that relationship, and the more she will be able to articulate this in her artworks. O'Connor claims in the essay "On Her Own Work": "Belief, in my own case anyway, is the engine that makes perception operate."[7] That is, belief informs not only the way that she understands the world, but how she represents it to others.

At the same time, O'Connor is aware that her readers' circumstances and needs are particular to them, and that the writer (or artist) needs to appeal to or address them if the reader is to take any notice of what the writer says. Maritain's analysis provides O'Connor with a great deal of relief when she realizes that she does not need to deal with explicitly Catholic subject matter in order to express her believer's vision.[8] That perspective will naturally emerge, whatever she writes about. Still, she needs to keep her audience in mind. They are, she finds, particularly devoid of religious sensibility, numbed by the modernist belief that reason can answer every question, address every problem, and that faith is always unreasonable. O'Connor makes a specific choice in her fiction, so that those shocked by the violence and grotesqueness of O'Connor's imagery are at least waking up a little, and responding to her dictum that "[f]or the hard of hearing you shout, and for the almost-blind you draw large and startling figures."[9] Parker works similarly, though with less initial reflection. He could find no more startling a figure than the Byzantine icon of Christ. When he sees it, it is as though he had been looking for this particular image all his life. He is convinced that this image will finally seize his wife's attention, and compel her to move in the right direction. The difference between O'Connor and

---

5. O'Connor, *Habit of Being*, 93, 258, 335, 343, 365, 367, 439. For more on the ways in which O'Connor draws on Thomas, see: Bauerschmidt, "Shouting in the Land of the Hard of Hearing."

6. O'Connor, *Habit of Being*, 216.

7. O'Connor, "On Her Own Work," 109.

8. See Elie, *Life You Save*, 151–52.

9. O'Connor, "The Fiction Writer and His Country," 33.

Parker is mainly of degree: O'Connor knows better than Parker why he constantly seeks beauty in the world, and how he finally sees Christ. However, she is aware that she will never fully understand all that this entails; this is what constitutes Christian mystery. She comments that "[m]uch of [her] fiction takes its character from a reasonable use of the unreasonable, though the reasonableness of [her] use may not always be apparent."[10] Rather than capitulating to the modernist tenet that everything must be completely rational, explained utterly through reason taken alone, like Parker she submits to faith. That assent makes them both like martyrs in the analogous sense that Thomas Aquinas proposes; namely, that someone who refuses, on the basis of faith, to adopt an otherwise attractive philosophical or heretical argument, is wise and in some ways like a martyr.[11]

Again, it is helpful here to recall that O'Connor thinks that Parker's wife, Sarah Ruth, is a heretic. Sarah Ruth's refusal to recognize images of God in the world—in particular of the loving and suffering Christ that her husband searches out so earnestly and almost blindly—is sustained by her belief that God is pure spirit. Sarah Ruth denies the reality of the incarnation that both the Catholic life and the Catholic artist seek to express. Parker never submits to Sarah Ruth's particular deformation of belief—even if it would make his life somewhat easier. This indicates that his approach conforms better to the proper relationship between faith and reason: with faith indicating to reason a horizon over which the latter cannot travel alone.

In contrast to his wife then, Parker's desire to make his body a thing of beauty, even though he does not seem to understand either why this is important or quite how to accomplish it, is an act of faith. His recognition of Christ and selection of Christ's image for the final tattoo of the story, on the last piece of canvas that is his skin, is inspired by a desire to communicate with the woman he loves (even though he really cannot understand why he does love her, outwardly unattractive as she is). Both O'Connor and Parker wisely and courageously defy untruths about reality. According to Thomas's reasoning, this makes them like those martyrs whom Catholics venerate as models of the Christian life. For Thomas, the key to understanding the martyr is the virtue of fortitude, understood within its proper context—which is that of a whole Christian life.[12] Nicholas Lombardo points out the connection between fortitude and martyrdom in Thomas's thought. Namely, Thomas "agrees with Aristotle that fortitude is most properly

---

10. O'Connor, "On Her Own Work," 109.

11. Aquinas, *Summa Theologica*, Vol. III–Part II, Second Section, II–II Qu. 2 art.10 ad.3; 1182.

12. See Lombardo, *The Logic of Desire*, 148; De Young, "Power Made Perfect in Weakness"; Herdt, "Aquinas's Aristotelian Defense"; Clark, "Is Martyrdom Virtuous?"

concerned with the dangers of death in warfare. Nonetheless, Aquinas presents the warfare of martyrdom, rather than physical combat, as the paradigm of fortitude."[13] The charity that motivates martyrdom makes the latter the action that most exemplifies what it means to be courageous. For, rather than remaining on an immanent plane, the martyr sees further, and can rise up to converge with the ultimate personal meaning of the entire cosmos: Christ. This point will be explained below.

Demonstrating again the relationship between faith and reason, Thomas's understanding is that Christian courage is transformed by the theological virtues of faith, hope, and love, so that its inner meaning is oriented toward God[14]—the Omega point with which O'Connor is concerned in this series of stories.[15] As faith guides reason, then, it also influences the way that one responds to dangerous situations in the world. Lombardo explains that for Thomas "[f]aith and hope widen natural horizons and make room for the possibility of supernatural charity, and then charity permeates all the powers of the soul, ordering and elevating the moral virtues."[16] In other words, the Christian martyr acts with courage that is motivated by charity, because the Christian sees more of the ways in which the world is shaped by such love, and responds to that vision with his or her entire life. As will be seen, Thomas intimates that persons can become *like* martyrs by submitting to that view of reality.

At the same time, analysis of Thomas's proposal that a martyr is the most courageous person brings one closer to understanding how O'Connor might be speaking, in "Parker's Back," about what it means to be a Catholic writer (or Catholic artist).[17] Thomas argues that the main proof of the mar-

---

13. Lombardo, *Logic of Desire*, 181.

14. Lombardo, *Logic of Desire*, 181. For other discussions of Thomas's uniquely Christian approach to fortitude, see also De Young, "Power Made Perfect"; Herdt, "Aquinas's Aristotelian Defense"; Clark, "Is Martyrdom Virtuous?"

15. See also Zubeck, "Alpha & Omega."

16. Lombardo, *Logic of Desire*, 150.

17. O'Connor's emphasis that both faith and reason are needed, in daily life as well as in the work of the artist, are still not always understood. See for instance Haddox, "Something Haphazard and Botched." Haddox states that "[t]he discrepancy between O'Connor's letters, with their detailed discussion of Catholic theology and their apparent endorsement of both reason and faith, and O'Connor's fiction, with its frequent rejection of reason . . . points to a fundamental tension in her work" (ibid., 420). This interpretation, I would argue, overlooks O'Connor's own understanding of the relation between faith and reason, which is Thomistic in foundation and implication. For discussions of what constitutes catholic fiction as such, the reader might find the following of interest: Contino, "Fiction and Catholic Themes"; Breslin, "The Open-Ended Mystery of Matter." Specifically on O'Connor as a Catholic writer: Kinney, "Flannery O'Connor and the Fiction." Less helpful in understanding O'Connor's vision for

tyr's courage is in endurance when persecuted. The martyr is self-reflective enough to know that the point of courage is not foolhardiness: intentionally placing oneself in harm's way without just cause is wholly unreasonable. Instead, the martyr finds himself in a dangerous situation because threatened by those who want him to renounce Christ. That renunciation would be completely unreasonable, given that the purpose of human life is to witness to the reality of Christ, but renunciation need not only occur in the form of the refusal to confess to one's faith. Thomas explains that:

> the truth of faith includes not only inward belief, but also outward profession, which is expressed not only by words, whereby one confesses the faith, but also by deeds, whereby a person shows that he has faith. . . . Thus all virtuous deeds, inasmuch as they are referred to God, are professions of the faith whereby we come to know that God requires these works of us, and rewards us for them: and in this way they can be the cause of martyrdom.[18]

Thomas continues to say that John the Baptist died because he spoke against adultery, rather than because he specifically refused to deny his faith in God. Thus, what we do matters when seen in the context of the inner life of faith, because it enacts and makes known that faith—perhaps not only to those who see, but also to the one who performs the action. Martyrdom can happen in so many situations because one can give witness to faith in multifarious ways. Human deeds matter in the life of faith because of the final goal of the virtuous Christian: to be like Christ in this life and even more like him in the next, where the true Christian will see him "face to face."[19] O'Connor expresses her faith through her writings. Parker witnesses to his slowly adjusting vision of what is most important about being human by constantly, though unwittingly, looking for the perfect image of what it is to be human. He finally finds this in the face of Christ.

Virtuous deeds, then, constitute a connection between what Christians believe and how that belief is made manifest. Nonetheless, this claim only makes sense if the reason, or cause, of an action is love of God that strives for perfect fulfilment in eternal life with him. For any person of faith, the inner significance of an action is magnified, making the exterior world not less, but more, important for understanding the actions of a martyr. Faith alone, says Thomas, is not enough to explain those who give their lives entirely for Christ. Outward witness is essential. Most crucially, what

purposes of contemporary thought is: Blue Lemay, "God's Back."

18. Thomas Aquinas, *Summa Theologica*, II–II 124 Art. 5, 1713.

19. 1 Cor 13:12.

the martyr witnesses *to*, and what he sacrifices in so-doing, give the act of courage its inner worth. To emphasize this, when speaking of martyrdom as the greatest perfection, Thomas claims that the act of endurance of death is not praiseworthy in itself. It is only because it is an act of virtue "such as faith or the love of God . . . that this act of virtue . . . is better."[20] Further, he argues that martyrdom is a perfect act because it stands as a proof of perfect love.

Such perfect love unites with faith in things unseen, which does not contradict reason, but it may provide philosophical challenges to those who cannot quite understand what is at issue. Here, the point that Thomas makes, when discussing the question of whether "reason in support of what we believe lessens the merit of faith," is most pertinent. Thomas observes that the wise can be *like* martyrs, when they do not renounce their faith because of philosophical or heretical arguments. In other words, reason can sometimes be called upon to give up its immanent horizon, for the sake of something greater—which it does not understand, but still entirely accepts through faith. This can be better appreciated through an analogue. Thomas argues in the *Summa* that "a man's love for a thing is proved to be so much the greater, according as that which he despises for its sake is more dear to him. . . . But it is evident that of all the goods of the present life man loves life itself most."[21] Thus, being willing to give up that which he loves most in this life for the sake of a love that exceeds the limitations of death is the finest proof of love. Life is what we most value on earth, and so dying for something else is the highest proof of love. The comparison comes here: the wise person loves reason; when he or she is willing to give up an idea that *seems* reasonable, but which contradicts what is known by faith, then the faulty truth claim can be sacrificed. This sacrifice is like the action of a martyr. Here, what appears to be true is known to be false according to what one believes by faith. Reason might thereby seem to give up something of itself, but in fact the believer is brought to a greater level of appreciation of reality.

This is what happens in the case of Parker, who now knows that his life has been about so much more than he previously realized. For, in the case either of real or analogous martyrdom, the person can see that there is more at stake than this life on earth. Such vision is captured in Rebecca Konyndyk DeYoung's words: "[m]artyrdom models in a concrete act both sacrificial love and the right ordering of goods, teaching that even the highest human goods (even those sometimes worth dying for) are not ultimate."[22] "Parker's Back" is published in O'Connor's short story collection entitled *Everything*

---

20. Aquinas, *Summa Theologica*, II–II, Qu. 124, Art. 3, 1711.
21. Aquinas, *Summa Theologica*, II–II, Qu. 124, Art. 3, 1711.
22. DeYoung, "Power Made Perfect," 158.

That Rises Must Converge. Within that book, characters either succeed or fail to sacrifice what *seems* wise according to a worldly perspective, for the sake of the demands of faith in a vision of Christ-centred reality. The book thus offers an extended reflection on the nature of Christian martyrdom.

3. The Context of Convergence

The Christ-centered nature of the concept of "convergence" that O'Connor employs in the collection brings one closer to understanding O'Connor and Parker as martyrs for their art. The phrase "everything that rises must converge" comes from Teilhard de Chardin's thought. O'Connor claims in a letter that it describes "a physical proposition" with multiple dimensions.[23] As Robert H. Fitzgerald explains, Teilhard's concept of convergence demonstrates that "generations, social classes, and races are slowly rising and converging in greater knowledge and love, in other words, becoming more and more personal."[24] Fitzgerald argues that the title of the collection provides an architectonic for the whole collection of stories, whereby any character capable of rising upward moves toward the Omega point—Christ—described by St. Paul.[25] Convergence refers to the idea that everything material has spiritual significance, which defies the rationalistic belief in materialism: that material forces explain everything that exists. For Teilhard, materialism denies the reality of love in the universe, and the understanding that love finds its completion in Christ. To reach the Omega point, then, is to live with Christ's love at the center of all, in community with everything else in the cosmos that has similarly risen, in order to converge with all that has existed, exists, and will exist, by the end of time. Martyrs, then, can be understood as persons who, motivated by Christ's love, are rising up to meet him; at the end of time, they and all others who have loved Christ, will converge. Throughout the collection of short stories under consideration, other characters think of themselves as martyrs, without fulfilling either the Thomistic criteria of martyrdom or the Teilhardian prerequisite for convergence: they have neither faith nor love.[26] Parker stands in contrast. He does

---

23. O'Connor, *The Habit of Being*, 438.

24. Fitzgerald, "Flannery O'Connor's 'Everything that Rises,'" 37.

25. Fitzgerald, "Flannery O'Connor's 'Everything that Rises,'" 37. See also Zubeck, "Alpha & Omega."

26. By way of example, in "Greenleaf," Mrs May thinks herself a martyr to her sons, for whom she works to provide a living—she dies when gored by a bull; the grandfather in "A View of the Woods" idolizes progress—his granddaughter dies in revolt against his tyranny; Asbury of "The Enduring Chill" wants to be a martyr for his writing and his ideals, but thinks of life with his mother as a kind of martyrdom—his knowledge

not think of himself as a martyr, but he wants to love and be loved; and he sees with the eyes of faith.

The main character in the short story entitled "Everything That Rises Must Converge" provides the key to reading Parker as a true, rather than a false, martyr, by providing his opposite, in the character of Julian, a son who is convinced that he gives up every noble ambition for the sake of his mother, and that this constitutes his martyrdom. Julian also thinks that he is superior to his mother, in submitting to her without loving her. Only at the moment of her death are his eyes opened. O'Connor makes the most explicit reference to false martyrdom when she describes Julian as "pinned to the door frame, waiting like Saint Sebastian for the arrows to begin piercing him."[27] Julian is a failed writer, who now sells typewriters to earn some money, seemingly only to save face, since in fact his mother supports him. The irony of a self-proclaimed writer selling to others the tools with which to write is impossible to overlook, and stands in contrast to Parker, who gives everything he has—his very flesh—as a canvass; in this way he offers himself fully and indelibly to what he wants to be: an artistic life-project. One character displaces his artistic responsibility, while the other is fully committed to it.

According to a Thomistic understanding, every dimension of a martyr's life is involved in expressing the love of Christ. In contrast, we find in Julian the epitome of distancing oneself from the world. O'Connor describes Julian as often retreating into his own perfect world, which we are told was:

> the inner compartment of his mind where he spent most of his time. This was a kind of mental bubble in which he established himself when he could not bear to be a part of what was going on around him. From it he could see out and judge but in it he was safe from any kind of penetration from without. It was the only place where he felt free of the general idiocy of his fellows.

---

that he will not die, after all, at the end of the story is devastating to him; another son dependent on his mother, Thomas in "The Comforts of Home," ends up inadvertently killing her due to his inability to confront his own limitations (which he blames on others, and on circumstances); Sheppard in "The Lame Shall Enter First" is so intent on saving a delinquent that he neglects his son, who dies to be with his dead mother; Mrs Turpin in "Revelation" is convinced that she knows exactly where everyone fits in the social scale, and dies railing against God, who has sent her what she thinks of as a "message," from a girl in a waiting room fed up with her snobbery. The girl claims that Mrs Turpin is a "wart-hog from hell." The rage at such effrontery finally kills her, but it is then that she sees things as they really are. Finally, "Judgment Day" sees Tanner, who understands himself a martyr to the old (racist) values of the south confront a new order, killed by a mocking Negro far from the plot of land where he wants to be buried.

27. O'Connor, "Everything That Rises Must Converge," 271.

His mother had never entered it but from it he could see her with absolute clarity.[28]

Julian creates all the conditions that he needs to be unaffected by factors outside of him. He closes himself to the possibility of seeing something new. We have the image here of a bubble, floating above but without the possibility of converging, because Julian refuses to love what he sees; and only those who love will rise toward the Omega point. Fittingly, Julian's attitude is the polar opposite of that of a Catholic artist. According to O'Connor:

> ... when you write a story, you are [not] supposed to forget or give up any moral position that you hold. Your beliefs will be the light by which you see, but they will not be what you see and they will not be a substitute for seeing. For the writer of fiction, everything has its testing point in the eye, and the eye is the organ that eventually involves the whole personality, and as much of the world as can get into it. It [the act of writing] involves judgment ... that begins in the act of vision, and ... when it becomes separated from vision, then confusion exists in the mind which transfers itself to the story.[29]

O'Connor considers that principles, or beliefs, should not cut the reader off from the world. Julian is in an "inner compartment," a "mental bubble" from which he refuses contact with his surroundings. In contrast, O'Connor gives us the image of an eye, which she considers both a physical and a spiritual means of contact with the world. The "act of vision" that O'Connor encourages immerses the writer in a world illuminated by inner beliefs. For the Catholic, this is ultimately an act of love of Christ, in apostolic communion. This involves him or her in a community of saints, aware of the ways in which persons near and far are loveable images of God's divine love.

In the short story "Everything That Rises Must Converge," O'Connor dramatizes the tragic loss that can result when unreflective judgements remove us from the world. As described, Julian judges his mother from a dissociative chamber, and decides that she is "clever enough"[30] and with the "right premises"[31] would go far; but that she lives in a fantasy world: she is unreasonable, and so unlovable. He can put up with her, and this makes him a martyr in his own eyes. What he cannot see, until it is too late, is how

---

28. O'Connor, "Everything That Rises," 276.
29. O'Connor, "Writing Short Stories," 91.
30. O'Connor, "Everything That Rises," 277.
31. O'Connor, "Everything That Rises," 277.

much she loves him, and he loves her. He is forced to this realization of what is really important, and of how blind he has been, at the moment of her death. With a touch of irony, the mother's view of another type of "rising"—that of the Negroes rising—is the non-proximate cause of her death. Julian and his mother are sitting together on a bus, and the latter is dismayed that right across from her is an African American who is wearing the same hat as herself. Julian's mother has proclaimed earlier that she does not mind if the Negroes rise up, so long as they do so on their own side of the fence. Now, she is faced with a Negro mother acting as her black double, and the sight displeases her. In an act that she thinks to be charitable, whereas Julian sees only another form of prejudice and naïveté, Julian's mother gives the Negro son—Julian's double in another sense—a penny. Outraged at perceived condescension, the child's mother strikes Julian's mother, instigating a stroke in the latter. It is only now, at the very end, in a moment where his mother has apparently died for her belief, or principle, that Julian realizes how much he relies on and actually loves her. Moments earlier, he had walked along, "saturated in depression, as if in the midst of his martyrdom he had lost his faith."[32] His mother's new hat and all that it represented of her character had been the cause. Now he sees that this was not faith at all—that he has been an ideologue and an egoist with no grasp of truth. Unlike O'Connor's ideal writer, he has until now judged only from afar, and so not known how connected he is to the world, how much he is indebted to those around him. As will now be seen, Julian is unlike Parker. Whereas Julian thought of himself as a martyr, his selfishness could only deny him that honor; Parker has no sense at all that he is a martyr, but his love makes him *like* one, in Thomas's sense.

4. Parker as Martyr for the Beatific Vision

Perhaps the best way to understand the contrast between Julian and Parker is to consider the image that O'Connor gives of martyrdom in each of their stories: false and true respectively. In "Everything That Rises Must Converge," Julian is cast as a negative image of Saint Sebastian (who was martyred by being shot with arrows) pinning himself against a door-frame. At the end of "Parker's Back," the protagonist sees "a tree of light burst over the skyline" and falls "back against the door as if he had been pinned there by a lance."[33] Julian's martyrdom is actually meaningless: a martyr does not

---

32. O'Connor, "Everything That Rises," 272.

33. O'Connor, "Parker's Back," 441. It is noteworthy that Sarah Ruth screams "Idolatry! Enflaming yourself with idols under every green tree!" (ibid., 442). She thinks that

martyr himself. Instead, standing up for what he believes, he is subjected to martyrdom. Parker, on the other hand, receives martyrdom in a Christ-like way. A lance pins him, like the lance that pierced the side of Christ after he had died on the cross. Furthermore, the tree Parker sees has biblical resonances. It is like the one he has already encountered, not so long ago, after it burst into flame when he drove into it. Shoes thrown off his feet and wild-eyed at having almost died, Parker seemed then like Moses before the burning bush. That earlier incident and his near escape had performed "a great change in his life, a leap into a worse unknown, and . . . there was nothing he could do about it."[34] After this, Parker chooses his final tattoo. He does not coherently understand his motivations when he does this—that comes later when he reasons that all he has ever really wanted is to "please"[35] Sarah Ruth. There is something more, though, to Parker's actions. He chooses an image of God that strikes him, not realizing that Sarah Ruth is, like Julian, unable to connect a belief in principles with an ability to see and love others in the world.

In her own way, Sarah Ruth has refused to look at the world, and especially at the person with whom she lives, and who loves her. O'Connor has explained that all of Parker's life has been motivated by the desire to make his body a beautiful canvass of moving images. She describes how, at the age of fourteen, Parker had experienced a moment of wonder, when he saw from a distance a man whose entire body was tattooed. To Parker, this was beautiful. The narrator tells us that this is the first time that he has ever "felt the least motion of wonder in himself"[36] and in his existence.

From this moment onwards, he is as a "blind boy [who] had been turned so gently in a different direction that he did not know his destination had been changed."[37] Parker is from this point forward firm in his conviction that he can make his body beautiful by having it tattooed. His wife constantly ridicules this articulation of inner belief. She claims in contrast only to want to know God. Her abstract faith, though, means that she cannot find God in the world: she cannot recognize his image anywhere. More than this, she refuses to do so, and proves herself completely unreasonable. The picture of the Byzantine Christ strikes Parker to his innermost core, and he wants Sarah Ruth to see the same image and become so captivated that

---

he finds the opportunity for idolatry everywhere. It would be better to say that he finds the opportunity for moments of revelation of God, through images, everywhere.

34. O'Connor, "Parker's Back," 434.
35. O'Connor, "Parker's Back," 440.
36. O'Connor, "Parker's Back," 427.
37. O'Connor, "Parker's Back," 427.

she will no longer turn away from the one who bears it. Seeing an image of Christ, she will finally see her husband's self-giving. As he reasons to the tattooist: "[s]he can't say she don't like the looks of God."[38] Having the icon on his back rather than where he can see it expresses his desire to wake her up, to offer something beautiful for her, and not himself.

However, Parker has not appreciated that his wife's iconoclasm makes her unable to see and hear. He shouts, he whispers, and he has his back painted with a startling figure, but she remains able to appreciate neither beauty, nor her husband's love for her. Sarah Ruth does not want to look at images. Most poignantly, she cannot recognize the face of Christ.

5. Looking at Parker's Back: On Being Able to Recognize Martyrdom

O'Connor's artistic sensibility is infused with the grace of faith that sees, presents, and saturates unexpected moments and details. This is because she thinks that everything here and now indicates what transcends. Her world is one of "mystery,"[39] in which unlikely heroes have moments of conversion, though often when it seems too late. In "Everything That Rises Must Converge" and "Parker's Back," each protagonist is alerted in different ways to the significance of this life in light of the next. Charity is the key to each story, for proper love is directed toward Christ as the Omega-point. Only with such love can human persons rise up to be united with the entirety of creation. In "Parker's Back," the protagonist both literally and figuratively converges with Christ. He now has Christ's image on his back; and his vision finally coincides with that of a Christian martyr—who sees that he must sacrifice some of what he wants, for the sake of what he knows at a deeper level, actually matters. Finally, "Parker's Back" provides an explicit—"startling"— image of how being Christ-centred entails being *like* a martyr in Thomas's sense discussed above.

In the last moments that we see him, Parker is pinned against a doorframe, transfixed by a vision. He then whispers his baptismal name to his wife, through a keyhole and, having shown her his final tattoo, is beaten and we see him crying against a tree. The face of Christ looks at us, flagellated, disfigured, bleeding, on Parker's exposed flesh. The final image that O'Connor gives us is of a suffering Christ-figure. Sarah Ruth has seen the tattoo on Parker's back, called her husband an idolater, turned him from the house and beaten him until welts form on the face of the image of Christ.

38. O'Connor, "Parker's Back," 438.
39. Hence the title of her collected essays: *Mystery and Manners*.

We witness him "leaning against a tree, crying like a baby."[40] As a boy, seeing the tattooed man, Parker had been like a blind boy whose direction has been changed. He saw then a depiction of dynamic beauty, where all the parts worked together to form a beautiful whole. Every new tattoo has been a quest for such completion—but until now he has not known that what he desired was love—from his wife, but also from the one with the all-seeing eyes. Crucially, Parker has faith in the vision that has led him toward what he knows, deep down, is the fitting completion of the artwork on his body. He has given himself up to that work, and at the same time found the significance of his life.

In fact, not until Parker has the tattoo of Christ on his back does he really consider the significance of his life. After a bar-room brawl instigated by friends mocking his new image, he sits outside in an alley, "examining his soul." As O'Connor puts it, "[h]e saw it as a spider web of facts and lies that was not at all important to him but which appeared to be necessary in spite of his opinion. The eyes that were now forever on his back were eyes to be obeyed. He was as certain of it as he had ever been of anything."[41] Parker is forced to consider the implications of his actions, as a kind of artwork held up for scrutiny. Finally, he makes it home to Sarah Ruth. As he stands against the door hoping she will let him in, just after he whispers his real, Christian, name to her, Parker "[feels] the light pouring through him."[42] Because he now obeys Christ, even though he cannot entirely reason as to why he does so, his inner world is transformed. Faith has guided him here, with a certainty that he cannot know through reason, because he does not have enough points of reason with which to work. Instead, he is more aware of the coordinates that faith has offered him all along. This reflective faith, though, takes him toward reason, because it has opened up inner dimensions; formerly Parker had taken these aspects to be no more significant than his vision of the tattooed man in the circus long ago. But now he knows that something more had always driven his desire for beauty and for love. He feels "light pouring through him, turning his spider web soul into a perfect arabesque of colors, a garden of trees and birds and beasts."[43] It is as though inside, he has become like the paradise he has constantly sought to have inked into his flesh. Thomas's point, that a martyr is not constituted as such because of his suffering, but rather by that *for which* he is suffering,

---

40. O'Connor, Parker's Back," 442.
41. O'Connor, Parker's Back," 440.
42. O'Connor, Parker's Back," 441.
43. O'Connor, Parker's Back," 441.

provides a key to understanding Parker; and at the same time, it explains what the Catholic artist seeks to express.

6. How Is Parker Like a Martyr?

Before concluding, a strong objection to the idea that Parker is a martyr needs to be considered. Namely, since Thomas thinks the martyr's death to be essential to martyrdom, it should follow that Parker cannot be deemed a martyr. Nonetheless, Thomas's analogous sense of martyrdom, whereby a person gives up a philosophical or heretical idea that contradicts faith, holds true here. Parker does not literally die in the story, but he can still be thought as a martyr in Thomas's analogous sense. Parker has fortitude in the face of persecution. He is misunderstood, unloved, beaten, for what he knows is true. He gives up an easier life for the sake of greater gain.

More than this, Parker in the end witnesses to his willingness to give up what is most important about his life for the sake of something else. He has from his time as a young boy wanted to know that his body carried beautiful and integrated images. He has also wanted his wife to love him. What constantly amazes him, and what he cannot fathom, is that these two earthly desires prove mutually incompatible. Sarah Ruth will never love him, with his love of images and his body the way that it is, because she is firmly convinced that any image—whether of creation or of God—is an abomination. An image of God is the final straw for her, because she believes that God has no image. In other words, according to O'Connor she is not actually Christian; she does not recognize that God has a human face. So committed is Parker to the truth that everything has an image, and in particular that Christ can be seen, that he has a Byzantine Christ tattooed to his back as the final argument that will make Sarah look at Christ, see God, and love her husband. From the perspective of his faith, what he does is reasonable. He does not count on the fact that what Sarah Ruth takes to be faith is neither reasonable, nor recognizable as faith.

Another reason for choosing the final tattoo inserts itself within the story: that is, that this image of Christ has redemptive power; now a Christ-bearer, Parker experiences his life as having meaning, because now he knows that he needs to and can obey the all-demanding eyes of Christ. Parker's life-story is one of redirected desires. When he begins to have tattoos, he starts to think that only painful things are worthwhile.[44] Increasingly, he wants tattoos that are more life-like.[45] Having something tattooed

---

44. O'Connor, Parker's Back," 428.
45. O'Connor, Parker's Back," 428.

to his back, where he cannot see it, is a sacrifice for Parker, who had up until now seen no point in not being able to see each new image.[46] After the tractor accident and getting the final tattoo, Parker knows that he wants, with Sarah Ruth, to experience his renewed life. His martyrdom consists in this: in aiming for God, he ends up losing his wife entirely; but at the same time he finds the overall purpose of his life. Parker has witnessed to the reality of image and incarnation, and now appreciates very deeply—if not yet completely reasonably—their meaning.

To understand Parker as a martyr is to accept the approach of Thomas who argues that in the face of philosophical or heretical arguments, a wise person can become a kind of martyr to faith. Parker's faith in Christ fulfils his faith in images. He can recognize Christ in an image that completes his self-image, illuminating it from within. Reason can now work with what faith knows on a very personal level. The all-demanding eyes of Christ make Parker feel translucent, and harmonized as had not been previously possible. He realizes that through obedience he can become whole; and only then, when he realizes how much sacrifice this will demand, is the analogy with martyrdom accomplished.

In the end then, if the courage of endurance in the face of persecution is the virtue of a martyr, and a virtue is a disposition toward action, then Parker again acts as a kind of martyr. His disposition toward endurance is manifest when he faces Sarah Ruth at the end. According to Thomas's understanding, such action is possible because of the presence of faith, and also because the martyr has the vision and the insight to know that human action is ultimately for human goods that extend beyond what we can see in this world. A virtue for Thomas is far from merely being an external and mindless activity. Instead, it is a disposition that provides a reasonable response to one's human situation.[47] We know that Parker has received the mark of faith, in baptism, within the earlier context of his revealing his true name to Sarah Ruth when they were courting. The narrator tells us that: "[h]e had never revealed the name to any man or woman, only to the files of the navy and the government, and it was on his baptismal record which he got at the age of a month."[48] A baptismal registry, which documents that a Christian has received the mark of the theological virtue of faith, is the first official place where Parker's Christian name is found. That faith has always worked within him, but only now can he begin to confront what a

46. O'Connor, Parker's Back," 429.
47. Pinckaers, "Virtue is Not a Habit"; Lombardo, *The Logic of Desire*; Clark, "Is Martyrdom Virtuous?"
48. O'Connor, "Parker's Back," 431. For more on the significance of the name, see: Leigh, SJ, "Suffering and the Sacred," 375.

difference it has made. He demonstrates perseverance motivated by faith, and this gives him the marks of analogous martyrdom.

After all, Parker has already demonstrated that he has faith; even though he does not quite understand what he is doing, he certainly tries to. Unlike any of his other tattoos, this one of Christ expresses the sense of purpose he feels especially strongly when thrown from a tractor in a blaze of fire during a farming accident. The tattoo also enables further action, and interior perspective. It is as though everything that he saw from a distance as a boy has finally taken root within him, but only because of his obedience to Christ's "all-demanding"[49] eyes. Parker's reason is slowly catching up with his faith, and this is, according to Thomas, a way that faith and reason can work together. Thus Thomas states that:

> Faith cannot altogether precede understanding, for it would be impossible to assent by believing what is proposed to be believed, without understanding it in some way. However, the perfection of understanding follows the virtue of faith: which perfection of understanding is itself followed by a kind of certainty of faith.[50]

There is no faith at all without understanding "in some way," and at the same time there is no faith if what one believes in can be fully rationalized, thereby running the risk of being explained away.

In contrast to his faith in the power of this image, and the one whom it represents, Sarah Ruth's iconoclasm, which O'Connor describes as "the notion that you can worship in pure Spirit,"[51] is as lifeless as it is disembodied. Catholic thought emphasizes that embodied humans need to worship with more than spirit. To say that one is worshiping without using the senses to do so is impossible, according to a Christian vision in which actions in the world matter, because of the interior disposition accompanying them. In striving to overcome and counter Sarah Ruth's insistence that she cannot see God in the face of Christ, Parker endures persecution. Parker, without fully understanding this point intellectually, witnesses to Christ when he insists that this is an image of God, and as such should be recognized; to him this is self-evident and reasonable. He becomes, especially at the end of the story, a martyr. O'Connor's vision, which unites faith and reason, enables her to see this and to attempt to represent that insight in her final piece of Catholic fiction. O'Connor and Parker are both artists who draw out the somewhat startling implications of the complementary relationship between faith and

---

49. O'Connor, "Parker's Back," 436.
50. Aquinas, *Summa Theologica*, II–II, Q. 8, art. 8, ad. 2, 1204.
51. O'Connor, *The Habit of Being*, 594.

reason. Thomas Aquinas appreciates the courage demanded of those who take this complementarity seriously. O'Connor's fictional work depicts such courage in action—both in the strength of her writing as well as in the actions of her main character. In contrast, the reader is struck by the anaemic quality of Sarah Ruth's heretic denial of Christ's incarnate presence in the world through an image of love. Her husband's back is intended as a gift to her; but she cannot accept it. Ultimately, the Catholic artist's vocation is to express the relationship between faith and reason, emphasizing that Christian love is all-demanding, like the eyes of the Byzantine icon that Parker insists be forever on his back.

3

LOGOS AND LOVE

Reason's Tentative Understanding of the Doctrine of the Trinity

—Paul Morrissey

The Mystery of God revealed in Jesus Christ by the power of the Holy Spirit is a mystery of *ekstasis*, love, communion and mutual indwelling among the three divine persons; a mystery of *kenosis*, the relinquishing of the form of God by Jesus in his incarnation, so as to take the form of a slave (cf. Phil 2:5–11); and a mystery of *theosis*, human beings are called to participate in the life of God and to share in "the divine nature" (2 Pet 1:4) through Christ, in the Spirit. When theology speaks of a negative path and of speechlessness, it is referring to a sense of awe before the Trinitarian Mystery in which is salvation. Though words cannot fully describe it, by love believers already participate in the Mystery. "Although you have not seen him, you love him; and even though you do not see him now, you believe in him and rejoice with an indescribable and glorious joy, for you are receiving the outcome of your faith, the salvation of your souls" (1 Pet 1:8–9).[1]

The focus of this chapter is the greatest mystery of the Christian faith. "Greatest" is applied here because the Trinity is the Christian doctrine that treats of God in and of himself. All other Christian mysteries concern God's relation with creation. Though the Christian tradition has consistently held that God's existence is knowable through human reason alone, the doctrine

1. International Theological Commission, *Theology Today*, n.98.

of the Trinity is revealed truth. Without Christ revealing God as Father, Son, and Holy Spirit we would have no access to this teaching. There have been notable exceptions to this, such as Abelard's attempt, using Plato, to demonstrate that reason's grasp of God's power, wisdom, and goodness is a witness to God as Father, Son, and Holy Spirit. More notably still there were those medieval theologians—Anselm, Richard of St Victor, and Bonaventure—who argued apologetically for the necessity of the doctrine of the Trinity on the grounds that a God who is perfectly good must be immanently communicative because the good is diffusive of itself.[2]

Much recent Trinitarian theology has been motivated by a noble desire to make the doctrine of the Trinity more relevant. This theology sees the truth in Karl Rahner's quip that Christians are, in their practical life, "mere monotheists" and should the doctrine of the Trinity be dropped as false, much of Christian literature would remain unchanged.[3] In their quest for "relevance," many have seen it necessary to move away from the western theological tradition, which is stereotyped as overly focused on God's essence, tending toward the abstract and metaphysical. This tradition, so the argument goes, is insufficiently biblical, neglectful of the economic Trinity, and is only secondarily concerned with the distinction of persons in God. The key thinkers in this classic tradition are Augustine and Aquinas. In the quest for more relevance, a new type of orthodoxy has arisen in western Trinitarian theology, sometimes described as social Trinitarianism.[4] We also see in the giants of twentieth-century Trinitarian theology (Barth, Rahner, Moltmann, Balthasar) a similar trend, not so much in terms of seeking relevance, but certainly in terms of distancing themselves from the classical tradition.

The classical western Trinitarian tradition deserves, I believe, to be more widely known and may represent an approach uniquely attractive to the contemporary believer. This is because of its anthropological emphasis and its highlighting of the unique dignity of our subjectivity. This chapter aims to show that the western tradition, through looking at the Trinitarian theology of Aquinas, does indeed have significant resources with which to make the Trinity "relevant." A resource with arguably the most potential is the teaching of the processions in the Trinity, a teaching that links the revelation of Scripture and philosophical reflections on the human person.

---

2. See the discussion in Emery, "The Doctrine of the Trinity," 46, 47.

3. Rahner, *The Trinity*, 10–11.

4. See Kilby, "Perichoresis and Projection"; on contemporary trends in Trinitarian theology see also, Marshall, "The Unity of the Triune God."

In what follows I will focus on Aquinas's discussion of the divine processions and missions. Logos and Love are the processions in God. The Logos (the Word, the Son) proceeds eternally from the Father; the Holy Spirit is love *proceeding* eternally from the Father and the Son. The divine processions are analogically processions of knowledge (the Son) and love (the Holy Spirit). If we say that our defining characteristics as human persons are to know and to love, then the doctrine of divine processions give, by way of analogy, a depth to the doctrine of the *imago Dei*: we image God in the way we reason (intellect) and love (will). Furthermore, the divine missions (invisible) of the Son and Holy Spirit to individual souls reflect the eternal processions of the divine persons: the Son is the graced soul's wisdom; the Spirit is the graced soul's love.[5]

It would also seem that approaching the Trinity through this teaching on processions counters somewhat the common stereotype of western Trinitarian thinking. This doctrine is based in Scripture; it can be reconciled with modernity's turn to the subject (in that it is understood by way of analogy with the human person); and the immanent and economic modes of the Trinity are taken seriously and brought into harmony.

1. Faith, Reason, and the Doctrine of the Trinity

All theology needs humility, but this is especially the case with the Triune God. As the International Theological Commission recently stated: "Theology rightly intends to speak truly of the Mystery of God, but at the same time it knows that its knowledge though true is inadequate in relation to the reality of God, whom it can never 'comprehend'. As St Augustine said: 'If you comprehend, it is not God' (*Sermo* 117, 3, 5)."[6] It is sometimes said that Aquinas in his exploration of the mystery of God is too confident in the ability of human reason to grasp the ungraspable; that he is too philosophical and neglects revelation, especially in relation to his use of the psychological analogy of the Trinity. However, it is worth reflecting on what Aquinas saw as the basic motivation or need for doing theology.

The very first article of the first question of the *Summa theologia* addresses the need for theology (*sacra doctrina*). The *telos* of the human person

---

5. This chapter is particularly indebted to the recent *resourcemment* in Thomistic Trinitarian theology especially as found in the work of the French Dominicans, Jean-Pierre Torrell and Gilles Emery. See especially, Torrell, *Saint Thomas Aquinas, Volume 2*; Emery, *The Trinitarian Theology of St. Thomas Aquinas*, and *The Trinity*. I'm also indebted to Matthew Levering's important book, *Scripture and Metaphysics*.

6. International Theological Commission, *Theology Today*, n.97.

needs to be known so that the thoughts and the actions of the person can be directed to this end: "Hence it was necessary for the salvation of man that certain truths which exceed human reason should be made known to him by divine revelation."[7] Even though human reason can know divine things unaided (philosophical wisdom), this knowledge is limited, prone to error, and available to only a few. Furthermore, our "whole salvation," which is in God, depends on knowing the truth of God. "Therefore, in order that the salvation of men might be brought about more fittingly and more surely, it was necessary that they should be taught divine truths by divine revelation. It was therefore necessary that besides philosophical science built up by reason, there should be a sacred science learned through revelation."[8] This statement, right at the beginning of his great *Summa* of theology, is a far cry from the common stereotype of St. Thomas that holds that his theology was merely a dressed up philosophy. And this is especially true of his Trinitarian theology where he expertly explicates the data of sacred revelation with the aid of metaphysical realism.

2. Processions in God

Aquinas roots his Trinitarian theology in the doctrine of processions, which has its origins in Scripture.[9] The tradition holds that procession is the word usually reserved to describe the origin of the Holy Spirit "who proceeds from the Father (and the Son)." However, from Scripture, Thomas sees procession as applicable to the origin of the Son as well as the Holy Spirit. The procession however is necessarily different, for if both simply proceeded from the Father they would not be distinct. The procession of the Son is one of generation, for the Son proceeds from the Father by nature. The Holy Spirit proceeds not by way of nature but by way of love and is called spiration since it is the procession of the Spirit.[10] Aquinas is careful to point out that procession in God cannot be understood in any created sense, for example when one thing may proceed from one place to another. Procession

---

7. Aquinas, *Summa Theologiae* (hereafter *ST*), Ia, q.1, a.1.

8. Aquinas, *ST*, Ia, q.1, a.1.

9. "I have come down from heaven, not to do my own will, but the will of him who sent me." Also, John 13:20 "He who receives any one whom I send receives me; and he who receives me receives him who sent me." "But when the Counselor comes, whom I shall send to you from the Father, even the Spirit of truth, who proceeds from the Father, he will bear witness to me." (John 15:26).

10. Aquinas, *ST*, Ia, q.27, a.4.

and origin in God are words used to describe the eternal distinction between the divine persons, their relation of emanation.[11]

In his affirmative answer to the First Article of Question 27, "is there procession in God?" Aquinas underscores that this procession can only be understood as being immanent, it is not outside of God. Seeing procession as somehow to be going forth from God is the mistake of both Sabellius and Arius, albeit in different ways.[12] Procession only exists in God himself.[13] This inward procession corresponds, by way of analogy, to the activity of our human intellect: "Whenever anyone understands because of his very act of understanding, something comes forth from within him, which is the concept of the known thing proceeding from his awareness of it. It is this concept which an utterance signifies; we call it the 'word in the heart,' signified by the spoken word."[14] This analogy has its scriptural basis in the Son's identification as the Logos, the Word. "In the beginning was the Word, and the Word was with God, and the Word was God. . . . And the Word became flesh and dwelt among us, full of grace and truth; we have beheld his glory, glory as of the only Son from the Father" (John 1:1, 14). Aquinas calls this procession of the Word "generation," correlating to the formula of faith that the Son is born of the Father before all ages. When that which the intellect reproduces is the likeness of the thing understood, the knower and the known are one. In God, to be and to understand are identical so when the Father conceives the Son he eternally begets nothing other than his divine

---

11. Emery, *Trinitarian Theology*, 53 referring to St Thomas Aquinas, I *Sent.* d. 13, q. 1, a.

12. "This procession has been differently understood. Some have understood it in the sense of an effect, proceeding from its cause; so Arius took it, saying that the Son proceeds from the Father as His primary creature, and that the Holy Spirit proceeds from the Father and the Son as the creature of both. In this sense neither the Son nor the Holy Spirit would be true God: and this is contrary to what is said of the Son, 'That . . . we may be in His true Son. This is true God' (1 John 5:20). Of the Holy Spirit it is also said, 'Know you not that your members are the temple of the Holy Spirit?' (1 Corinthians 6:19). Now, to have a temple is God's prerogative. Others take this procession to mean the cause proceeding to the effect, as moving it, or impressing its own likeness on it; in which sense it was understood by Sabellius, who said that God the Father is called Son in assuming flesh from the Virgin, and that the Father also is called Holy Ghost in sanctifying the rational creature, and moving it to life. The words of the Lord contradict such a meaning, when He speaks of Himself, 'The Son cannot of Himself do anything' (John 5:19); while many other passages show the same, whereby we know that the Father is not the Son. Careful examination shows that both of these opinions take procession as meaning an outward act; hence neither of them affirms procession as existing in God Himself . . ." (Aquinas, *ST*, Ia, q.27, a.1).

13. Aquinas, *ST*, Ia, q.27, a.1.

14. Aquinas, *ST*, Ia, q.27, a.1.

nature: "Hence the procession of the Word in God is called 'generation', and the Word itself proceeding is called 'Son.'"[15]

In his discussion of the second procession in God, Aquinas also begins with Sacred Scripture: "I will ask my Father and he will give you another Advocate" (John 14:16). The procession of the Holy Spirit is not, as noted, a generation. He is not another Son of the Father. The Holy Spirit is equally God, he also proceeds as one with the divine essence: God from God. The procession is what makes the Spirit distinct. For Aquinas the logical step is to continue from the analogy of the Word as an intellectual procession with the other interior procession involving the will. And this procession is called love.

> Now in us there is another spiritual process following the action of the will, namely the coming forth of the love, whereby what is loved is in the lover, just as the thing expressed or actually understood in the conceiving of an idea is in the knower. For this reason besides the procession of the Word another procession is posited in God, namely the procession of Love.[16] The analogy is key for Aquinas to understand the distinctiveness of the two processions. Love does not proceed by way of generation as it does not "reproduce" the likeness of something understood, as the intellect does when it understands something when the likeness is conceived. Rather the will is moved by love when it tends toward what it wills, the beloved. The will is moved towards

---

15. Aquinas, *ST*, Ia, q.27, a.2. "The very object that is known to the divine intellect is God himself. 'As the Father knows me and I know the Father' (Jn 10:15) In the act through which God knows himself the unity of the divine intellect and the word is the most intimate. Thus we can arrive at some understanding of how a procession occurs within a substantial unity without separation or diversity." Emery, *Trinitarian Theology*, 59. It is sometimes thought that Aquinas, in his use of the analogy of the human soul, is too motivated by an attempt to rationally demonstrate a doctrine of faith. Emery answers this charge: "Has one then fallen for the rational temptation to *prove* an article of the Creed and *demonstrated* the personal being of a Word in God? St Thomas' answer to this would be 'No', because 'the analogy with our minds does not constitute a sufficient proof to demonstrate something about God, because reason does not exist univocally in God and in us.' (*ST* I, q. 32, a. 1, ad 2). It is a matter of an 'argument from congruity', a 'persuasive reason' which enables one to grasp only what has been received from revelation, that is to say the faith, made known to us. But, using an analogy which gets to grips with the content of the confession of faith, one has disclosed how we can get to grips with the generation of the Word in God. This analogy preserves a profound respect for God's spiritual nature, since it draws on the word's spiritual procession. It attempts to illuminate believers' minds by starting from what is closest to them, the word in our own human mind, to open the door a little way onto the mystery of the divine generation of the Word" (Emery, *Trinitarian Theology*, 185).

16. Aquinas, *ST*, Ia, q.27, a.3.

something and this is its procession; in God this procession is a breathing of spirit, a word that "indicates a living motion and impulse, as when somebody is said to be driven or impelled by his love to do something."[17]

Aquinas in describing the divine processions as analogous to the intellect and will reminds us that the analogous nature of understanding divine things is necessary in order to protect the oneness and simplicity of the divine nature of God. God's will and intellect are not distinct properties: God is God's will; God is God's intellect. There cannot be division in God. So when St Thomas speaks of the Son as wisdom proceeding and the Holy Spirit as love proceeding, he is not saying that the Son is the limit of God's knowledge or the Holy Spirit is the limit of God's love. Rather, everything in God is one perfect eternal act. The doctrine of divine processions is related only to understanding the data of divine revelation, namely that within this one perfect divine act that is God there exists three distinct, equally divine persons. Aquinas further underlines this distinction when he states that there is a certain order in the procession related to the order of knowledge and love. We love only in connection to that which we have first known. Thus, "though in God will and intellect are the same, nevertheless because the very meaning of love implies an issuing forth from what the mind conceives, the procession of Love in him is distinct by its connection with the procession of the Word."[18]

3. A Trinitarian Understanding of the Imago Dei

How then is the doctrine of processions relatable to the life of the believer? Aquinas, I think, would answer that the immanent processions in God of knowing and loving relate to us as created in his image, as knowers and lovers. This point is outlined clearly by Thomas:

> Now the processions of the divine Persons are referred to the acts of intellect and will, as was said above (Article 27). For the Son proceeds as the word of the intellect; and the Holy Spirit proceeds as love of the will. Therefore in rational creatures, possessing intellect and will, there is found the representation of the Trinity by way of image, inasmuch as there is found in them the word conceived, and the love proceeding.[19]

17. Aquinas, *ST*, Ia, q.27, a.4.
18. Aquinas, *ST*, Ia, q.27, a. 3.
19. Aquinas, *ST*, Ia q.45 a.7. Aquinas further explicates: "Image means a likeness which in some degree, however small, attains to a representation of the species.

Aquinas's connection of the divine processions and the *imago Dei* is a very striking example of how he integrates divine revelation, speculative theology, Christian anthropology, and spiritual theology.

Aquinas's teaching on the *imago Dei* has been described by Jean-Pierre Torrell as a key component in his spiritual theology as well as a description of the *exitus* (creation) and *reditus* (recreation and glorification) of the rational creature.[20] Aquinas sees the image of God in the human person in three ways: First in a way common to all human persons in that they have a natural aptitude to understand and love God through the spiritual nature of their soul. Second, in so far as the human person knows and loves God in conformity with grace. Thirdly, there is the *imago Dei* when the human person knows and loves God perfectly, a likeness of the blessed in glory.[21] Thus, as Aquinas notes, there is a threefold *imago Dei* of creation (common to all), recreation (the just conformed to God's image by grace), and of "likeness" itself (the blessed).[22] This teaching is intimately linked to Aquinas's Trinitarian theology, especially in relation to the temporal missions of the Son and Holy Spirit, who indwell the human soul drawing it back to the Father.

Wherefore we need to seek in the image of the Divine Trinity in the soul some kind of representation of species of the Divine Persons, so far as this is possible to a creature. Now the Divine Persons, as above stated (AA[6],7), are distinguished from each other according to the procession of the word from the speaker, and the procession of love from both. Moreover the Word of God is born of God by the knowledge of Himself; and Love proceeds from God according as He loves Himself. But it is clear that diversity of objects diversifies the species of word and love; for in the human mind the species of a stone is specifically different from that of a horse, which also the love regarding each of them is specifically different. Hence we refer the Divine image in man to the verbal concept born of the knowledge of God, and to the love derived therefrom. Thus the image of God is found in the soul according as the soul turns to God, or possesses a nature that enables it to turn to God. Now the mind may turn towards an object in two ways: directly and immediately, or indirectly and mediately; as, for instance, when anyone sees a man reflected in a looking-glass he may be said to be turned towards that man. So Augustine says (De Trin. xiv, 8), the 'the mind remembers itself, understands itself, and loves itself. If we perceive this, we perceive a trinity, not, indeed, God, but, nevertheless, rightly called the image of God.' But this is due to the fact, not that the mind reflects on itself absolutely, but that thereby it can furthermore turn to God, as appears from the authority quoted above" (Aquinas, *ST*, Ia, q.93, a.8).

20. Torrell, *Spritual Master*, 90.
21. Aquinas, *ST*, Ia, q.93, a.4.
22. Aquinas, *ST*, Ia, q.93, a.4.

4. The Trinitarian Mission to the Human Soul

Aquinas's exposition of the divine missions is, I think, a tremendous resource with which to contemplate the economic Trinity, God's Trinitarian life present to the world. To speak of the mission of the Trinity is to speak the language of the Bible. Aquinas cites, among other texts, "It is not I alone, but I and the Father who sent me" (John 8:16) and "When the time had fully come, God sent forth his son, born of a woman" (Gal 4:4). St Thomas clarifies many points regarding the mission of the divine persons: they are temporal and not eternal; they involve only the Son and Spirit, the Father is not sent; the missions are visible and invisible; and their purpose is revelatory as well as salvific (divinizing).[23]

The Father is not sent, as he does not proceed. It is the Son and the Holy Spirit who are sent into the world.[24] The Son is visibly sent in the incarnation. The Son assumes a human nature in the unity of his divine person. When the Virgin conceives in her womb the eternal Son of God becomes human, becomes visible. This visible mission unveils in a corporal way the mystery of the Triune God. The visible mission of the Holy Spirit is not corporal as such, but includes the baptism of Jesus and Pentecost: the Spirit is manifested to witnesses and apostles.[25]

Aquinas attests that God is "in" creation, present to it, sustaining it as the cause through which effects participate in his nature and goodness. But above and beyond this universal presence,

> There is one special mode belonging to the rational nature wherein God is said to be present as the object known is in the knower, and the beloved in the lover. And since the rational creature by its operation of knowledge and love attains to God Himself, according to this special mode God is said not only to exist in the rational creature but also to dwell therein as in His own temple. So no other effect can be put down as the reason why the divine person is in the rational creature in a new mode, except sanctifying grace. Hence, the divine person is sent, and proceeds temporally only according to sanctifying grace.[26]

---

23. Aquinas, *ST*, Ia, q.43, a.1–8.

24. This is not to say that the Father is not "in" creation or is not also in the souls of the just. The Father is fully "in" the Son and fully "in" the Holy Spirit; the three persons are one God. See, Aquinas, *ST*, 1a, q.43, a.5.

25. On the visible and invisible missions in Aquinas, see Emery, *Trinitarian Theology*, 373.

26. Aquinas, *ST*, Ia, q.43, a.3.

The Son and the Spirit come together into the hearts of the just—the divine person is sent by the one from whom he eternally proceeds (both Son and Spirit). It is truly the divine, uncreated person that dwells in the soul and there is the created effect of this, namely sanctifying grace. "The gift of grace empowers the intelligent being not only to have this created gift at his ready disposal, but also for loving union with the divine person. The gift of grace, therefore, explains how there is an unseen mission, but the divine person himself is the one who is sent."[27]

Aquinas teaches that the divine person who is sent conforms the soul to himself according to his distinctiveness as a person.

> Hence for a divine person to be sent to anyone by grace, there must needs be a likening of the soul to the divine person who is sent, by some gift of grace. Because the Holy Spirit is Love, the soul is assimilated to the Holy Spirit by the gift of charity: hence the mission of the Holy Spirit is according to the mode of charity. Whereas the Son is the Word, not any sort of word, but one who breathes forth Love.[28]

Here we see in Aquinas the connection between the doctrine of processions in God (an aspect of the immanent Trinity) and his teaching on the temporal missions (economic Trinity). As the Son proceeds eternally as Word (knowledge) so the effect of his mission in the soul is that of wisdom related to knowledge of God. As the Holy Spirit proceeds eternally as love so the effect of his mission in the soul is that of charity.

There are two aspects of the invisible mission, namely that associated with sanctifying grace, an indwelling of the divine persons, as well as a "quality of newness brought about by grace."[29] The invisible mission takes place also when the soul grows in virtue or increases in grace. Aquinas cites Augustine to support the idea that the eternal Son is sent to someone whenever he perceives or knows the Son. Also, "there is a special instance of an invisible mission based on an increase in grace when someone advances to a new act or new stage of grace, e.g. to the grace of miracles or prophecy or to delivering himself in the fervor of his charity to martyrdom or to renunciation of all he possesses or to taking up any sort of heroic task."[30] This, I believe, to be a crucial teaching of Aquinas. Every movement of knowing and loving God is a result of an invisible and very personal mission of the divine persons to the individual's soul. When I renounce personal pleasure

27. Aquinas, *ST*, Ia, q.43, a.4.
28. Aquinas, *ST*, Ia, q.43, a.4.
29. Aquinas, *ST*, Ia, q.43, a.6.
30. Aquinas, *ST*, Ia, q.43, a.6.

or material gain to better follow God; when I am drawn to prayer; when I sacrifice a good for a greater good; when I forgive; when I am faithful in my vocation; when I do the right thing even when it is difficult; in any act that brings me closer to God, it is the Son and Spirit "on mission" in my soul drawing me to the Father.

Conclusion

Is then Aquinas's and, in more general terms, the classical western tradition of Trinitarian theology still "relevant"? The answer, I think, is very much so. Far from being an abstract exposition of a divinity removed from his creation, Aquinas's teaching seeks to contemplate the biblical God who deigns to create, recreate, and glorify. Yes, this contemplation is grounded in realist metaphysics, including a philosophy of the human person; however, this philosophy is always the handmaiden of sacred doctrine. What is particularly striking is how St Thomas relates the Trinity to the human person: first to his creation as *imago Dei* and second to his recreation through sanctifying grace. It is in the Trinitarian image that the human person is created; it is the Trinitarian processions that visit us and sanctify us. We come from God: Father, Son, and Holy Spirit. We return to dwell eternally with God the Father through the Son and Holy Spirit who visit our souls as Logos and Love.

4

RECENT DEVELOPMENTS AS AN EXAMPLE OF DIALOGUE BETWEEN FAITH AND REASON

—Sr Moira Debono

As an understanding of Revelation, theology has always had to respond in different historical moments to the demands of different cultures, in order then to mediate the content of faith to those cultures in a coherent and conceptually clear way. Today, too, theology faces a dual task. On the one hand, it must be increasingly committed to the task entrusted to it by the Second Vatican Council, the task of renewing its specific methods in order to serve evangelization more effectively.

On the other hand, theology must look to the ultimate truth which Revelation entrusts to it, never content to stop short of that goal. Theologians should remember that their work corresponds "to a dynamism found in the faith itself" and that the proper object of their enquiry is "the Truth which is the living God and his plan for salvation revealed in Jesus Christ."[1]

According to the above excerpt from *Fides et Ratio* (FR) 92, theology is meant to be at the service of the Church. The work of theologians is to make the elements of faith understandable to the people of their time. The theologian has the responsibility not only to endeavor to explain the faith, but by doing so he or she points to the living God of that faith. This essay will consider how those responsible for the liturgical language of the Mass[2] influ-

---

1. Congregation for the Doctrine of the Faith, *Donum Veritatis*, 8: AAS 82 (1990).

2. The Mass is the most significant form of worship in the Catholic Church; it is also referred to as the Eucharist in this essay.

ence the understanding of members of the Mass assembly. Specifically, we will consider how the two-fold task outlined in FR 92 is attempted through the contemporary public worship offered by the Church in the third edition of the *Roman Missal* published in 2010.[3] In other words, how do the wings of faith and reason, beating together, provide understanding sufficient to carry believers to the Truth through this new edition?[4] We will look at elements within the third edition of the RM to answer this question.

By using the venerable axiom, *lex orandi, lex credendi*,[5] I believe we can illustrate the complementarity of faith and reason which leads to a mature and sound faith. With such a faith, the personal encounter with God in liturgy can be profound and thus, enduring and transformative in its effects. Some preliminary definitions and principles will first be presented as stepping stones to the argument at hand.

Faith is an act of personal assent of intellect and will to the encounter with God; it is an act of submission, one could say.[6] The *Catechism of the Catholic Church* uses the Letter to the Hebrews 11:1 to back up its statement: ".Faith is the assurance of things hoped for, the conviction of things not seen." Reason is not opposed to, but rather differentiated from faith; it is described as the "general human 'faculty' or capacity for seeking truth and problem-solving."[7] Thus faith and reason can be understood as complementary responses to the encounter between the revelation of Jesus Christ and the human person who is seeking the truth, such that "the response of [the] human person to the stirring of this encounter is by acts of intellectual assent and by acts of wilful entrustment, acts of love, releasing further questions."[8]

---

3. For the purposes of this Australian publication, when reference is made to either the *Roman Missal* (RM) or "General Instruction of the Roman Missal" (GIRM), the authorized Australian edition of this publication will be the source of citations and this according to section numbers. It contains the words and rubrics of celebrating the Mass (*Roman Missal*).

4. Cf. John Paul II, *Fides et Ratio*. The image of wings used by St John Paul II acknowledges not only the complementarity between faith and reason, but together faith and reason are capable of elevating hearts and minds to an understanding of the truth of God.

5. *Catechism of the Catholic Church*, 1124 (hereafter CCC). CCC 1124 accents the axiom, noting it to have been abbreviated from *legem credendi lex statuat supplicandi* (the law of praying establishes the law of believing) attributed to the fifth century writer Prosper of Aquitaine.

6. Cf. CCC 150.

7. "Reason" as defined in *Oxford Companion to Philosophy*.

8. Allen, "Person and Complementarity," 43.

Faith and reason are both at work in the believer at a liturgical celebration. This public, organized worship of the Church is understood to be a participation in the unending praise of God taking place in heaven. Jesus Christ, the Son of God sitting at the Father's right is the Head of the Church he founded. Whether they are in heaven or still on earth, the faithful, the Body of Christ are associated with him in this worship of the Father.[9]

The most effectual participation in this public worship or liturgy is in the celebration of the Church's seven sacraments, which are moments of real encounter with Christ.[10] They are not simply understood as symbolic rites, but, indeed, as events composed of signs, symbols, and words which communicate a true event. The effects of the sacraments are remedies for human weakness as well as empowerments to live the Christian lifestyle. This essay will consider the sacrament of the Eucharist within this context of encounter with Christ.

1. Some Background: Prior to Sacrosanctum Concilium (1963)

As probably the most notable event in recent Church history, the Second Vatican Council (1962–65)[11] will be the pivot point for these introductory remarks. While *Sacrosanctum Concilium* (SC)[12] was the liturgical document of the Council promulgated in 1963 and the basis for later liturgical reform, we recognize that there was pioneering work accomplished beforehand which was foundational to the document. The so-called Liturgical Movement,[13] begun in the monasteries and university chaplaincies of Europe, was gaining momentum in the early to mid-twentieth century and at the same time there were liturgical innovations and reforms carried out by popes in the years before the Second Vatican Council. These alterations or developments in the liturgy were primarily based in pastoral care. Popes or parish priests saw the need to promote a more profound involvement of the laity in the liturgical actions. This more profound involvement will be elucidated later in this essay.

---

9. 1 Cor 12:27.
10. CCC 1153.
11. For a brief history, see Carbone, "Vatical Council II," 1.
12. Second Vatican Council. *Sacrosanctum Concilium* (hereafter SC).
13. The Liturgical Movement was a pastoral initiative which arose especially to assist the laity to comprehend and enter into the worship of the Church in a more informed or enlightened manner.

2. Sacrosanctum Concilium of the Second Vatican Council

Sacrosanctum Concilium or "The Most Holy Council" was a somewhat unusual title for a liturgical constitution. The time-honored tradition of the Church is that the authors of major magisterial documents typically craft the first Latin sentence in such a way as to place a crucial identifying phrase at its beginning and this becomes the title. Yet in this case, liturgy was not addressed, but rather the Council itself. However, introducing the Council and its goals (as the document did lay them out) was an excellent segue to demonstrate the close relationship between the liturgical worship of God (celebrating liturgy) and the daily activities of members of the Church (living out the liturgy). This relationship would be among the major emphases during the Council from varied perspectives.

The four aims or goals of the Council as stated in SC, were to increase the holiness[14] of its members, to update what could and should be renewed within the liturgical life of the Church, to nurture ecumenism, and to improve methods of evangelization.[15] These aims each came to play important roles in in post-Conciliar liturgical renewal. The purpose of the renewal, and of the Second Vatican Council itself, was to make liturgical worship more accessible to the faithful in their call to holiness. A more profound understanding of the significance of the effects of liturgy in the lives of the faithful underpinned the updating of the various sacramental rites. The increased use of Sacred Scripture in the liturgy opened the treasures of the Bible to the Catholic faithful by acknowledging its close connection with liturgy and catechesis. Further, use of Scripture was a gesture of ecumenism welcomed by non-Catholic Christians, who were often among the more Scripture-based ecclesial communities. This change in liturgy was intended to draw the members of the various Christian communities together. The evangelizing strength of the liturgy was acknowledged in the reform as well. All these aims of liturgical reform can be seen as deepening the faith life of individuals and of parishes. They were steps toward enhancing the faith and reason dialogue.

Since a good fifty-plus years has passed since the promulgation of SC, a detailed historical study is outside the limits of this essay. In summary, we acknowledge that a major post-Conciliar thrust was the renewal of liturgical

---

14. "Holiness, whether ascribed to Popes well-known to history or to humble lay and religious figures, from one continent to another of the globe, has emerged more clearly as the dimension which expresses best the mystery of the Church. Holiness, a message that convinces without the need for words, is the living reflection of the face of Christ" (John Paul II, *Novo*, 7. See also CCC 1709).

15. SC 1.

(or public or communitarian) worship of the Church indicated by SC but already initiated in the previous decades. This is the context to consider the experience of liturgical celebrations today.

3. The Faith and Reason Dialogue in the Liturgy

Returning to *lex orandi, lex credendi*, this axiom is literally translated as "the law of prayer [is] the law of belief." The first item for us to note is the use of the term "law." Law typically indicates an ordered system of rules, regulations, and established principles. For example, we speak of the "law of gravity" or the "laws of physics." Since "law" also underlies the use or practice of ritual, a basic term when we speak of the Church's public worship, the relationship of ritual to law suggests that ritual has an important rational—as well as religious—aspect.[16] Ritual reveals meaning and value at the deepest level and, by definition, is ordered, repetitious, established by a community over time.[17] Typically, within this orderedness, there is a determined vocabulary.[18] In our case, we have the language of public prayer (liturgy) that is given by the Church in the liturgical books and that eventually enters the hearts and minds of believers, ideally with thoughtful engagement. We naturally ask: What words are used by the Church in public prayer? Where do they come from? What do the words mean? What gestures accompany these words? What do the gestures mean? How do the words and gestures affect the members of the assembly as individuals and as a community?

These are questions that the Church has addressed in various ways over the centuries. Rituals, words, and gestures have been retained, changed, eliminated, and adapted according to historical contexts or local situations. In the Church's more recent history, this adaptation has occurred as anthropological and cultural considerations have taken on greater importance in theological study. We will be looking at possible differences in the liturgical experience since the introduction of the Third Typical Edition of the *Roman Missal* (RM).

---

16. Fagerberg, *Theologia Prima*, 138.

17. Augé, *Liturgia*, 85–86.

18. The Western secular ritual of a presentation of a cake with candles and song on an individual's birthday provides an illustration.

4. What Is Liturgy?

Saint Thomas Aquinas (d. 1274) identified public worship with the twofold expression that the praise of God leads to the Christian's holiness. Saint Thomas explained that humanity's worship is not needed by God, but worship is important for the faithful. Worship brings believers into a proper relationship with him and, thus, leads to their perfection.[19] By worshipping God, each individual cannot but become better because worship is the proper role of humanity before its Creator. In extrapolation, a community that worships together grows in communion and in holiness, becoming more like God. At the same time, the individual or community who does good works for the sake of God is giving glory to God.

To carry on laying the context of our discussion, we'll use an explanation of the Church's public worship or liturgy from the *Catechism of the Catholic Church*:

> In Christian tradition it [liturgy] means the participation of the People of God in "the word of God." (Jn 17:4) Through the liturgy Christ, our redeemer and high priest, continues the work of our redemption in, with, and through his Church.[20]

The Redemption was accomplished through Christ's passion, death, resurrection, and ascension, known collectively as his paschal mystery. It is re-presented to the faithful in Eucharistic celebrations so that they become in some mysterious way participants at the foot of his cross.[21] Through the centuries and the circumstances of liturgical history, this truth lost its potency for many of the faithful. As the understanding of Latin decreased and a sense of the sacred became excessively exaggerated, the reasoning underpinning the Eucharistic celebration became less apparent to the faithful and hence they became less engaged with the liturgical realities. Proponents of the pre-Conciliar liturgical movement desired that their work would lead to a more profound involvement of the faithful in this tremendous mystery of the loving self-emptying of Jesus Christ.

Increased involvement of the faithful is key to the present discussion. Pope Pius X first drew the attention of the Church's faithful to "active participation" in a 1903 document discussing liturgical music. This theme can be found in later magisterial writings. It was probably most famously used in SC 14. In that section of the Liturgical Constitution, the laity are encouraged to engage with the liturgy in "fully conscious and active participation

---

19. Aquinas, *ST*, II/II q. 81, art. 7, later reiterated by SC 10 and CCC 1077ff.
20. CCC 1069.
21. CCC 1370.

(*actuosa participatio*)." The word *actuosa* has the sense of "actual participation" or more "complete participation." Active participation goes beyond knowing the exterior words and gestures used in liturgical celebrations; it signifies understanding their meaning so that one can enter deeply into the mysteries being celebrated by way of words and gestures. The goal was that believers would engage with the liturgical mysteries with a more informed faith, a more reasoned and mindful faith.

But what was to be renewed in the liturgy if the paschal mystery is an unchanging reality? CCC 1145 can assist us here:

> A sacramental celebration is woven from signs and symbols. In keeping with the divine pedagogy of salvation, their meaning is rooted in the work of creation and in human culture, specified by the events of the Old Covenant and fully revealed in the person and work of Christ.

Thus, liturgical language does not simply consist of words, it is made up of signs and symbols. We must have some knowledge of that language, that is, the words, signs and symbols, if we are to appreciate what is being communicated. All three elements must have a link with Tradition or Sacred Scripture and yet also be understandable to the people using those words, signs and symbols.[22] But what is it that liturgical language is meant to communicate? Primarily, the faith of the Church is conveyed through liturgy. As a vehicle of Tradition, liturgy assists in the handing on of the faith. As it is succinctly put in CCC 1124, "the Church's faith precedes the faith of the believer who is invited to adhere to it."

5. The Believer as Theologian

As noted above, the believer is considered a theologian and the community members of a local church are acknowledged to be primary theologians. It is they who are immersed in the mysteries of salvation when they participate in liturgy and find themselves "face-to-face" through faith with the living God. On the other hand, "academics" at their desks are secondary

---

22. Tradition, used here with a "T," is defined in the CCC's glossary as: "The oral preaching of the Apostles, and the written message of salvation under the inspiration of the Holy Spirit (Bible), are conserved and handed on as the deposit of faith through the apostolic succession in the Church. Both the living Tradition and the written Scriptures have their common sources in the revelation of God in Jesus Christ (75–82). The theological, liturgical, disciplinary, and devotional traditions of the local churches both contain and can be distinguished from this apostolic Tradition (83)" (CCC, page 901).

theologians who describe the content and experience of faith of the primary theologians.[23]

6. Introducing "Christopher"

While liturgy is a corporate or communal event with a common experience,[24] the primary theologian will have a personally unique experience at the ecclesial event of the liturgy. It will be helpful to have a character who embodies the elements that we are discussing. Thus, in like manner to Aidan Kavanagh who gave us Mrs. Murphy to consider as a personification of the faithful in the pews,[25] I now introduce a similar character who personifies the process of integrating faith and reason in the liturgy. Let us give a name to this believer who is invited to that integration of faith and reason: Christopher. As a member of the Church, he belongs to a community of faith. It is a community called to be "like a sacrament," that is to be "a sign and instrument of both a very closely knit union with God and of the unity of the whole human race.[26] By his Baptism, together with other believers Christopher is to be an image of the communion of persons of the Most Holy Trinity. He represents the believer in the pew, spiritually formed[27] as he enters into the celebration, hearing and speaking of liturgical language, participating in its gestures. Thus, a blind faith is not at work, but rather faith that interacts with reason, faith that can perfect the intellect.[28]

Further, to understand liturgical language, Christopher will engage heart, body, and mind. He does not enter into "mindless ritual."[29] Liturgical language, the *lex orandi*, or law of prayer will inform Christopher, not only in the liturgical moment, but in his life generally. The Church's public prayer has long been known to affect those apt to encounter God. For example, the experience of St. Anthony of the Desert comes to mind, when he heard the words of the Gospel of St Matthew spoken directly to him: "Go and sell . . . , then, come follow Me . . . ."

Christopher (a name meaning "Christ bearer") is a child of his times, the fruit of spouses who would have been new parents sometime in the

---

23. Kavanagh, *On Liturgical Theology*, 146ff.
24. I clarify "common" to mean the objective event that occurs before the assembled community.
25. Kavanagh, *On Liturgical Theology*, 146.
26. *Lumen Gentium* (LG hereafter), ch. 1, 1.
27. Albeit, this formation is unique to each individual.
28. Aquinas, *ST*, II/II, q.1, art. 3, ad 1.
29. Fagerberg, *Theologia prima*, 138.

mid-1980s. He had a Catholic school education of the time, and received baptism, penance, Eucharist and Confirmation (in that order). His experience would be wholly with the *Novus Ordo*,[30] the Catholic Mass as celebrated in a renewed manner and in a vernacular language after the Second Vatican Council. He comes to Sunday Mass not only with that background, but with the influences of his family life, cultural background, including the various parishes to which he has belonged, and his personal prayer life. In addition, we cannot forget the societal pressures that individuals experience when they identify themselves as Catholic in our post-Christian society; Christopher will have his share of those pressures.

We also cannot overlook the sacramental effects that Christopher has received knowing that he is "fully initiated." He did not simply experience rites of passage, but Christopher carries with him the effects of Christ's paschal mystery. As baptized, he is a child of God; he participates in the family of the Trinity and he has received the gifts of the Holy Spirit, the theological virtues of faith, hope, and charity and the graces of baptism, which allow him to fulfill his vocation to holiness. All the sacraments he has received have had effects on Christopher. The principle popularized by the saying of St Thomas, "grace perfects nature,"[31] is at work in him.

These effects are available to Christopher because, once marked with the sacramental characters of Baptism and Confirmation, he has been changed forever. He is ontologically marked by God as his child.[32] Consequently, Christopher has privileges and consequent obligations within the Church. He is disposed to the actions of the Holy Spirit in his life. While the character of Baptism opens him to the right to participate in liturgical worship, through Confirmation he has obligation in that worship to pray for others. A fuller description of this character and its effects is outside the limits of this essay.[33] Nevertheless, because of both his faith and reason, he has the privilege and obligation to worship and to grow in understanding of what it means to worship.

Having set the stage and introduced Christopher, let us look at what the Church now presents in the living language of liturgy in recent times. In broad brushstrokes, we will consider examples of language and gesture in the contemporary *Novus Ordo*, asking how the liturgical prayers, signs

---

30. Literally, the "new order" of Mass; this is the shorthand term referring to the Mass promulgated as a result of the post conciliar reforms.

31. Aquinas, *ST*, I, q. 1, art. 8, ad. 2.

32. CCC 1274.

33. For more discussion of the sacramental character, see O'Neill, *Meeting Christ*, 155–56.

and symbols, in other words, the *lex orandi*, influence the *lex credendi* for Christopher and all whom he represents.

7. One Element: Vernacular Language

In addition to the gestures and symbols used in worship, the use of vernacular language became an important issue of liturgical reform. SC 36 encouraged a moderate introduction of the vernacular languages into liturgy, but Latin was not to disappear. However, as committees met and bishops' conferences asked for a broader use of vernacular languages within the liturgy, an increasingly wider scope was permitted; until eventually the Sacred Congregation for Divine Worship allowed "for the use of the vernacular in all parts of the Mass" in 1971.[34] Yet, even the most recent edition of the GIRM still insists that the faithful should be comfortable with at least some of the Mass being celebrated in Latin.

This positive tension between becoming familiar with and understanding the proper prayers[35] through the use of the vernacular and the encouragement that a portion of the Mass be prayed in Latin is reasonable. The practical expression of the *lex orandi, lex credendi* principle would be more effectively addressed by the more precise translation of terms from the Latin *and* the use of the religious language of the Church, which helps the Catholic to recall the universal nature of the liturgy. One of the good side effects of the newest promulgation of the RM was the chance for bishops to initiate some faith formation for Christopher and all his fellow Catholics. A quick browse of the internet indicates the many dioceses that have taken the opportunity as the third edition was introduced to promote adult faith formation in relation to the Mass. Consequently, both faith and reason can be engaged profitably with proper formation or catechesis for Christopher.

This faith formation gives opportunities for nuances of the original Latin texts to be explained to the faithful. For example, the more faithful translation of the original Latin (that for arguably pastoral reasons was not used previously in the English translation) now found in the Second Eucharistic Prayer offers an opportunity to deepen an understanding of the Holy Spirit through scriptural and Patristic images.[36]

---

34. Sacred Congregation of Divine Worship, *Notification*, 4.

35. The proper prayers are the specific prayers of a particular feastday, such as Christmas.

36. A discussion of translation theory and Church authority for translations is beyond the limits of this chapter. Much ink has been spilled on the subject. The recent liturgical document on translation, Pope Francis' *Magnum Principium*, may incite further interest in the topic.

The translators of the English language third edition of the RM were guided by the 2001 document *Liturgiam authenticam*, (LA) promulgated by the Congregation of Worship and the Discipline of the Sacraments.[37] Using principles indicated by LA,[38] the translators provided texts that more closely followed the original texts than earlier editions of the RM. Critiques that led to the re-evaluation of earlier editions included the loss of metaphors and the exchange of vocabulary for the sake of inclusive language. Obviously, the danger was that the faith could not be appreciated in its depth and breadth if the vocabulary was watered down, deleted, or substantially altered in meaning. Christopher has a right to the riches of the faith so that he can develop a more profound understanding. The newly translated texts replaced those which had earlier compromised the theology expressed in Latin.

The precision of expression of the translation according to the guidelines of *Liturgiam authenticam* was greeted with appreciation by some and apprehension by others.[39] While we can cite a number of changes in the translation of both the proper prayers and the Order of Mass,[40] we will limit the examples to the latter.

8. Words Make a Difference

Among the translation changes within the Nicene Creed, some of the faithful were taken aback by the exchange of the long familiar "*one in being* with the Father" with "*consubstantial* with the Father." This latter phrase is the more accurate rendering of *consubstantialem Patri*. "Consubstantial" was considered an obscure theological term by the critics. True, it is not a word found in Christopher's everyday vocabulary. It is a term used to define an intricate doctrine that is unique to God and hence one can argue that the use of unfamiliar language is beneficial in liturgy. We do not use this word for any other relationship and it most closely follows the *consubstantialis* of the original text.[41] It identifies the relationship of God the Father and Jesus according to the declaration made by the Council of Nicaea in 325. The Church was in the throes of controversy at that time and the term captured

---

37. Congregation of Worship and the Discipline of the Sacraments, *Liturgiam authenticam*.

38. LA, 56.

39. McManus in "Translation theory in *Liturgiam authenticam*" gives an account and observations of translation theories.

40. The Order of Mass is the frame of the rite, and the proper prayers are specific to each celebration.

41. Turner, *Understanding the Revised Mass Texts*, 22.

the careful and precise description that was adopted to clarify our understanding of the Son of God. In his use of this term, Christopher will not be shortchanged regarding his understanding of this tenet of the faith. Those in teaching roles within the Church have the obligation to inform Christopher of the truths of the faith as precisely as possible.[42]

Another replacement within the Order of Mass is within the priest/assembly dialogue: "The Lord be with you" and the response, "and *with your spirit.*" The response of the people supersedes the less exact translation "and *also with you*" of the earlier editions.[43] Monsignor Bruce Harbert, Executive Director until 2009 of ICEL,[44] grounds this liturgical dialogue in Gal 6:18 and 2 Tim 4:22 and the baptismal bond Christians have with another through the Holy Spirit. The dialogue is not simply a ritual exchange or even a personal exchange. The celebrant has a particular relationship with God through his priestly ordination and this is what Christopher acknowledges in the exchange. The exchange also implicitly acknowledges Christopher's relationship with God, which allows him in faith to make that reply.[45] The less exact "and also with you" kept the relationship on a horizontal level while the more faithful translation communicates the original and fuller meaning of the ecclesial relationship we have with the celebrant, which is rooted in the biblical text and in our vertical relationship with God.[46]

This is another example of liturgical language that is meant to be distinctive from our everyday communication. The use of this language can either provide an opportunity for Christopher to ask the question, "What does this mean for me?" as a Christian (child or adult) or at least stimulate curiosity that might awaken him to a deepened understanding. The direct link to the phrase's origin in Sacred Scripture would allow an uplifting of hearts and/or alert individuals to their ignorance of biblical texts. In doing so, the uniqueness of liturgical language is accentuated once again.

At the Rite of Holy Communion, the celebrant shows the Host to Christopher for adoration with the words, "Behold the Lamb of God, behold him who takes away the sins of the world. Blessed are those called

---

42. On the other hand, one can argue that the phrase "one in being" is not really any more accessible than "consubstantial" was thought to be at the time of the earlier translation.

43. English was the only modern language to translate *Et cum spiritu tuo,* in this way. See the United States Conference of Catholic Bishops website: https://www.usccb.org/prayer-and-worship/the-mass/order-of-mass/and-with-your-spirit

44. ICEL: International Commission for English in the Liturgy.

45. Australian Catholic Bishops' Conference, DVD *One Body One Spirit in Christ.*

46. "Vertical" is used in the sense of a relationship not with peers (other humans) but with God himself.

to *the supper of the Lamb.*" The previous edition of the RM required the celebrant to make this declaration: "This is the Lamb of God who takes away the sins of the world. Happy are those who are called to *his supper.*" While this latter acclamation was true, it was not as accurate a rendition of the Latin as is the current translation. Hearing the earlier version, Christopher was told first of all, "This is . . ." and through the movement of the Mass, the assembly is progressively taken deeper into the mystery. However, this simple statement, true as it is, seems to cause the movement to falter in comparison to the revised translation which seems to draw Christopher into a relationship: "Behold the Lamb of God . . ."[47] Christopher is invited both to direct his gaze, as were John's disciples in John 1:29, and to approach the reception of Holy Communion.

The latter part of the statement: "who are called to *his supper*" lacked the theological depth of the Latin. Christopher could examine his conscience and know himself disposed to receive Holy Communion at this Eucharistic celebration. That is entirely reasonable, but there is more to the liturgical moment. The current rendition directs one's thoughts to the celebration of the here and now, and, more importantly, gives the biblical vocabulary of the wedding feast of the Lamb of Revelation: "Blessed are those called to the marriage supper of the Lamb!" (Rev 19:9) Not only is one prepared to receive Holy Communion at that moment, but one is reminded of the Eucharist as the "pledge of future glory" described by St Thomas Aquinas.[48] Christopher is confronted with the obligations required for the blessedness towards which our Christian life tends. This is further highlighted with Christopher's response: "Lord, I am not worthy that you should enter under my roof, but only say the word and my soul shall be healed." This clear scriptural reference is the centurion's response to Christ's offer to enter his home (Luke 7:6–7). The previous translation had been thinned down to such an extent that some did not recognize the scriptural source and even ridiculed the correction. However, relatedness with the centurion allows Christopher to claim: "Those are now *my* words." The faith of the centurion has been passed on, and as Christ rewarded him, so now may a similar faith be rewarded.

These last examples are illustrative of the anamnetic or memorial nature of the liturgy. The great works of God are recalled and in some way made actually present to Christopher in his liturgical experience.

---

47. This is more faithful to the Latin original which is: *Ecce Agnus Dei, ecce qui tollit peccata mundi. Beati qui ad cenam Agni vocati sunt.*

48. Taken up in SC 47 and CCC in various sections on the Eucharist.

An example of how liturgical language (*lex orandi*) as the spoken word and gesture can enhance Christopher's understanding is found in GIRM 5. There we find a description of how the royal priesthood of the faithful is properly matched with the ministerial priesthood in the liturgy.[49] There are prayers and roles within the Mass specifically of the priest and of the laity illustrating this.[50] GIRM 69 is one example as it indicates that the General Intercessions or Universal Prayer allow "the people [to] respond in some sense to the Word of God which they have received in faith and, exercising the office of their baptismal priesthood, [to] offer prayers to God for the salvation of all." The General Intercessions are to be introduced by the celebrant, but announced by "the deacon or by a cantor, a reader, or one of the lay faithful" and then concluded with a prayer by the celebrant. It is an act of the service of the laity in the liturgy to lead the Universal Prayer. The prayers are to include the needs of the world and the community at large before turning to the more local needs. This example of *lex orandi* illustrates the belief discussed in *Lumen Gentium* and later in the Conciliar decree *Apostolicam Actuositatem*[51] that the laity in the world have a specific role in uplifting and consecrating the world by their prayers and actions. Rational reflection on having this role during the celebration of liturgy can assist individuals to associate the work of liturgy to their daily life. The beating of the wings of faith and reason are thus synchronized and lift individuals in flight.

Besides the Order of Mass, the GIRM contains directives for the content of music at various points of the Mass.[52] As Cardinal Ratzinger (later Pope Benedict XVI), well known for his love of music, instructs: "Whenever man praises God, words do not suffice. Conversation with God transcends human speech and ... it has called to its aid music, singing ... instruments."[53] In pride of place are the antiphons of the RM. However, these scriptural passages may be replaced with other texts that have approval of the Bishops' Conferences.[54] While this key statement, "other texts that have approval of the Bishops Conferences," was already in the GIRM of 1975, it was not

---

49. As baptized, every Christian has a participation in the priesthood of Christ. The ordained or ministerial priesthood is a unique sharing in that priesthood. See CCC 901ff for a fuller explanation.

50. SC 28: "In liturgical celebrations each person, minister or layman, who has an office to perform, should do all of, but only, those parts which pertain to his office by the nature of the rite and the principles of liturgy."

51. See especially LG 33–35 and AA 2.

52. GIRM 48, for example.

53. Ratzinger, "Liturgy and Sacred Music," 377.

54. GIRM 48.

always adhered to and some hymn texts were introduced that did not do justice to the liturgy.[55] In *A New Song for the Lord* Pope Emeritus Benedict XVI discusses a particularly poignant point of the misdirected focus of the liturgy when the *Opus Dei* is obscured by the autonomy of the assembly. He points out that this misdirection allows the focus to become the assembly itself, rather than God's action, which is forming the community of worshippers.[56] The praise is shifted from the Creator towards the creature, thus negating the purpose of the liturgical celebration.

Such a musical approach will have effects on Christopher. For example, as the celebration moves to the Preface dialogue and the priest bids the assembly: "Lift up your hearts," Christopher replies: "We have lifted them up to the Lord!" However, Christopher and the rest of the faithful, already focused on themselves after identifying with a misdirected entrance hymn, have to first adjust their "flight pattern" back to the Lord before they can raise their hearts. The intended attitude of raising one's heart does not reach its potential but falters, and it becomes obvious that the *lex credendi* can then be skewed to a less than complete response.

The utilization of certain hymns at the time of the reception of Holy Communion is another example of a needed coordination of the wings of faith and reason. Some texts commonly heard in parishes through the years speak of bread and wine and fellowship, but not the clear Catholic teaching of the real presence of the Body and Blood of Christ under the forms of bread and wine offered to us by our Lord through the hands of the priest. Clearly, if a teaching is not presented in its fullness, the faithful are likely to have a less than adequate understanding, especially if this inadequate presentation is heard often.[57] Such texts are insufficient for as a catalyst to Christopher's own spiritual flight. Christopher will only fly so high if the teaching he received is inadequate. Thus the GIRM spells out the requirements for appropriate music for the purpose of the faithful gaining transcendent altitude.

The logic of the Mass introduces the faithful to a trajectory of the mystery to be experienced. The elements of the Mass as a whole are designed to assist Christopher to deepen his prayer (the *lex orandi*); the elements are ordered so that as individuals and as a worshipping community the faithful enter into the paschal mystery and are progressively brought deeper into

---

55. We won't enter into the discussion of the appropriateness of the music arrangements.

56. Ratzinger, *A New Song for the Lord*, esp. 146–50.

57. Campbell, "Pastoral Issues in the Translations of Liturgical Text," 104–5.

the mystery. These elements are not haphazard actions and are not meant to take attention away from the Trinity.[58]

9. Another Characteristic: Signs, Symbols, Gestures

Besides spoken words, signs, symbols, and gestures, other actions are also part of liturgical language and play a role in heightening Christopher's experience. Actions coupled with the words can amplify the liturgical experience. As we know, a warm handshake will intensify a greeting, an embrace even more so. In the press conference held at the promulgation of the Latin language third edition, Cardinal Medina Estevez affirmed that the

> ... liturgical books express the *sensus fidei* of the Church, not by means of dogmatic-style formulas, but by means of a classic style of liturgical language, which is nourished not only by words but also by gestures and signs that come from Revelation itself.[59]

Now we will consider instances regarding particular action or gestures which can contribute to the altitude Christopher's wings allow him to reach.

GIRM 160 indicates that the faithful are to make a gesture of reverence by bowing or even genuflecting and to respond "Amen" at the minister's declaration, "Body of Christ/Blood of Christ," before receiving Holy Communion. This rubric had actually been in the previous GIRM, but was rarely carried out. Its frequent omission was probably due to ignorance of its existence rather than to dissenting from its practice. By the addition of the bow,[60] Christopher's response of "Amen" was given a distinctive meaning at this point in the Mass: "Yes! It IS the Body/Blood of Christ" and deserves the honor of a bow. This intentional reverential gesture increases the interior reverence behind the "Amen" of the communicant. The faith of communicants is complemented by their reason for uttering words and undertaking bodily action as both reflect reverence for what communicants are about to receive.

The encouragement of the reception of Holy Communion under both species is another example of the *lex orandi* strengthening the *lex credendi* of

---

58. Cf. CCC 1077ff.

59. Jorge Arturo Cardinal Medina Estévez's intervention at press conference for the Presentation of the Third Typical Edition of the New Roman Missal, 18 March 2002. (Author's translation)

60. As the more common posture in Australia is standing while receiving Holy Communion, we read: "The faithful bow in reverence of the Sacrament they are to receive." GIRM 160.

Christopher. The GIRM of 1975 stipulated fourteen specific occasions when the reception of Holy Communion under both species could be received by the laity.[61] The present GIRM extends those possibilities to the point that the local Bishop may "establish norms in his own Diocese."[62] GIRM 281 acknowledges that "[h]oly Communion has a fuller form as a sign when it is distributed under both kinds" so that the form of a banquet is recognizable. The use of the word "banquet" refers both to the feast spread before us in the Eucharistic celebration and the eschatological marriage supper of the Lamb of the book of Revelation. It can be noted here that GIRM 327–32 instructs that the vessels used for the liturgy are to be of precious metal, artistic, and "distinguishable from vessels intended for everyday use." Such noble vessels will communicate without words the veneration due to the cherished contents.

Nonetheless, GIRM 282 also states the faithful are to be "as fully aware as possible of the Catholic teaching [on concomitance]."[63] Thus, an optional action is not necessarily to be implemented unless it enhances the faith of the people. This might mean that, for the sake of informed faith, a more thorough catechesis is required before reception of both the Body and Blood of Christ is introduced in a parish. The "fuller sign" is really the best sign when those involved understand in some way the theological principle of concomitance *and* the sign value of eating and drinking at a meal as well. We see in this section of the GIRM a good example of how the authors have endeavoured to enrich the understanding of the faithful for a growth of faith through reason.

Conclusion

Most likely lacking an academic degree in theology, Christopher is nonetheless acknowledged by the Church as a primary theologian. Engaging his faith and reason in the liturgy, he experiences an encounter that is like none other and thus he learns about God. Through the supernatural relationship he has with the Trinity and the Church due to his Baptism and the reception of the other sacraments, he listens for the Lord's words communicated to him through liturgical language. Attentive with the eyes and ears of faith, he trusts his relationship with Christ and counts on Mother Church for the

---

61. GIRM of 1975, 242. Before the *Novus Ordo*, the occasions were even more restricted.

62. GIRM 283.

63. Concomitance is the Catholic understanding that under the form of either the bread or the wine that Christ, his Body, Blood, Soul, and Divinity, is wholly present.

authentic transmission of the faith and the development of his understanding through rational reflection. Through a few representative examples, we saw that the Third Typical Edition of the *Roman Missal* can reveal rich treasures for Christopher. His faith and reason can work together to enrich his relationship with the Living God revealed by Jesus Christ and to enhance his understanding of the truth of God. Christopher can be drawn into the paschal mystery of Christ in a manner that transcends a mere study of the liturgical celebration. The theologian's task as outlined in *Fides et Ratio* begins in the experience itself and continues as the dismissal is given: "The Mass is ended. Go in peace."

5

FAITH AND REASON AND METAPHYSICS

—Angus Brook

Introduction

In a time when many philosophers have claimed that metaphysics is dead, and many others in contemporary analytic philosophy who pursue metaphysical questions no longer subscribe to the basic questions or objectives of traditional metaphysics, it is perhaps an oddity that the centrality of traditional metaphysics, particularly the traditional questions of first principles and the first cause of the unity and order of the cosmos, is maintained and promoted in many (if not most) Catholic universities. Part of this can be explained by reference to the centrality of and focus on the philosophy of St Thomas Aquinas, for whom metaphysics was both the beginning and end of philosophical investigations. However, I would suggest that metaphysics was important to St Thomas and remains important to Catholic universities, for more than this reason. The Catholic approach to the integration of faith and reason also provides a justification of the centrality of the philosophy of St. Thomas in Catholic thought, and in particular of the essential place of metaphysics in both philosophical and theological endeavours.

In this chapter I will attempt to justify and provide evidence for the claim that the integration of faith and reason plays a foundational role in understanding the metaphysical system of St. Thomas Aquinas, and further, goes some way to explaining the importance of metaphysics in Catholic universities. The chapter will attempt this justification via an examination of the objectives of metaphysics, the role of faith and reason in metaphysics, and finally, the various possible ways of constituting the relationship between faith and reason as a basis for philosophical investigation of reality. Finally, the chapter will offer some broad observations about how the commitment of the Catholic Church to the integrity of faith and reason also entails a commitment to metaphysics.

1. Re-examining metaphysics

Metaphysics is traditionally defined as the science of first principles and causes.[1] It is a science that begins with human everyday experience of the world as a unified ordered whole and then moves from the particulars of the experience to the universal (principles and causes)[2] through a series of questions about the "reasons why" there is this apparent unity and order. Metaphysics then generally terminates in two discrete, but interrelated, approaches to the question of the explanatory cause of this apparent unity and order in the universe: ontology, the science of being qua being; and natural theology, the science of the identity or identifiable explanatory cause of the unity and order of reality.

First principles are ultimate and universal "reasons why" reality is a unified and ordered community of entities. First principles are ultimate insofar as there are no possible prior or explanatory "reasons why" that unify and order reality underlying them. First principles are universal inasmuch as they must provide the "reason why" of everything and anything, the particular and the ordered relationships between particulars. A first principle orders and unifies through determination and\or differentiation and yet will itself remain indeterminate and undifferentiated.[3] A first principle explains how reality, as a community of entities, is unified and ordered, and yet at the same time, is only knowable or intelligible through our experiences of particular entities and the relations between them. The final thing to note about first principles, at this stage, is that first principles cannot themselves be entities inasmuch as entities are always determinate (and first principles cannot be). A first principle must be something like a concept, or activity, or effect, rather than an entity. A first principle is the foundation of thinking about the ordered and unified reality we experience, and as such, serves as the limit or boundary of what can be thought and experienced.

---

1. Aristotle, *Metaphysics*, Vol.II, Book I, 982b8–10.

2. A principle in this sense is universal. Causes, while determinate, have universal effects. Thus a primary or first cause is universal in effect without being a universal.

3. See Aristotle's discussion of principles in Book V of the *Metaphysics* (1012b32–1013a23).

The question of first principles and causes is a question that faces any philosopher who wants to provide an account of reality irrespective of the approach taken to reality or philosophy. Every science and all attempts to know reality begin with, and depend upon, first principles. It is particularly interesting that most of the "great thinkers" in the philosophical tradition have sought to address the same questions, e.g., that of first principles and causes, and have all begun with everyday human experience, and yet many of them have arrived at markedly different solutions to these questions. Examples of these differences in relation to the notion of the first cause are immediately evident when we glance at the history of philosophy: the demiurge of Plato, the first cause of Aristotle, the cosmos itself in Stoic thought and later in Spinoza, the One in Plotinus, God in medieval philosophy, Absolute Spirit in Hegel, humans ourselves in existentialism, and arguably the universe\multiverse in contemporary analytic philosophy of science.

These differences are not arbitrary and appear to coincide with differences in the very history of the tradition of metaphysics or changes in the way that people have understood or related to reality within history. The Ancient philosophers sought to understand the first principle via a presupposition that perfection unified and ordered the cosmos. In the medieval period, the first principle was clearly grasped within the context of the presupposition that the cosmos is created. With the rise of modern science, the first principle came to be grasped within the presupposition that the cosmos is empirical and physical and thus being came to signify existence in a new way. There is obviously something more going on; something more at stake, in the question concerning first principles and causes than appears at the outset. It is worthwhile, then, briefly returning to the question of what first principles and first causes are. This discussion, in turn, may serve as a basis for defining more precisely what constitutes the "something more" of first principles and causes.

By comparison with first principles, a first cause is an identifiable determinable explanation that serves as the ultimate reason why humans experience reality as a unified and ordered community of entities. The first cause must be thought of as an entity, or something like an entity, for all causes are determinate and determining in their explanatory power.[4] Part of the issue at stake here is knowledge. It is helpful to go back to Aristotle's claim that we can only really know substances, or at the very least, that substances are the framework and limits of human knowledge.[5] To think about

---

4. Aristotle, *Metaphysics*, Book V, 1013a24–1014a25.
5. Aristotle, *Metaphysics*, Book VII, 1028a30–1028b3.

something, we must think about it as something to think about: an identity, a substance.

The problem of the first cause is that it sits at the very boundaries, if not beyond the boundaries, of the human capacity to think. The metaphysician is therefore stuck in an *aporia* of sorts; we have a concept of first cause which is necessary for the explanation of all human knowledge: on the one hand, first principles must be conceived of as an effect of some prior determinate act, and on the other hand, we must think of the first cause as an entity (or substance) to be able to say anything about it at all. Yet, if we are honest we cannot be sure that the first cause should be properly thought of as an entity or whether it is an entity in any sense that we understand entities. This is the case inasmuch as a first cause cannot be physical and thus limited nor can a first cause be defined by an essential definition.

Nonetheless, there is an overarching, if vague, consistency in the posited relationship between first principle and first cause throughout the history of the tradition of metaphysics; there must be inasmuch as first principles are necessarily an effect of an entity or identity of some kind. The only other possibility is to deny that a philosopher has any access to the first cause whatsoever. One consequence of this possibility is the claim that no-thing explains the first principle; that in fact there is no-thing—except freedom perhaps—underlying our understanding of reality as a unified ordered whole.[6] At best, this position proposes a kind of via-negation account of the first cause, i.e., that we cannot know or understand the first cause and thus cannot name it properly. This amounts to a negative theological position that encompasses what remains "un-sayable," a position that is often attributed of philosophers like Pseudo-Dionysius, Maimonides, Heidegger, Derrida, and others.

It is also important to note here that since the notions of subjectivity and objectivity achieved dominance in post-Cartesian philosophy, the question of first principles has generally come to be posed as the question of the a priori principles of the possibility of experience within the structure of the thinking subject (the principles of reasoning). First principles, as such, are assumed to belong to the intellect and are thought to be the 'ground' of experiencing reality. This then leads to an inevitable disjunction between the intellect and reality and raises the question of whether thinking and reality can be unified in any way that grounds the possibility of truth. In this case, the question of first cause cannot be answered insofar as the human

---

6. See Heidegger's works: *The Principle of Reason* (1991), 113; "On the Essence of Ground," in *Pathmarks*, 134, as examples of this kind of argument.

intellect cannot escape its own boundaries to ask the question intriguing us: what is the first cause of the unified and ordered structure of reality?

2. Faith as the Ground of Our Experience of Being

The quest to discover and know first principles and causes begins with our ordinary experience of the world and the basic sense, in our experience, that reality is unified and ordered. This fundamental unity and order of experience is something so self-evident that we rarely ask ourselves how it is possible or why it is the case. When we do, as philosophers, ask questions as to how and why the apparent unity and order of reality we experience is to be explained we find that there are two basic possible responses: (i) that reality is indeed unified and ordered and our experiences reflect reality as it is, or (ii) that it is our intellects that unify and order our experience of reality but that reality may not really be unified and ordered—the appearance of unity and order is an effect or by-product of the activity of the intellect.

We could use reason to evaluate these two possible explanations; in fact, the history of philosophy is arguably nothing much more than an attempt to evaluate these possible explanations of the appearance of unity and order in our experience. Nonetheless, a variety of evaluations have been offered in the history of philosophy and many contradict each other. Reason alone, it seems, is insufficient to arrive at a conclusion about which explanation is true and how that truth is to be justified. There are two dimensions of the problem at this point: (i) the question of how we would go about determining the ground of this apparent unity and order of reality as it is experienced, and (ii) the question of how we would go about evaluating the various, often seemingly mutually exclusive, approaches and arguments offered to explain the unity and order of reality.

This is the point at which the importance of faith emerges as a theme of investigation. Faith, in a general sense, is a kind of trust that serves as the basis for our pursuit of truth. By way of example, the general means by which we learn about science in a classroom is our faith in our teachers and textbooks. In this case, if we did not have faith in either our teachers or the textbooks they provide us with, we would not be open to the truths they are attempting to teach us. As such, we need to note that all of our attempts to explain the unity and order of our experiences entail a prior relationship and commitment to reality that shapes our understanding of experience and therein our explanation of the unity and order of experience. Inherent in this prior relationship and commitment to reality is our capacity to establish a relationship of trust of some kind with the world. I will argue, in fact, that the establishment of this reasoned relationship—what we call philosophy—is grounded in faith in this sense.

3. Faith and Reason and the First Principle (Being)

Metaphysics begins with an experience of being as the ground or first principle of the unity and order of reality. The interpretation of this experience, in turn, is grounded in faith. In this respect, however, faith takes on two key characteristics: a prior trust that there is some kind of truth available to human beings, and additionally, faith in some means or method of attaining that truth, e.g., some kind of *logos* or reason. Faith, as such, proves to be the ground of our experience of being in at least two ways:

(i) Faith as a capacity intrinsically connected to the desire to know why reality appears to be a unified ordered whole

Let us say for the moment that faith in the most general sense (not in the sense of the infused theological virtue nor in the sense of religious faith) can be determined to be intrinsic to the human capacity for the truth insofar as any grasp of truth is grounded upon trust or at least assent to the possibility of truth. It is clear, in this case, that faith must express some capacity of the human intellect to be directed towards the truth as something beyond the individual operations of reason. By this I mean that intrinsic to our desire for truth is: a) an assent to the truth as referring to something extrinsic in some fashion to our intellects, and b) an assent in the actual operations of our intellect to rules of attaining the truth that we do not, as individuals, make up as we go along. We cannot desire or seek the truth, if you will, without a corresponding faith in the truth as the object of our desire, and without a corresponding faith in some characteristic or method\operation of the human intellect that rules and measures our efforts to attain it.

Given that the question of metaphysics is that of the first principles and causes of the unity and order of our experience of reality it follows that the truth that is desired by the metaphysician is an explanatory account of the appearance of that unity and order in our experience. It also thus the case that in the most general way faith will be intrinsic, or at least implicit, in the reasoning of a metaphysician in two ways. In the first instance, we must be open to the possibility that there is some explanation of the apparent unity and order of our experience of reality for metaphysical reasoning to occur. Likewise, it is a requirement of metaphysical investigation that there is in the human intellect a proper method of getting to the truth of the unity and order of our experience of reality. The very possibility of metaphysics, in the most general sense then, requires an assent to the possibility of truth. However, it is also somewhat obvious that this account of faith as a capacity to assent to truth is insufficient to explain the fact that, in approaching metaphysics, and even in asking proto-metaphysical questions, humans have generally already decided or already assented to some kind of preconception about the world of experience. This suggests a second way in which to conceive of faith as the ground of our experience of being:

(ii) Faith as a common or communal relation of trust with reality via a "first cause" and the means by which the first cause is known

It is worth taking note of the fact that philosophical investigation, and especially metaphysical investigation, is undertaken by human beings who have been educated, or formed, within a community. Human beings are social animals in the sense that we are dependent, at almost every level of our existence, upon a community for our well-being and flourishing, not least with regard to the formation of our intellect.[7] It could be argued that the acceptance of the necessity of faith in the human quest for truth, or goodness, or beauty, has its experiential or existential origins in our intrinsic and essential dependence upon community. This is so given the fact that our well-being, flourishing, and intellectual formation as children are only possible on the basis of assent. Children trust—for good or ill—their parents, their caregivers, and the wider community of which they are part, with their very identities and potentialities. This is not per se a conscious assent; it is certainly not free consent, but it is nonetheless assent.

That adults apparently maintain this faith in an active way hides the roots and undercurrents of faith, even in adult life. Faith at its roots is to a certain degree passive and this passivity remains, whether one is conscious of it or not, throughout life. Growing up within a community; being formed intellectually within a community, and therein, forming our orientation towards truth within community requires at least an undercurrent of faith. It is this dimension of community that more often than not forms our prior commitments to the world, which in turn shape the interpretation of our experience of being and orient us towards philosophy in a particular way.

Our community, of course, does not appear ex nihilo. Communities are embedded in history, which in turn is embedded in tradition (or rejection thereof), and the relations between traditions; whether they be relations of conflict or synthesis, fragmentation, unity, or pluralism. Tradition clearly provides the foundation of our preconceptions of reality in all of its basic aspects. In this respect, tradition serves as a reasonable or reasoned

---

7. MacIntryre, *Dependent Rational Animals*, 63–79.

foundation for our orientation to reality; tradition guides and encompasses the communal dialogue and the passing down of common truth claims which are generally held on the basis of well established and long standing rational debate. Likewise, it is also clear that the foundation of this "handing over" or "passing down" of truth claims found in traditions rests upon faith: the capacity of the human being in community to assent to and trust in the wisdom and knowledge of its community.[8]

We may conclude, therefore, that like any other human tradition, current/modern metaphysics is the result of a communal dialogue passing down through history common truth claims about first principles and first cause. This dialogue implicitly contains within itself a preconception of being and further, a prior commitment to explaining the unity and order of our experience of reality. The traditional formulation of metaphysics (as onto-theology; the relation of principle and cause) was established on the basis both of reasoning and of faith: reasoned dialogue and trust\assent.

4. Three Basic Modes of Faith as the Possible Grounds of Philosophical Endeavour

Our attempts to explain the unity and order of our experience of reality begin with a faith orientation towards reality, which in turn serves as the interpretative basis of our experience of being, and thus our preconceptions about reality. In looking at faith as the ground of philosophy, and in particular, the ground of metaphysics, we need to begin with the way faith gives rise to preconceptions of the relationship between thinking, experience, and reality. Three simplified, but historical, philosophical examples may serve to illustrate this point.

The first of these I will call "rationalism." By this I mean the tradition of thought that becomes prominent in the thought of Parmenides, then Pythagoras, later Plato, and which then becomes a prominent approach to metaphysics in the history of philosophy. Rationalism in this sense is a position contrary to modern epistemological rationalism, in that it prioritizes thinking and thoughts with respect to the nature of reality. In what I am calling rationalism, the relationship between thinking, experience, and reality is preconceived as a relationship grounded upon reason itself. It is reason as such that makes sense of experience and the reality grasped in

---

8. Both Cicero and St. Thomas Aquinas appeal to faith as the basis of community in the broadest sense: "the foundation of justice, moreover, is good faith—that is, truth and fidelity to promises and agreements." Cicero, *De Officiis (On Duties)*, Book 1, 23; Aquinas, *Summa Contra Gentiles*, Book 1, Chapter 5.

our experience. Consider asking the question: what makes something real? If the immediate response to this question is based on the preconception noted above then "our idea or conception via reason" provides the ground of the reality of something. It is our ideas that serve as the ground of explaining why individuals are what they are. This preconception then gives rise to two further explanations of ground; what we might call "idealism," where we conclude that reality must be in, or the product of, some intellect, or dualism, where we conclude that there must be two kinds of reality—the intellectual and the physical—both of which will be explained by some prior "reason" for their distinction, e.g., an explanation of evil, corruption, or change, the immortality of the soul, and so on. . . . In rationalism, metaphysics tends to become dogmatic (as Kant calls it in the *Critique of Pure Reason*).[9]

The second example I will call "empiricism." Like rationalism, empiricism finds its roots in Ancient Greek thought and is always marked by a prioritization of the objects of experience with respect to the nature of reality. Empiricism, in metaphysics rather than epistemology, has also always tended towards a focus on the material composition of the objects of experience. In what I am calling empiricism, the relationship between thinking, experience, and reality is preconceived as a relationship grounded upon experience. It is experience herein that makes sense of thinking and reality. We may again ask the question, what makes something real? In an approach analogous to that taken above in relation to "rationalism," the answer that follows from the preconception noted is generally: it is the individuals (individual entities) that we experience that serve as the ground for our thinking and our account of reality. This enables us to infer that the products of the mind, especially concepts or universals, are simply words or at best social constructs, which describe our experiences. Nonetheless, this preconception of the relationship will generally give rise to the conclusion that reality is simply to be explained by the physical individuals that we experience and that universals, or indeed, any claim to a unified and ordered reality is an illusion—or at best—a feature of calculated statistical probability. Within this preconception metaphysics becomes an illusion.

In moderate realism, or what we might call the "Aristotelian tradition," the relationship between thinking, experience, and reality is preconceived as a synthetic relationship; a relationship in which unity and order is prior to any apparent differences. It is "being" as the preconceived unity of thinking, experience, and reality that makes sense of the relationship. When we ask the question: what makes something real? the answer that emerges

---

9. Kant, *Critique of Pure Reason*, 424, 591–92.

from this preconception is that "being" is the ground (or first principle) of reality. From this, a metaphysician will infer that individuals are real; that universals are real in individuals (substantial and accidental forms) and in the relationships between individuals (e.g., concepts such as justice, causal laws of nature, etc.); and that reality is an ordered unified community of individuals in relation with one another. In short, traditional metaphysics (onto-theology proper) is only possible on the ground of a preconception of a synthetic relationship between thinking, experience, and reality.

In each of these—admittedly simplified—philosophical examples, it is a preconception of the relationship between thinking, experience, and reality that serves as the ground of a philosophical account of reality. In each case, however, these preconceptions are themselves grounded upon prior commitments towards reality. A rationalist has a prior commitment to reason; an empiricist a prior commitment to sense experience; and a moderate realist a prior commitment to unity and order. In each case, the prior commitment serves as a hermeneutic key; a foundational principle for the investigation of reality.

It is important to note at this point that we can only understand these prior commitments in terms of some kind of trust or assent that justifies our prior commitments. We only hold commitments, in this sense, on the basis that we already believe that what we desire can be gained through that commitment and through no other prior commitment. This phenomenon, of grounding our preconceptions of the world on the basis of trust (or faith) is so widespread it would be difficult to find an example of its absence.

5. Faith as a Relation of Naming the First Cause

Let us say for a moment that all humans—especially those with philosophical or metaphysical inclinations—have an experience of some identifiable cause of "being"; the unifying and ordering principle of our experience of reality. The experience itself might be vague, it might be almost unnoticeable and so remain un-thought, or it might be mystical. No matter the quality of the experience, it nonetheless must be assented to, even if merely passively, if it is to serve the basis of our investigation of reality. This experience, then, will give rise to the possibility of an intellectual relation to the first cause in the form of naming it as an identity. However, because of the very nature of the experience that underlies the origins of metaphysics—the experience of unity and order, and further, the fact that the very subject matter of metaphysical investigation is being itself—there are really only a limited number of modes of faith that can serve as the necessary preconception of metaphysics.

It is important to note that these possible modes of faith, in this respect, are markedly different to those we passively accept from our tradition or community. These are modes of faith that arise out of a more considered and informed engagement with our experience. They are modes of faith that in effect mark a reflective response to a certain amount of experience and a degree of intellectual engagement (or disengagement) with the tradition\community in which we have been formed. One could argue that these modes of faith, which constitute an intellectual naming of the first cause arise out of something like an intellectual conversion experience. Certainly, this appears to be the case with a philosopher like Martin Heidegger, whose early phenomenological interpretations of philosophy clearly arise out of a sustained quasi-religious-intellectual conversion experience of sorts.[10]

These modes of faith must nonetheless be intrinsically connected to those modes of faith that serve as the ground of philosophical endeavours. However, in the case of metaphysical investigation, they tend to operate as a way of 'naming' the first cause inasmuch as the first cause becomes apparent through a more reflective approach to the experience of being. The boundaries of the experience and the nature of being itself suggest the three following possible modes of faith:

(i) That we assent to a likeness (or analogy) between being and the first cause

(ii) That we assent to a disjunction or difference (equivocation) between being and the first cause

(iii) We assent to an identity (univocity) between being and first cause

If we look at the history of metaphysics, we can clearly identify these three modes of faith. Most forms of rationalism assert a univocity of being and first cause and most forms of physicalism\empiricism assert an equivocity of being and first cause. Classical philosophers in the pre-enlightenment, who take a moderate realist approach to metaphysics, ergo: Aristotle, Averroes, Maimonides, and Aquinas, all assert some kind of analogy between being and first cause; and all likewise assert the integrity of faith and reason.

Thus far, this chapter has covered the role of faith in philosophy in a variety of ways. While each of these ways is related, each underpins the possibility of a particular approach to metaphysics, as is evident in the history of the tradition of philosophy. Within this tradition we also find that the

---

10. See van Buren, "Martin Heidegger, Martin Luther" or Theodore Kisiel, "On Becoming a Christian."

faith through which our experience of being and first cause are interpreted also informs our account of the relationship between faith and reason.

There are, as such, at least four ways of talking about faith that are relevant to metaphysics. The first is what might be called our ordinary or everyday faith; the faith constituted by an assent to our community and to reality that forms our orientation towards the truth in a general sense. The second is faith as it serves as a mode of interpreting our experiences of being that then serves as the ground of various philosophical accounts of reality, e.g., rationalism, empiricism, and moderate realism. The third is faith as a mode of interpreting our experience of the first cause as an identity to be named, whether it be a relation of univocal, equivocal, or analogical naming. Finally, then, we also talk about faith in the context of the way in which we constitute its relationship with reason.

6. The Relation between Faith and Reason in Philosophical Approaches to Reality

The question about the relationship between faith and reason is entirely dependent on how we have already made sense of the unity and order of our encounters with reality and the mode of faith we bring to our philosophical endeavours. The mode of faith we bring to our philosophical endeavours determines, in advance, how we will define faith and reason and in turn our account of the relationship between them. There are, in the end, only four primary ways of relating faith and reason.

The chapter has thus far only been discussing faith and reason in the broadest of senses. However, when we turn to accounts of the relationship between faith and reason in philosophy it is important to note that these accounts are almost always constituted within the discussion of a relationship between religious faith and reason. I would suggest that this is not a problematic transition to make inasmuch as the distinction between ordinary faith and religious faith is not one of form, but rather, of the object of faith. In both ordinary and religious faith, we trust in a source of truth; in both, we trust in a means to get to the truth; and in both we assent to a particular kind of authority for the acquisition of truth.

If we have faith, at the outset, in our immediate experience as a literal source of truth as is found in empiricism, physicalism, and various forms of religious fundamentalism we will inevitably define faith and reason in a particular way. Religious faith will be defined, as it is in some of Søren Kierkegaard's writings, as purely subjective; something that is personal, private, and involves a passionate and committed relationship with God.[11] In a corresponding way, reason can be constituted as "scientific rationality"; an objective rationality that refers stringently to a method of description and explanation of physical change and movement. In this account of faith and reason, both faith and reason have been reduced; faith to a purely subjective relation to God, reason to mere empirical explanation and description. "Fideism," or literalism, leads to a reductionist account of both faith and reason, and yet at the same time, rests solely on a faith in experience.

If we begin with a faith in reason itself as the source of truth, as in rationalism, we invariably find a consequent subsuming of faith into rationality itself. In Kant, for example, the consideration of religion within the bounds of mere reason leads to a conception of "pure religious faith" that is at the same time, a "plain rational faith"; a faith reduced to rational beliefs in God, the freedom of the will, the principles of good and evil, and the hope for the immortality of the soul.[12] Religious faith, as such, is merely reason as it refers to necessary but non-objective rational principles.

Another approach to the relationship between faith and reason involves a kind of dualist account of reality, sometimes referred to as a "double truth"[13] account of human attempts to explain the unity and order of reality. This account takes on board the perceived strengths of "fideism" and "rationalism," attempting to hold both faiths in the same account of reality whilst still holding faith and reason to be completely distinct from each other. As such, this dualistic account of the relationship between faith and reason holds that we can get to the truth via a faith in experience and via a faith in reason. However, the truths we arrive at separately in both arenas may well contradict each other. Attempts to resolve these contradictions often then lead to a distinction between kinds of truth or aspects of reality, e.g., a distinction between "subjective" and "objective," between religious truth and truths about the world, between necessary and contingent truth, or eternal and temporal, and so on. . . . The dualistic approach to the relationship of faith and reason does not tend to lead to a very coherent account of reality or human persons, and also tends to lead to overly complex explanations of how both kinds of faith can be held at the same time.[14]

11. Kierkegaard, *Concluding Unscientific Postscript*.

12. Kant, *Religion within the Boundaries of Mere Reason*, 112.

13. The paradigmatic example of 'double truth' is found in Averroes's investigation of the intellectual soul in which he finds no philosophical grounds to support the Islamic belief in individual immortal souls, but rather, that there is only one intellectual soul shared by all. See Campanini, *An Introduction to Islamic Philosophy*, 113–22.

14. I am thinking here of Duns Scotus as an example, who held that the meaning of being is univocal (existence), that the relation between first principle and first

If we begin with a faith in unity and order as the source of truth, as in the Aristotelian approach to metaphysics, we invariably find a consequent harmony or integrity of faith and reason. In the thought of St. Thomas, this integrity is marked by an analogy between faith and reason in the unifying and ordering of the objective of truth; religious faith supplements and fulfils (but also increases and transforms), without contradiction, the truths found by reason.[15] Reason, in this sense, is the human intellectual capacity to grasp being and the activity of pursuing universal truth (primarily first principles and the first cause). Equally, faith expresses the human capacity to assent to the truth; to trust in the source of truth.

If we look generally at the history of philosophy we find that there is a pattern and structure to the various accounts of the relationship of faith and reason that follows from the faiths that underpin it. The table below is intended to provide a simplified overview of this pattern:

Mode of Faith	Account of the primary feature(s) of reason	The relationship of faith and reason	Primary way of saying "being" in relation to first cause	Expressions of this mode of faith
Faith in sense experience	Description, calculation, probability, naming	Fideism (faith in experience alone—literalism)	Equivocity	Scientism, religious fundamentalism, empiricism\physicalism
Faith in reason	Ideas, universal unchanging forms or concepts	Rationalism (the subsuming of faith within reason)	Univocity	Platonic realism, gnosticism, rationalism, idealism, pessimism, some forms of dualism, etc.
Faith in unity and order	The activity of unifying and ordering. Reason rules and measures.	The integrity of faith and reason	Analogy	Traditional metaphysics (onto-theology) Aristotle, Ibn Rushd, Thomas Aquinas, etc.

cause is equivocal, and that analogical naming only pertained to the unity and order of creation as intelligible by the human intellect. See Duns Scotus, *Philosophical Writings*, 2–5, 15–16.

15. Aquinas, *Summa Contra Gentiles*, Book 1, chapter 5.

Dualism of faith and reason	Thinking, ideas, universal unchanging concepts	Faith and reason are disjunctive (either\ and\or). The attempt to include both faith and reason while holding them to be completely different	Being = univocal Universals drawn from experience = analogical Naming first cause = equivocal	Avicenna, Duns Scotus, Heidegger, etc..

It is impossible for a human being, and therefore a philosopher and metaphysician, to avoid having faith in the various senses explored thus far, just as much as it impossible for a human being to avoid reason. It is impossible, at least in part, because the human intellect cannot: a) get behind itself to demonstrate its own first principles, making faith in certain self-evident principles necessary in any system of knowledge, and b) cannot escape the boundaries of reality as we experience it to provide demonstrative understanding of the first cause, making faith in a causal explanation of reality necessary for any system of knowledge production. In short, we cannot pretend to get rid of faith in our systems of knowledge production, our quest for truth, any more than we can get rid of reason. The only question concerning faith and reason in philosophy and in metaphysics is: *which account of faith and reason is true?* In answering this question, we are trying to establish which account is actually faithful to the reality of our quest for truth, and which account is most reasonable? This is, whether we are aware of it or not, the matter at stake in the various philosophical accounts of reality and the debates in the history of philosophy about how to get to the truth.

Conclusion: Faith and Reason and Metaphysics in the Catholic Tradition

At the beginning of this chapter I claimed that the integration of faith and reason plays a foundational role in understanding the metaphysical system of St. Thomas Aquinas, and further, goes some way to explaining the importance of metaphysics in Catholic universities. At this point I think I have shown, at the very least, that a prior faith in the unity and order of reality gives rise to a commitment to the integration of faith and reason, which then goes hand in hand with a commitment to traditional metaphysics. Inasmuch as traditional Christian communities (also traditional Jewish and Islamic communities) assent to a shared experience of a unified and ordered reality that expresses the creative act of a personal God, those communities will also be committed to the integration of faith and reason and will likewise tend to commit to a moderate realist metaphysical account of reality.

A Final Point

There has always been a close and intrinsic relationship between the concept of universals and the notion of unifying and ordering. It is arguable that universals (ideas\forms) in philosophical accounts of reality are nothing other than unifying and ordering principles, e.g., the idea of human nature refers simply to the reality of what it is to be human and is that which unifies and orders individual humans in all of our activities. Likewise, we talk about a universe or a university precisely because they are unified and ordered communities; they are "one" insofar as they are unified and ordered aggregates, rather than being one individual entity. A faith in unity and order, as such, is first and foremost a fidelity and assent to reality itself as it shows itself to us in experience as a cosmos—a community of individuals which are unified and ordered; not merely as the individuals present to our senses nor as universal ideas manifest as shadows on the wall of our experience, but rather, what really is there and given to us in all forms of experience.

The thought of Thomas Aquinas and metaphysics are important in a Catholic\Christian university because metaphysics is an inevitable expression of the integration of faith and reason. It is clear in the light of the Encyclical *Fides et Ratio*, that this integration is a necessary condition of being a philosopher in a Catholic context. However, I would suggest that the thought of St. Thomas and the discipline of metaphysics are important beyond this commitment to the integration of faith and reason. After all, this commitment only makes sense if we already have faith in unity and order, if we already have faith that reality really is at least analogous to how it appears to be. To have faith in unity and order is to think with fidelity and to be humble in assenting to reality. The truth that we seek in both faith and reason is not something of our own creation. Rather, the truth is found only when our thinking conforms to how reality is, and when our thinking conforms to what shows itself when we pay attention to reality.[16] In summary, the objective of faith and reason—truth—is found when the human

---

16. Aquinas, *Disputed Questions on Truth*, Volume 1, Question 1, Article 1: What is Truth? See also St. Augustine, *Of True Religion*, xxxvi.

intellect faithfully conforms itself to reality; this is the point of origin of the integration of faith and reason, of metaphysics as a discipline, and of the priority of both in a Catholic University.

6

COMPASSION AS A RESOURCE FOR PLURALISTIC SOCIETIES

—Annette Pierdziwol

One of the major challenges facing contemporary democratic societies is how to foster social stability—and, perhaps even more, flourishing—in the face of their increasing pluralism.[1] The deep-seated internal diversity characteristic of democracies is viewed, on the one hand, with pride as their great achievement—"the inevitable outcome of free institutions"[2]—and, on the other hand, with growing anxiety as the cause of increasing disagreement, division, and even violence.

Interestingly, these worries and accompanying diagnoses of the problems of pluralism are ones in which deep religious commitments are often assumed to be key culprits. What Rawls called "comprehensive views" about "highest things: for religion, for philosophical views of the world, and for moral conceptions of the good"[3]—but perhaps especially religious doctrines—are thought to be held with the kind of passionate commitment that generates irreconcilable clashes with competing views. As such,

---

1. Earlier versions of this essay were presented at the Australian Political Theory and Philosophy Conference at the University of Sydney, the ASCP Annual Conference at the University of Tasmania, and a workshop on Political Liberalism and Emotion with Professor John Haldane organised by the Institute for Ethics & Society (IES) at The University of Notre Dame Australia. I'm grateful for helpful comments from these audiences, as well as for feedback from the reviewers and editors of this volume and from my IES colleague Timothy Smartt. This project was supported by a research grant from the Australian Research Theology Foundation.

2. Rawls. *Political Liberalism*, 4.

3. Rawls. *Political Liberalism*, 4.

questions about faith and reason are more often than not questions about faith, reason, *and society*. Epistemological debates consistently morph into moral, social, and political concerns.

In this chapter, I begin by sketching the historical context surrounding narratives about faith, reason, and society in western thought—from the Enlightenment to today. By highlighting some of the assumptions made by these narratives, I show that the task of specifying the nature and causes of the problems faced by contemporary pluralistic societies is more complicated than is often countenanced. In the second section, I consider the potential "solutions" and resources that have been offered thus far by philosophers. I argue that much recent philosophy has focussed almost exclusively on fashioning a *political* solution to the challenges posed by radical pluralism, seeking to carefully specify the role the state must play in order to secure social stability. The dominance of this approach in political philosophy has, I argue, led to a wider tendency to overlook potential resources to be found elsewhere at the social level, especially in the affective realm and in the emotional and motivational resources of human psychology. To develop this point, I draw on some of Martha Nussbaum's recent work in *Political Emotions* (2013). In the final section, I extend Nussbaum's approach by developing one example of this kind of resource, namely, that of cultivating compassion or empathic concern with those in need. A further interesting pay-off of the argument will be to show that while, as noted, religion is often assumed to be one of the key causes of conflict in pluralistic societies, it turns out that the key emotional resource Nussbaum draws to our attention has a great deal in common with the emphasis of certain faith traditions on cultivating love of neighbor.

1. Faith, Reason, and Society

Debates about the relation between faith and reason in modern thought are often depicted as occurring on epistemological terrain. Standard narratives of modernity encourage us to imagine Enlightenment thinkers concerned about truth, justification, knowledge, and the rational foundations for religious knowledge as they grappled with redefining rationality in the new scientific age. These narratives depict philosophers engaged in battles to expose religious faith as non-rational, passionate and even fanatical.[4] Meanwhile counter-narratives put forward examples of those who sought to defend the

---

4. For a brief overview of the rise of the religious fanatic as "one of the stock characters of modernity," see Cavanaugh, "The Invention of Fanaticism."

idea of a reasonable faith and continued in the vein of premodern theories in which faith, reason, and the passions were inseparably intertwined.[5]

Yet, epistemological questions about the truth and rationality of faith were not the only questions vexing thinkers in the modern period, and these questions did not occur in a vacuum. Rather, as Jennifer Herdt has argued, they arose within a broader set of social and political concerns and in particular within a "concern over the relation between religious belief and institutions and society."[6] As Herdt contends, "the history of modern religious thought" is better understood "in terms of the whole course of reflection about the relationship between religion and society, which emerges out of a concern about how to secure peace in a world of pervasive disagreement over theological matters."[7]

At stake in reflections upon faith and reason, then, was never merely an intellectual "crisis of belief," as new kinds of scientific rationality clashed with "traditional intellectual authorities."[8] Rather, at the center of such debates were "practical concerns about the destructive effects of religious conflict."[9] Writing in the aftermath of the religious wars and the experience of increasing Christian disunity,[10] thinkers were interested in the consequences of certain religious beliefs and institutions; in what they meant for the moral character of individuals and communities, for social cohesion and designing political arrangements.[11] The question that motivated and gripped them, Herdt argues, was how to secure the peace, stability and even flourishing of society. And if, as many had begun to suspect, it was no longer possible nor desirable to return to the kind of religious homogeneity—the broadly Christian and Catholic culture—that had characterized Western Europe in the Middle Ages, then what were the available options

---

5. For some examples along these lines see contributions in Coakley, *Faith, Rationality and the Passions*. Summing up this counter-narrative, Coakley writes: "the Enlightenment presents no unified voice on these issues, then; and whilst it may have spawned one sort of problematic divide between religious fanaticism and reasonable 'religion,' there was no one way in which it consistently drove a wedge between reason and affectivity *tout court*. There remains a more complicated story to be told on that front." (Coakley, 'Introduction: Faith, Rationality and the Passions," 4).

6. Herdt, *Religion and Faction*, 226.

7. Herdt, *Religion and Faction*, 225.

8. Herdt, *Religion and Faction*, 225.

9. Herdt, *Religion and Faction*, 225.

10. John Haldane writes that "whereas in the Middle Ages, Western Europe formed a broadly Christian culture, and more specifically a Catholic one, religious homogeneity then gave way to Christian disunity which in turn became part of a greater diversity of belief and unbelief" (Haldane, *Faithful Reason*, 170).

11. Herdt, *Religion and Faction*, 226.

for securing stability and cohesion? Questions such as these go beyond the terrain of epistemological debate about the rationality of religious beliefs. They propelled modern thinkers into moral, social, and political philosophy—with all three often entangled.

Turning to the contemporary context, the relationship between faith, reason, and society continues to exercise us—and perhaps even more so as the internal diversity of democratic societies continues to increase. Such societies are no longer just dealing with the Christian disunity characteristic of the early modern period but with a much wider diversity of belief and unbelief, one which involves a thoroughgoing pluralism of comprehensive views on the meaning and purpose of life that coexist within the same nation, city, and neighborhood. In this context, discussions about the rationality of certain beliefs and values continue to be closely intertwined with practical concerns about their social implications. What might this or that comprehensive view mean for our precarious social fabric—our ability to live and act together?

Most political theorists and social actors within contemporary Western democracies worry that an increasing pluralism of mutually opposed comprehensive views poses a serious threat to social stability. Some worry that pluralism might water down the motivation to help those in need and undermine the willingness to make sacrifices for the sake of the common good, both within one's society and even more so when it comes to assisting those beyond it. For instance, many collective action problems—that is, problems which can only be solved by a group action rather than an individual action, such as reducing carbon emissions or ending slavery—require all or most social actors to agree on what's morally good or important. Others worry that the disagreement characteristic of pluralistic societies might cause physical conflict. Concerns about the social consequences of pluralism thus range across a spectrum from worries about disagreement and disunity, through to social tension, discrimination, and injustice, and then to fears of violence and even civil war. Conditions of radical pluralism seem, at best, to pose challenges to the mutual flourishing and civic virtue of society, and at worst, to fundamentally undermine the basic preconditions for the stability, safety, and very existence of society.

Interestingly, even within the contemporary recognition of a more wide-ranging pluralism of views, religious beliefs continue to be singled out as particularly concerning. Perhaps still under the influence of a certain Enlightenment legacy, religious views are assumed to be one of the most problematic contributors to the depth of disagreement and severity of division that we see in contemporary society. Suspicions still linger about the sub-rational nature of religious belief and the kinds of passionate disagreement thought to be typical of arguments about what Rawls called "highest things"—disagreements which people of faith are thought to be particularly prone, and whose worst excesses are taken to be evidenced in the actions of extremists of varying stripes. In popular literature against religion, "new atheists" warn about the spectre of violence and religious wars arising within western pluralistic societies.[12]

In the contemporary context then, much as Herdt argued for modern religious thought, concerns about faith and reason are still bound up with concerns about society. Discussion about the rationality or irrationality of religious belief, of their grounds and justifiability, are intertwined with and motivated by practical concerns about their social implications for our common life.

2. The Challenges Facing Pluralistic Societies

At this point, two significant questions arise. The first relates to the nature of the *problems* faced by pluralistic societies and the need to better understand their causes. The second question relates to the *solutions* these require and the resources available for constructing them. It is the solutions that are my primary interest in this chapter, but first a few words on the problems in order to clarify the terrain.

The first question relates to some key assumptions that are at play in accounts of the *causes* of social disagreement, division, tension, injustice, conflict, and violence—as well as the implied causal links between these. For instance, one might wonder whether it is indeed the case that disagreements over "highest things" have been the major casual driver historically of division and conflict. John Haldane raises this objection in relation to Rawls' assumption that it is philosophical disagreement which gives rise to political disagreement. Haldane writes:

> This invites two questions. First, is philosophical disagreement as widespread and as extensive as a reading of Rawls would suggest? Are philosophical issues present in the very midst of political life? Second, even to the extent that they may be present in the background, do they actually yield political disagreement?
>
> If one thinks about the circumstances of political dispute as those pose challenges for political regimes, there is certainly a good range of grounds of disagreement. One such involves issues of cultural diversity. This need not be about competing

---

12. For example, Harris, *The End of Faith*.

comprehensive doctrines; rather it may relate to behavioural and life-style differences arising from the mixing of cultures.[13]

Another example is issues of economic disparity and inequality serving to create division in society and politics. Haldane raises the idea that there are a wide range of grounds for disagreement that impact upon the possibility of securing a peaceable political order—all of which may not be causally reducible to clashes of competing comprehensive doctrines.

Further doubts about the causal connection between religion and social discord are raised within the work of William Cavanaugh, which focuses in particular on scrutinising the role that religious disagreement is often thought to play in causing violence. Cavanaugh seeks to carefully trace the historical emergence of the idea that "religion has a dangerous tendency to provoke and exacerbate violence" and the explanatory assumption this idea often contains that religion "has this lamentable tendency because it is an essentially non-rational impulse, a passion that frequently eludes or exceeds the attempts of reason to tame it."[14] Cavanaugh traces what he terms "the invention of fanaticism" through Enlightenment thinking to our own time and queries the purpose this narrative has served. He writes that "[r]eligion as passionate and non-rational is not a fact but a construction of the modern West"; religion is "not a transhistorical and transcultural dimension of human life, but a category with a history tied up with the rise of the modern state in the West."[15] In this connection, Cavanaugh seeks to show how "the construction of 'religious fanaticism' can promote secularist rationales for violence."[16] Charges of fanaticism and religious violence can be mobilized to justify the power of civil authority, and even to authorize and excuse certain kinds of violence on behalf of the secular nation-state, particularly towards those taken to be beyond the bounds of reasonableness and persuasion.

Cavanaugh's account raises an interesting question about the challenges facing pluralistic societies. Most contemporary work on pluralism and social stability seems to take for granted a fundamental motivation to avoid conflict and violence and to secure peace and stability for society as a whole and each of its members. Cavanaugh's reading, however, raises a suspicion about whether violence is in fact our greatest worry or whether it is perhaps only certain types of violence we mind: "Religious violence is fanatical and irrational; secular violence is rational and peace-loving."[17] He

13. Haldane, *Practical Philosophy*, 247.
14. Cavanaugh, "The Invention of Fanaticism," 29.
15. Cavanaugh, "The Invention of Fanaticism," 30.
16. Cavanaugh, "The Invention of Fanaticism," 30.
17. Cavanaugh, "The Invention of Fanaticism," 38.

reminds us that violence comes in many forms and is done in the service of many "gods." His own work highlights the often overlooked (and frequently justified) violence of the state, but once we start looking, we may well identify other forms of society-undermining violence with which liberal democracies have made an uneasy peace.

Questions could also be raised about the common assumption that disagreement inevitably leads to conflict. We might wonder whether this is really the case and, where it appears to be so, whether there any other important factors involved. It is not unusual to find people with deeply held disagreements who yet remain close, whether with family members, colleagues or neighbors. Psychologist Alison Gopnik raises a similar question about the causes of political and cultural divides in the US when she notes the way marriage counsellors advise that relationships can weather fundamentally different values and misunderstanding, but what they cannot survive is contempt. As in interpersonal relationships, so too on the larger scale of social relationships, she argues that the real problem may be the loss of "a background of trust and commitment that allows conflict without contempt."[18] In other words, what's needed may have less to do with minimizing disagreement and more to do with cultivating bonds of affection and mutual commitment. I will return to this theme in section four.

The critical analyses raised above suggest that questions remain about our understanding of the *causes* of social division and violence, and about the specific role which philosophical and religious disagreements about comprehensive doctrines play in this problem. Arguments from Haldane, Cavanaugh, and Gopnik give us reason to think religious disagreements are often given too much weight in contemporary accounts of social instability. A more careful study of these causes would be one area worthy of further investigation for those interested in untangling narratives around faith, reason, and their relation to the problems of pluralism being discussed in contemporary social and political philosophy. Careful historical and empirical work is needed to provide a better understanding of the challenges facing contemporary democratic societies, and of the unique ways their stability and motivational resources are being threatened. As this work continues, critical engagement with the assumptions underlying the narratives we currently rely upon can help us avoid jumping to simplistic diagnoses of the challenges pluralism presents and, likewise, proposing quick fixes that miss the mark. Instead, greater understanding of the nature of these challenges and their causes can help inform more nuanced solutions. This is work largely yet to be done—or at least yet to be integrated into philosophical

---

18. Gopnik. "When Truth and Reason Are No Longer Enough."

discussion of these topics. In the next section, I briefly survey the main answer which has been proposed thus far by philosophers and consider its limitations.

3. The Political Solution for Pluralistic Societies, and Its Limitations

Within contemporary political philosophy, the most prominent and influential articulation of the challenges posed by pluralism can be found in the work of John Rawls and the brand of political liberalism it inspired.[19] Rawls argues that the "fact of pluralism," which he views as a positive and necessary feature of democracy, presents a fundamental practical challenge to the possibility of a decent society. As he famously formulates it: "how is it possible for there to exist over time a just and stable society of free and equal citizens, who remain profoundly divided by reasonable religious, philosophical, and moral doctrines?"[20]

For Rawls and his followers, the answer lay in fashioning a *political* solution. Given, they argue, that the idea of society as a unified community (or communitarian state) is no longer feasible or desirable, what is needed is to carefully specify the role the state must play in order to secure social stability. The task is to find those fundamental political principles and constitutional ideals that can form the basis of an overlapping consensus in a radically pluralistic society. As Martha Nussbaum sums up this strand in her own career: "My own work, like a lot of philosophical work in the past few decades, has discussed political institutions and laws, making general arguments about what justice is and what basic rights or entitlements all citizens have."[21] The achievement of political liberalism was to inaugurate this change of focus: "The scene of action shifts from society as a comprehensive whole to the political realm itself, and to its strategies to makes its ideals prevail in a world of pluralism."[22]

---

19. For a recent comprehensive history of this brand of political liberalism, see Forrester, *In the Shadow of Justice*.

20. Rawls, *Political Liberalism*, 4.

21. Nussbaum, *The Monarchy of Fear*, 12. Or, as she puts it elsewhere: the focus is on "the fundamentals of its own conception of justice (such as the equal worth of all citizens, the importance of certain fundamental rights, and the badness of various forms of discrimination and hierarchy). We might say that a liberal state asks citizens who have different overall conceptions of the meaning and purpose of life to overlap and agree in a shared political space, the space of fundamental principles and constitutional ideals." (Nussbaum, *Political Emotions*, 7).

22. Nussbaum, *Political Emotions*, 132.

Thus, while philosophical debate over these "strategies" has continued, there has been a point of broad agreement in terms of approach. Discussion about the challenges, resources, and prospects (whether pessimistic or hopeful) for contemporary democratic societies has largely occurred on the terrain of the political. Solutions to Rawls' question of the possibility of "a just and stable society" are pursued via attempts to explicate the fundamental political principles and constitutional ideals such a society would need to have. The idea being that if the political legitimacy of the state's arrangements and coercive laws could be demonstrated—namely, if we could find a political conception of justice that could be accepted by all citizens from within the perspective of their own competing comprehensive views—then we would have our solution. With this in place, justice and social stability would follow.

Questions have, however, been raised by some about whether this preoccupation with how to arrange and justify the ideal political order of the state is somewhat misguided. Even amongst those largely supportive of political liberalism, doubts have arisen about whether the now-thinned political sphere (the terrain of fundamental principles, constitutional ideals, rights, laws, and so on) is sufficient to ensure and sustain a decent society. One example of this kind of objection is raised by Martha Nussbaum. As noted in the quote from her above, much of Nussbaum's philosophical career has been spent working in the Rawlsian tradition, precisely on these questions of fundamental political principles. However, her work has also had another major focus, as she writes, "The other half of my career has focussed on the nature of the emotions and their role in our search for the good life."[23] For Nussbaum, this latter focus eventually led her to ask questions with regard to the former—both of which are brought together in her 2013 book *Political Emotions: Why Love Matters for Justice*. The key problem that she identifies in the history of liberalism is that not enough has been said to give us confidence in the stability and motivational sustainability of the just society it envisions. We could say, in the terms of Rawls' original formulation ("How is it possible for there to exist over time a just and stable society of free and equal citizens?"), that not enough has been said about the *"over time"* aspect. Nussbaum's work foregrounds the importance of this diachronic angle; asking whether liberalism is able to give us confidence that the just society can be sustained over time, and this by ordinary human beings.[24]

23. Nussbaum, *The Monarchy of Fear*, 12.

24. Note, on Nussbaum's reading, this is not an optional extra for Rawlsian and other liberal accounts. Rather, she sees this as an *internal* challenge that must be addressed: as "integral to the arguments justifying the principles of justice" (Nussbaum,

One of the ways Nussbaum approaches elucidating this diachronic, motivational dimension in *Political Emotions* is by way of a consideration of Plato's ideal city, which she thinks exhibits the logical conclusion of the desire for reliance on impartial principle in contrast to partial emotion. In Plato's city, local ties of family and kin are transcended for roles in which all impartially care for all. But, as Aristotle saw, this city then faces the problem of "*watery motivation*." In the *Politics* he writes "there are two things above all that make people love and care for something, the thought that it is all theirs, and the thought that it is the only one they have. Neither of these will be present in that city."[25] By seeking to overcome the intense attachments we have to particular persons, Aristotle argues that Plato ends up perilously diluting the love and care on offer all round. Instead of the intense bonds of affection characteristic of many close relations, such as most notably the love of parents for their children, one ends up with a dispersed and more "watery" care of all for all.[26] Instead of genuinely loving a few people, we're left being mildly benevolent to all people. Thus, while impartiality and justly proportioned care might sound good in theory, in practice and in terms of what "can move real people,"[27] it produces only tepid sentiments that fail to motivate action and thus threaten the stability of any society so organized.

Nussbaum argues in *Political Emotions* that Rawlsian political liberalism must come to terms with its own version of the problem of "watery motivation" and ask whether its principle-based account of political legitimacy ends up unconsciously cultivating sentiments that prove distant and anemic, thus leaving actual political actors within a liberal regime without the motivational resources to make their society stable over time.[28] Of course, as Nussbaum makes clear, Rawls is neither a Plato nor even a Habermas. Indeed, she thinks Rawls was unique in showing a nascent awareness of the need for cultivating sentiments that will support liberal principles and institutions, even if he fails to adequately develop this.[29] Nussbaum's project is to provide this supplement for liberalism, to which she remains committed. The task, she thinks, is to grapple with "the resources and the problems that

---

Political Emotions, 9). Nussbaum writes that, "Part of justifying a normative political project is showing that it can be reasonably stable" (ibid., 16); thus "showing that the just society can be stable is a necessary part of its justification" (ibid., 9).

25. Aristotle, *Politics*, 1262b22–23.
26. Nussbaum, *Political Emotions*, 219.
27. Nussbaum, *Political Emotions*, 221.
28. Nussbaum, *Political Emotions*, 220.
29. For instance, Rawls' early paper "The Sense of Justice"—much of which appears in Part 3 of *A Theory of Justice*—was carefully attentive to the tight connection between emotions, justice, and political stability. See Rawls, "The Sense of Justice."

human nature, insofar as we can know it, makes available"[30] in order to be able to offer "a blueprint for the cultivation of strong sustaining emotions."[31] As she puts it, "good laws and institutions need the *ongoing* support of real people's emotions—and need to be preserved from the corrosive effect of bad emotions."[32]

Of course, this is not a new idea. As Nussbaum acknowledges, there is "a long tradition stretching (in Western philosophy) from Plato through to modern thinkers such as Adam Smith and John Rawls" which has thought that "emotions have an important role to play in a decent political society. Emotions can destabilise a community and fragment it, or they can produce better cooperation and more energetic striving toward justice."[33] Nussbaum herself has drawn much inspiration from the Greeks,[34] but also from thinkers such as Smith and Rousseau among others, in her more recent work on political emotions. Thomas Dixon argues that excellent work on the role of the passions, sentiments, affections, and the like can be found in much of the history of social, moral, and political philosophy prior to the advent of the modern idea of "emotion" via nineteenth century psychology, which flattened all of affective life into the model of involuntary, non-cognitive impulses.[35] A turn to "the passions" then is not altogether new, but involves returning to explore philosophical and psychological terrain which has been out of focus in modern philosophy. The good news now, however, is that contemporary philosophers have access to vast new empirical data in these areas with which to engage. As Nussbaum writes:

> It is a propitious time to write on this topic, because cognitive psychologists during the past several decades have produced a wide range of excellent research on particular emotions, which, supplemented by the work of primatologists, anthropologists, neuroscientists, and psychoanalysts, gives us a lot of empirical data that are extremely useful to a normative philosophical project such as this one. Such empirical findings do not answer our normative questions, but they do help us to understand what may be impossible and what possible, what pervasive human

---

30. Nussbaum, *Political Emotions*, 137.
31. Nussbaum, *Political Emotions*, 219.
32. Nussbaum, *Political Emotions*, 136 (emphasis added).
33. Nussbaum, *Political Emotions*, 12.
34. See, for example, Nussbaum, *The Therapy of Desire* and Nussbaum, *Upheavals of Thought*.
35. Dixon, *From Passions to Emotions*.

tendencies may be harmful or helpful—in short, what material we have to work with and how susceptible to "work" it may be.[36]

Let us take stock. Nussbaum's argument in *Political Emotions* is one example of how we might raise questions about a purely political solution to the challenges facing pluralistic societies; that is, a solution that attempts to specify the right kind of fundamental principles and institutions for the liberal state, its constitutional agreements, coercive laws, basic rights and entitlements. While, as we've seen, Nussbaum agrees this is vital work and indeed she has done much of it herself, she also argues that on its own it will not adequately address the challenges faced by real people living in pluralistic societies nor answer how a decent society full of such people can be stable over time. For that, Nussbaum argues, other resources need to be explored beyond those which have been the preserve of liberal political philosophy. The key place she argues that philosophers need to be looking—in partnership with empirical psychologists, perceptive novelists, and others—is our emotional and motivational resources; "stability requires grappling with the complexities of real human psychology."[37] As she issues the challenge: "it isn't sufficient to create good institutions and then run away and hide.... We have to get our hands dirty by entering the feared emotional terrain."[38]

4. Emotional and Motivational Resources for Pluralistic Societies: Cultivating Compassion

In the final section of this chapter I want to move onto this "emotional terrain" and focus on sketching one potential resource for contemporary pluralistic societies, namely, that of cultivating compassion or empathic concern. This is a resource that Nussbaum highlights in her work, but also one that has featured prominently in the history of philosophy and is becoming increasingly prominent in contemporary psychology. In particular, I wish to highlight Nussbaum's addition of the "eudaimonistic thought" to the conception of compassion, and conclude by suggesting underappreciated links with faith traditions.

First, in choosing to focus on cultivating compassion, it should be noted that I am concentrating only on one side of the task, as Nussbaum conceives it. For her, developing "a blueprint for the cultivation of strong sustaining emotions" must address both the weaknesses and the opportunities

---

36. Nussbaum, *Political Emotions*, 15–16.
37. Nussbaum, *Political Emotions*, 210.
38. Nussbaum, *Political Emotions*, 214.

presented by the conative aspects of human nature. The blueprint needs to cover not only how to amplify helpful psychological tendencies, but also how to mitigate harmful ones. This two-sided analysis is evident in much of Nussbaum's recent work on the role of emotions in political life, for example, on the "negative side" in *The Monarchy of Fear* she examines the bad effects in democratic political life of fear, anger, disgust and envy.[39]

The "positive side" of the task is to harness and cultivate those emotional and motivational tendencies that might support a just and stable society. The key resource Nussbaum puts forward in her work on this front is *compassion*. For Nussbaum, the strong emotions and motives born of human beings' natural partiality and our particularized loves are key to any solution: "our erotic investment in the world, our attachments to our own team, our own love, our own children, our own life."[40] Rather than attempting to eradicate or in some way correct for the strong partial concern human beings tend to feel towards those in their immediate circle, Nussbaum argues we need to expand it. In particular, she thinks we should focus on the powerful psychological tendency people have to feel compassion for the suffering of those they love and strong accompanying motivation to help them when in need, even if this involves great sacrifice. According to Nussbaum, extending and channelling this emotion into the political realm is vital for a just and stable society. The state, Nussbaum argues, needs a blueprint for cultivating and expanding compassion in its citizens. It needs a plan for the political use of compassion.

So, what is compassion and how can it be cultivated? Nussbaum defines compassion as "a painful emotion directed at the serious suffering of another creature or creatures."[41] She is interested in the sort of compassion or concern for someone in need that produces altruistic motivation to help them. As she puts it: "we are after no mere tepid or detached sympathy, but, instead, something more closely akin to and periodically illuminated by love."[42] To help us fix the concept she has in mind, it is worth noting that her account of compassion draws on empirical results about how people are motivated to help others, especially from the pioneering work of psychologist C. Daniel Batson.[43] Pinpointing this emotion for which he prefers to use

---

39. See Nussbaum, *Political Emotions* and *The Monarchy of Fear*. There are a number of interesting theorists currently writing on these topics, including a number debating the benefits and dangers of seemingly negative emotions; for example, Amia Srinivasan argues for a positive political use for anger in her article "The Aptness of Anger."

40. Nussbaum, *Political Emotions*, 223.

41. Nussbaum, *Political Emotions*, 142.

42. Nussbaum, *Political Emotions*, 318.

43. For a summary of how Batson's work connects with a certain approach to

the term "empathic concern," Batson defines it as "other-oriented emotion elicited by and congruent with the perceived welfare of someone in need."[44] Compassion or empathic concern is felt in response to perceiving another in a situation of need, pain, grief or suffering of some kind. Furthermore, the link between this emotion of empathic concern and altruistic motivation has been subjected to extensive empirical investigation. Batson argues that ample evidence has emerged to confirm what he has labelled "the empathy-altruism hypothesis," which states that empathic concern "produces a motivational state with the ultimate goal of increasing that person's welfare by having the empathy-inducing need removed (i.e., altruistic motivation)."[45] So, feelings of compassion or empathic concern for a person in need produce motivation to help them.

Nussbaum holds that the philosophical tradition and empirical research has demonstrated that the emotion of compassion necessarily involves three thoughts. These are: (1) the thought of *seriousness*: the thought that the other is suffering in some way that is important and nontrivial; (2) the thought of *nonfault*: that the person's predicament is not chosen or self-inflicted; (3) the thought of *similar possibilities*: that the other is in some sense similar to me or that we share similar vulnerabilities.[46] To the above, Nussbaum adds a new, fourth thought as a necessary component of compassion, which she calls the *eudaimonistic thought*:

> This is a judgment or thought that places the suffering person or persons among the important parts of the life of the person who feels the emotion. It says, "They count for me: they are among my most important goals and projects." As I said in Chapter 1, the major human emotions are always eudaimonistic, meaning focussed on the agent's most important goals and projects, and seeing the world from the point of view of those goals, rather than from some impersonal vantage point. Thus we feel fear about damages that we see as significant for our own well-being and our other goals; we feel grief at the loss of someone who

---

thinking about compassion and benevolence in the history of philosophy, especially in the work of David Hume, see my "Cultivating Empathic Concern and Altruistic Motivation."

44. Batson, *Altruism in Humans*, 11–12.

45. Batson, *Altruism in Humans*, 29.

46. Nussbaum, *Political Emotions*, 142–44. Though, as Nussbaum notes, recent empirical work has shown the thought of similarity is less important than the tradition of work on compassion has previously assumed.

is already invested with a certain importance in our scheme of things.[47]

In adding the eudaimonistic thought as a part of compassion, Nussbaum highlights the key role it plays in both causing and strengthening feelings of compassion. We feel the most intense compassion for the suffering of those in our immediate circle of concern, those who already matter to us. And the stronger this thought of importance is, the stronger our emotion and motivation will be to help. Take, for example, the love of a father for his infant son. The son is right at the center of what matters for the father; everything that concerns the son is especially salient and vivid to him. When he witnesses his son in pain, the compassionate emotion and altruistic motivation will be much stronger than what he feels when he learns about the exact same pain experience by a distant stranger. As Nussbaum summarizes: "the things that occasion a strong emotion in us are things that correspond to what we have invested with importance in our thoughts, implicit or explicit, about what is important in life, our conception of flourishing."[48] The less a person is invested with a certain importance for us, the more "watery" our emotional and motivational responses with respect to them become.

The key implication of adding the eudaimonistic thought to the concept of compassion for Nussbaum is that cultivating compassion "will require creating a bridge between our current concerns and a broader circle of concerns that is still recognisably 'us' and 'ours.'"[49] Drawing on the terminology of Aristotle's criticism of Plato's ideal city, she writes:

> In short, to make people love something requires making them see it as "their own," preferably also as "the only one they have." This point, of course, is the point we have made all along: the major emotions are "eudaimonistic," tied to the person's conception of flourishing and the circle of concern that is involved in any such conception. To make people care, you have to make

---

47. Nussbaum, *Political Emotions*, 144–45. Another way of thinking about this could be via the idea of intrinsic valuing (see Batson, *Altruism in Humans,* 41–46). I also think it is similar to Hume's claim in *The Treatise* that thoughts which are closely connected with the thought of oneself always have a greater vivacity (see Hume, *A Treatise of Human Nature*, 316–24).

48. Nussbaum, *Political Emotions*, 145. Crucial to note on this: "Eudaimonism is not egoism. I am not claiming that emotions always view events and people as mere means to the agent's own satisfaction or happiness; indeed, I strenuously deny this" (ibid.).

49. Nussbaum, *Political Emotions*, 145.

them see the object of potential care as in some way "theirs" and "them."[50]

Thus, one important task for putting compassion to political use is to help citizens think the eudaimonistic thought about more people—*a lot more*, given the size and diversity of modern states and their globalized links with neighbors much further afield. Many more people will need to really matter to us and be "invested with a certain importance in our scheme of things."[51]

Is this possible? It is sometimes objected that human beings' circle of concern simply cannot extend this far. That it has natural limits, and we can typically only have that kind of intense particularized care for a quite limited number of people. Yet, we are all familiar with occasions where the circle does expand. One way this tends to happen automatically is via the vivid presentation of others' suffering and the strong emotional response this solicits. Some of Batson's experiments in this area have provided evidence for the common-sense observation that:

> The thought of importance need not always antecede the compassionate response; the vivid presentation of another person's plight may jumpstart it, moving that person, temporarily, into the centre of the things that matter. Thus, when people hear of an earthquake or some other comparable disaster, they often become very focussed on the sufferings of the strangers involved, *and these strangers really matter to them*—for a time.[52]

Thus, while the circle of concern does tend by default to be notoriously narrow, it is not static but possesses a great deal of flexibility: people can and do come to care about the sufferings of people they have never met.[53] Unfortunately, however, the feelings of compassion produced by processes like imaginative participation in others' situations tends to produce only "temporary salience" which is "wavering and inconstant, often diminishing over time and thus failing to sustain helping efforts required to address chronic problems."[54] The challenge then is to find a way to extend the eudaimonistic thought to more people in ways that are stable and sustainable.

50. Nussbaum, *Political Emotions*, 219.

51. Nussbaum, *Political Emotions*, 145.

52. Nussbaum, *Political Emotions*, 145. (Emphasis added) In this section, Nussbaum outlines some of Batson's empirical work supporting this claim.

53. Nussbaum, *Political Emotions*, 154.

54. Nussbaum, *Political Emotions*, 156. Nussbaum notes that this was something earlier thinkers also highlighted: "As Adam Smith already observed, however, using the example of an earthquake in China, this focus is unstable, easily deflected back to

Now, controversially, the main solution Nussbaum proposes to this challenge is the cultivation of patriotic love, arguing that "[w]e can extend compassion by attaching it to images and institutions that stand for the well-being of all people—preferably including people outside the nation itself. This is what a good form of patriotism does."[55] There are many critical questions that must be raised about the role Nussbaum gives to patriotism in *Political Emotions*, and she herself draws attention to the dangers of entering this territory and attempts to address them in the book. One part of her response is to argue that people defending liberal values simply cannot afford to "cede the terrain of emotion cultivation to fascists, or else they will certainly have to cede much more in the long run."[56] Drawing on lessons from Germany's history, Nussbaum writes, "imagine combating the canny propaganda machine of Hitler's Germany, so full of emotive devices, without any sources of love or emotional motivation."[57] Likewise, today, she highlights that there are many political leaders seeking to construct stories of a nation's past and public rituals designed to stoke and shape citizens' emotions towards certain ends. In view of this, Nussbaum contends that liberals ("people interested in relief of poverty, justice for minorities, political and religious liberty, democracy and global justice")[58] have little choice but to also enter into and contest the "feared emotional terrain." They too must tell stories of the nation's past, imaginatively project visions of its future, and develop rituals that will help shape good forms of patriotic love—forms which use the nation as a fulcrum to extend that love beyond itself. Another crucial part of Nussbaum's response to the dangers of invoking patriotic emotion is to emphasize that any attempt to cultivate it will also need to go hand in hand with the cultivation of the critical faculties in order to guard against the three key dangers of exclusionary values, coerced conscience and uncritical homogeneity.[59] These arguments need further examination and debate.

Without downplaying the importance of that debate, here I want to focus on making one point relevant to it, namely, I want to highlight the link between Nussbaum's turn to patriotism and her introduction of

---

oneself and one's immediate surroundings, unless more stable structures of concern are built upon it that ensure a continued concern with the people of that distant nation" (Nussbaum, *Political Emotions*, 145).

55. Nussbaum, *Political Emotions*, 210.
56. Nussbaum, *Political Emotions*, 222.
57. Nussbaum, *Political Emotions*, 213.
58. Nussbaum, *Political Emotions*, 256.
59. See the argument in the first part of Nussbaum, *Political Emotions*, "Teaching Patriotism: Love and Critical Freedom," 204–19.

the "eudaimonistic thought" discussed above. As Nussbaum defines it, "[p]atriotism is a strong emotion taking the nation as its object. It is a form of love, and thus distinct from simple approval, or commitment, or embrace of principles."[60] Though it should be noted she is also interested in other more local forms of patriotic love such as those addressed to the state, the city, the region.[61] Crucially, for Nussbaum, patriotic love involves the eudaimonistic thought "that the nation *is one's own*, and its rituals usually make reference to that idea."[62] For Nussbaum, the eudaimonistic thought explains why these loves are best placed to extend compassion in a stable way; namely, because they are forms of partial and particularized love. They exist on a continuum with the other partial loves that comprise our default circle of concern—they grab at our hearts and imaginations and can be motivationally efficacious. As Nussbaum explains:

> In all its forms, however, patriotic love is particularistic. It is modelled on family or personal love of some type, and, in keeping with that origin or analogy, it focuses on specifics: this or that beautiful geographical feature, this or that historical event. The *thicker* it is in these respects, the more likely it is to *inspire*.[63]

Yet, unlike our love for our nearest and dearest, these broader patriotic loves of region, city, state or nation include reference to much larger numbers of people. In this sense, Nussbaum argues that various forms of patriotic love can function as a fulcrum for extending compassion in a stable and sustainable way. If we can direct our efforts towards cultivating love for particular regions, cities, or countries that "stand for the well-being of all people," both within and even, at their best, beyond them, this will help sustain a broader compassion. It will create bridges from the intensity of our strong particularistic emotion for those in our immediate circle of concern to wider circles of loving concern towards our many and diverse fellow citizens. For Nussbaum, patriotic emotion will only work to extend compassion in this way if it is kept thoroughly eudemonistic. As she puts it: "If altruistic national emotion is to have motivational power, it needs to hitch itself to the concrete: named individuals (founders, heroes), physical particulars (features of landscape, vivid images and metaphors), and, above all, narratives of struggle, involving suffering and hope."[64] Only the

---

60. Nussbaum, *Political Emotions*, 208.
61. Nussbaum, *Political Emotions*, 209.
62. Nussbaum, *Political Emotions*, 208 (emphasis added).
63. Nussbaum, *Political Emotions*, 208–9 (emphasis added).
64. Nussbaum, *Political Emotions*, 209.

kind of strong emotion characteristic of particularized love will provide the required motivational stability.

It is interesting to note a contemporary example of political action that is in the spirit of Nussbaum's proposal. That is, we can think of the way some environmental and climate movements have started to make more unashamed appeals calling upon people's love for the living world, and of particular local regions (*this* creek, *this* woodland, *this* rainforest, *this* local colony of an endangered species and so on) in order to draw on emotional and motivational resources to sustain the larger-scale work they have in view. For example, drawing on Pope Francis' *Laudato Si: On Care for our Common Home*, the columnist George Monbiot writes that "Pope Francis reminds us that our relationship to the natural world is about love, not just goods and services."[65] He continues:

> Acknowledging our *love* for the living world does something that a library full of papers on sustainable development and ecosystem services cannot: it engages the imagination as well as the intellect. It inspires belief; and this is essential to the *lasting* success of any movement.[66]

Environmental movements have large collective action projects in view—ones that call for altruistic sacrifice for the long-term common good. It is interesting to note the move of some in these movements to appeal to cultivating love (for the natural world and for very particular parts of it, for other species and even for distant neighbors and future generations) as vital for making such projects motivating and sustainable.

Nussbaum's analysis would agree: calls to a common future must deploy imagination and emotion. And they must do so in full concrete, particular, and vivid mode, never shying away from seeking to foster strong emotions of compassionate and loving concern; or seeking to cultivate that kind of particularized, eudaimonistic love that works so well to move real people to action. This is something that Nussbaum thinks political leaders such as Martin Luther King Jr. understood in a way that too often eludes philosophers:

> People really don't fall in love with abstract ideas as such, without a lot of other apparatus in the form of metaphor, symbol, rhythm, melody, concrete geographical features, and so forth. Shrewd leaders understand this very well. Had Martin Luther King Jr. written in the manner of Rawls, world history would

---

65. Monbiot, "Why We Fight for the Living World."
66. Monbiot, "Why We Fight for the Living World" (emphasis added).

> have been very different. Vividness and particularity are crucial determinants of emotional response, and thence of altruistic action.... [B]y omitting the quirky ways in which real people are moved, Rawls omits both resources and potential dangers.[67]

The final section of this chapter has explored one of these motivational resources which human psychology has at its disposal, namely, that of cultivating compassion and altruistic motivation. There are no doubt other paths that could and have been used to get people to feel compassionate care for those beyond their immediate circle of concern, such as, for example, learning new information about their needs. But, for Nussbaum, the emotion cultivation path (tempered by the eudaimonistic thought) is unique in running with the grain of human beings' natural partiality and "the quirky ways in which real people are moved." *Pace* Plato's ideal city, the aim is not to correct or quarantine our natural partiality to those near and dear to us, but to enlarge it. The aim is to bolster and broaden this tendency. Rather than assuming that bonds of attachment, intrinsic valuing and their strong emotional and motivational responses are only of relevance for a small number of intimate relationships, the challenge, as Gopnik frames it by drawing on the ancient Chinese philosopher Mengzi, is "how to expand the mutual commitment and trust that define a family to the very different scale of a state."[68]

From one angle, it could sound like this argument has only made things harder. The liberal goal was a just and stable society and we were seeking resources to assist with the task of sustaining this kind of society over time. But now it turns out that justice needs love, and we need a blueprint for cultivating love for all those within and beyond the state. Hasn't the bar been raised impossibly high? Nussbaum disagrees:

> this project's demand for love, rather than ratcheting up the demands imposed by the political conception in a way that makes "overlapping consensus" more difficult to achieve, actually *ratchets the demands down*, by imagining emotions that do not presuppose full agreement on principles and institutions. ... Just as two people can be friends and even lovers when their religions, their political views, and their ultimate goals in life differ, so citizens in the society we are imagining, or many of them at least, can share the heterogeneous experiences we have

---

67. Nussbaum, *Political Emotions*, 222.
68. Gopnik, "When Truth and Reason Are No Longer Enough."

described—at least some of those experiences, and some of the time.[69]

It is interesting to note in conclusion and given the broader themes of this volume that the appeal to cultivating love is an avenue shared with a number of faith traditions that have long advocated for attempts and practices to expand the circle of care.[70] In Christianity, for example, the call to love one's neighbors, as well as strangers and even enemies, is given not just as a high bar for a few exceptional saints but to *all*.[71] *Everyone* is called to heed the injunction to "love your neighbor as yourself" and, in asking "Lord, who is my neighbor?" we are encouraged to discover neighbors we didn't know we had, as strangers in turn become part of the circle of what really matters in each person's scheme of things. Their needs begin to tug on our emotions, feelings of compassion arise in the face of their grief and motivate action to help. No prior limit is set on the scope of this circle of concern. The methods proposed in the Christian faith for cultivating this kind of neighborly love, as well as those that can be found in other religious traditions, merit further examination. As Batson notes from the empirical perspective, "the success of these different religious efforts is either questionable (Batson, Floyd, Mayer, & Winner, 1999) or yet to be systematically studied."[72] Yet the arguments outlined by Nussbaum above give us reason to be interested in further studies of this sort and what might be learnt from drawing on other traditions, which to date have paid greater attention to the challenges of cultivating love and compassionate concern for others than has modern political philosophy.[73]

The connections between Nussbaum's project in *Political Emotions* and traditional religious projects of cultivating love for one's neighbor (and even one's enemy) have at least two surprising upshots. First, for the religious believer, these connections provide encouragement that their practices of moral and spiritual formation might be of public and political force. That, given the link between empathic concern and altruistic motivation for which Batson argues, intentional efforts to cultivate compassion and love have a far wider significance than is commonly thought. They are not merely a matter of individual good deeds and local community service but can help ensure

69. Nussbaum, *Political Emotions*, 393 (emphasis added).

70. This point is made by Batson in *Altruism in Humans*, 181.

71. Batson (*Altruism in Humans*, 181) also briefly notes examples from "the contemplative traditions of the East, such as Tibetan Buddhism."

72. Batson, *Altruism in Humans*, 181.

73. One example of initial explorations in this area can be found in the work of Christian Miller on character; see "Improving our characters with divine assistance."

the stability and motivational sustainability of large and complex pluralistic societies.

Second, for the political liberal theorist, they have a reason to resist thinking of religious communities as necessarily antithetical to the liberal project. As the arguments of Cavanaugh and others canvassed in this chapter suggest, there needs to be an interrogation of assumptions about the causal connections between religion and social discord. And, as Nussbaum's arguments have shown, liberal political philosophy must also interrogate whether what I have referred to above as "the now-thinned political sphere" is sufficient to ensure and sustain the just society it envisions. And, if there is reasonable doubt here, to consider how it will address this problem of "watery motivation" while keeping firmly in view "the quirky, unpredictable humanity of the citizen who really feels and imagines."[74] Here then, returning to the point about religious communities, the political liberal theorist might go one step further: not only to resist thinking of them as antithetical to the liberal project and thus neutral, but to also consider what resources they might positively contain for it. Indeed, if as Nussbaum shows us love matters for justice, and if faith communities are one of the main places engaged in practices to cultivate and extend love, then perhaps we have a reason to entertain the thought that faith matters for justice too.

---

74. Nussbaum, *Political Emotions*, 396.

7

WHAT HAPPENS WHEN FAITH INTERRUPTS REASON?

Critiquing a Dominant Discourse from the Perspective of the Other

—Daniel J. Fleming

In the encyclical *Fides et Ratio*, St John Paul II famously posited that faith and reason "are like two wings on which the human spirit rises to the contemplation of truth."[1] This chapter seeks to understand what might happen when the operations of one wing (faith) necessitate the interruption of the operations of the other wing (reason). In other words, *what happens when faith interrupts reason*?

The chapter approaches reason through the lens of the twentieth-century continental philosopher Emmanuel Levinas. Following the atrocities of the Holocaust, Levinas declared that reason, in its attempts to understand the world, neglected ethics, exalted freedom, and in so doing provided no internal means by which to prevent such horrors from happening again. Since the time of Levinas' writings the world has witnessed yet more atrocities that underpin the salience of his argument: wars, terrorism, religious violence and persecution, massive financial fraud, ethnic cleansing, to name but a few. Of itself, reason too quickly becomes the handmaiden of ideologies that eventuate in violence, hence, it needs to be "ethically redeemed," its operations interrupted by a radical sense of responsibility for all other persons. The chapter begins by exploring key aspects of Levinas' thought,

---

1. John Paul II, *Fides et ratio*, 1.

and uses the case study of his critique of theodicy to demonstrate the implications of his method.

Drawing from Levinas' philosophy in dialogue with a Catholic understanding of conscience, the chapter argues that the moment of encounter with the other person presents a case of natural revelation by opening conscience up to "the voice of God." For people of faith, such a call necessitates the critical examination of reason through the paradigm of their religious tradition and its ethical teaching. Within the Christian tradition, such critical examination happens from the perspective of the gospel that requires reality be viewed through the eyes of the oppressed. As an example of this method of philosophical and theological critique, the chapter turns to the work of Cornel West and his interlocutors and analyses how—in critiquing reason from the perspective of faith—West shines light on previously unarticulated racist assumptions underlying modern discourse, an exemplary case of what Levinas warned against. Drawing from this method, the chapter offers suggestions for how it is that one part of the complementary relationship between faith and reason is openness to interruption of the latter by the former on ethical grounds.

1. Emmanuel Levinas and the Interruption of Reason by the Ethical[2]

Emmanuel Levinas had first-hand experience of the Holocaust. Levinas himself escaped the Nazi death camps but spent some time as a prisoner of war. Many of his family were exterminated along with millions of others during the Second World War.[3] From this horror, Levinas embarked on a search for answers: how could it be after thousands of years of philosophy and theology—those great examples of the exercise of human reason—that we did not have it within our means to prevent this violence? And, that being the case, what hope is there of preventing such violence from occurring again? Like a forensic investigator, Levinas interrogated the history of Western thought to locate the genesis for the violence expressed in the Holocaust. His cynical conclusion was that the exercise of reason typically justifies some form of freedom—for an individual or a group—at the expense of others.[4] Hence, reason justifies "my place in the sun" as against some-

---

2. Aspects of the analysis below are drawn from my fchapter "The Enduring Contribution of Religious Education to Reason's Good Functioning." I am grateful to Waxmann for allowing me to use this material here.

3. Malka, *Emmanuel Levinas*, 64–82.

4. Beyond Levinas' own historical context we can see examples of our concern

one else's, and relativizes my responsibility to any other person, inevitably leading to violence if someone gets in the way:

> My being-in-the-world or my "place in the sun," my being at home, have these not also been the usurpation of spaces belonging to the other man whom I have already oppressed or starved, or driven out into a third world; are they not acts of repulsing, excluding, exiling, stripping, killing?[5]

In the following paragraphs I will explore the line of argument that led Levinas to this point, and analyze his critique of theodicy as one example of his method at work.

Commentators on Levinas typically agree that he had one "big idea," namely that reason's functions will be redeemed only if ethics is positioned as "first philosophy."[6] By this, he meant taking on a manner of seeing the world—"an optics"—in which responsibility is central and all else flows from this.[7] Such a position changed everything in Levinas' eyes, because it stands in stark contrast to the typical operations of reason. Left unchecked, these are beset on understanding the world, encountering what is outside the self and directing it in ways which serve self-directed freedom. In his essay *Ethics as First Philosophy*, Levinas provided the following analysis: reason's mode of operation is *auffassen* (German: understanding) that "is also, and always has been, a *Fassen* (gripping)."[8] In this sense, reason is predisposed to take what is other and make it its own. Reason establishes its place at the expense of what is outside of it, and any ethics which has its origin in reason is subject to the same fundamental critique.

In Levinas' analysis, the encounter with the Other (understood as any other person) presents reason with a presence which it cannot properly *auffassen*. The Other is essentially and always mysterious to reason—outside of the four walls of its home—and hence interrupts its smooth functioning. To use a biblical metaphor, it is as if the Other is the stranger come to visit (Gen 18:2), and in the encounter with the Other reason is presented with the choice of asserting its freedom or welcoming the Other with hospitality and humility (Gen 18:3–8). In the former response, Levinas suggested that reason does violence to the Other by reducing her or his mystery into graspable

---

in new forms of radical liberalism, free-market capitalism, and political movements which hold as central the value of an individual group against all others.

5. Levinas, "Ethics as First Philosophy," 82.
6. Critchley, "Introduction," 6.
7. Levinas, *Totality and Infinity*, 23.
8. Levinas, "Ethics as First Philosophy," 76.

categories and forcing those into the "four walls" of reason's home.[9] This has been the unfortunate function of philosophy in Levinas' eyes—it has been too willing to categorize the world, to make sense of it, and to do so with a view to protecting the interests of certain individuals or groups, and in so doing overcome the mystery of many Others.[10] When such a stage is set, the conditions are in place for the violence of the Holocaust to be acted out. Such violence rests on a 'rational' foundation, a manner of engaging with the world and with Otherness, and hence for Levinas becomes inevitable.

However, there is another possible response, which rests on attending to the phenomenon of encountering the Other. On Levinas' view, the encounter with the Other is an ethical encounter precisely because it instantiates a challenge to the freedom of reason. When I am encountered by the mysterious Other a question is asked of me: will you continue to protect your freedom and your interests, or will you interrupt those in favour of welcoming me?[11] This question sits at the heart of Levinas' understanding of ethics. In his words:

> We name this calling into question of my spontaneity by the presence of the Other ethics. The strangeness of the Other, his irreducibility to the I, to my thoughts and my possessions, is precisely accomplished as a calling into question of my spontaneity, as ethics.[12]

This calling into question occurs on a pre-rational level—the operations of reason do not precede this encounter, they respond to it. This makes sense of Levinas' claim that ethics is an optics: we encounter the world on ethical terms, regardless of the way in which we respond to it.[13] Ethics in this sense is not to product of reason, but its antecedent. As distinct from René Descartes' "I think, therefore I am," Levinas' philosophy leads to the observation that "I think, therefore here I am."[14] The latter phrase is aligned with the Hebrew *hineni*, used by Abraham in answering "here I am" to God's call in Genesis 22.[15] The word carries connotations of presence, of presentation, and accountability: "I think, therefore here I am, presenting myself to you, accountable to you, responsible to you." Reason is in this sense an

---

9. Burggraeve, "Violence and the Vulnerable Face of the Other," 30–31.
10. Levinas, *Totality and Infinity*, 22.
11. Levinas, *Totality and Infinity*, 43.
12. Levinas, *Totality and Infinity*, 43.
13. Bernasconi, "What Is the Question to Which 'Substitution' Is the Answer?" 248.
14. Levinas, *Otherwise Than Being or Beyond Essence*, 114.
15. Putnam, *Jewish Philosophy as a Guide to Life*, 74.

exercise of our freedom in responding to an ethical call, and it is ethically redeemed only when it responds adequately to the call that animates it.[16]

Levinas' critique of theodicy provides a valuable case study in this regard, and is relevant to the overall topic of this chapter. A terminological clarification is in order here: for Levinas, a theodicy is any theological *or* philosophical attempt to explain human suffering, and so his use of the term is broader than the more narrow use typically found in theological studies.[17] Understood in this way, theodicy for Levinas is an example *par excellence* of reason's potentially troublesome operations. In the encounter with the suffering of the Other, it seeks to describe, explain, and ultimately abdicate itself from the suffering. White provides further clarification:

> In light of the Holocaust and other atrocities of the 20th century, Levinas claims that any kind of theodicy—whether this would be a natural or supernatural justification of suffering—is evil in itself: for quite apart from the evil of *causing* the suffering of others, the willingness to *justify* the suffering of other people is what allows an outrage such as the Holocaust to happen in the first place. In this respect, Levinas goes so far as to claim that, "the justification of the neighbour's pain is certainly the source of all immorality."[18]

The poignancy of this question for Levinas' own experience should not be underestimated, especially when it comes to theology: how could so many explicitly religious people become complicit with such horror? What kind of theological system would *not* interrupt this? Surely the Christian faith held by so many during this time would provide for some protection of those made vulnerable by the Nazi regime? As an activity of reason which reflects on faith, any theology which did not respond adequately to the call of the suffering Other in this case (and others) can be critiqued on these grounds. This is why Levinas argued that theology "will only ever be worthy of the name when it is attentive to the neighbour, that is, when it is ethically redeemed."[19]

---

16. Levinas, *Totality and Infinity*, 47. See also Levinas, "Ethics as First Philosophy," 84.

17. Levinas, "Useless Suffering," 160–61

18. White, "Levinas, the Philosophy of Suffering, and the Ethics of Compassion," 111. Here White quotes from Levinas, "Useless Suffering," 163.

19. Purcell, *Levinas and Theology*, 60.

2. The Call of Conscience, an Optics of Faith, and a Kierkegaardian Suspension

Elsewhere I have argued that Levinas' position aligns with Catholic teaching on conscience, and accentuates the insatiable ethical call that sits at the heart of Catholic faith.[20] To summarize, I proffer that Levinas' argument sits comfortably with one aspect of conscience as articulated in *Gaudium et spes*—the call to do good and avoid evil which is also the voice of God, echoing in the depths of a person.[21] The link with Levinas here highlights the insatiability of this call and its implications for the way in which reason is exercised. Furthermore, with Levinas it is possible to identify that it is in the encounter with the Other that the call of conscience (and the voice of God) are given prominence within Catholic faith. When the two positions are held together we can see that the way in which we respond to the question posed of reason is at once an ethical response and also a response to the voice of God. The combination of ethics and theosis here aligns with Matt 25:31–46, wherein the encounter with the vulnerable Other is also an encounter with God through Christ. Levinas comments directly on this passage of Scripture:

> I cannot describe the relation to God without speaking of my concern for the other. When I speak to a Christian, I always quote Matthew 25: the relation to God is presented there as a relation to another person. It is not a metaphor; in the other, there is a real presence of God. In my relation to the other, I hear the word of God. It is not a metaphor. It is not only extremely important; it is literally true. I'm not saying that the other is God, but that in his or her face I hear the word of God.[22]

What emerges from this description is that, if one takes the position of Catholic faith, then the call of conscience and the voice of God coalesce in such a way as to hold reason to account. The operations of reason are not free to be spontaneous, they are called to respond, to answer "here I am," and the manner of that response is given specific direction. If we take as a point of departure Matthew 25, for example, reason is accountable to the manner in which it responds to vulnerable others, especially in this case the hungry, the thirsty, the stranger, the sick, and those who are imprisoned (Matt 25:32). Hence, Catholic theology—as an activity of reason reflecting

---

20. Fleming, "Primoridal Moral Awareness: Levinas, Conscience and the Unavoidable Call to Responsibility."

21. *Gaudium et Spes*, 16.

22. Levinas, 'Philosophy, Justice, and Love', 171.

on the faith which inspires it—must allow itself to be open to the interruption of that ethical call stimulated by the encounter with the vulnerable other in order to ensure that it is adequately responding to it. To seek after truth without attending to this call opens theology up to a dangerous justification of the kind of violence about which Levinas issued a warning.[23]

Importantly, in the context of this article, the same should be extended to any exercise of reason which is actioned out of the framework of Catholic faith: it also is answerable to the ethical call, and hence it too may be interrupted in order to be hospitable to the Other and to overcome violence. There are precedents for approaches which privilege ethical responsibility over reason in Catholic (and more broadly Christian) theologies, such as the liberation theology movement which intentionally begins with the perspective of the poor and the suffering and offers critiques of social structures and their dominant discourses from that point of view.[24] Epistemologically, the argument underpinning this approach is that unless one analyses such structures from the point of view of the oppressed, one will see things only from the point of view of those for whom the structures work in favor.[25] Theologically, the argument is that God also sees reality from the side of the oppressed, through the paradigm of the cross, and this optics should be shared by those of faith. This manner of seeing takes precedence in the Christian worldview and may well interrupt what otherwise is seen as the good use of reason (cf. Levinas' argument that "ethics is an optics").[26] Spiritually, these functions are seen as part of the responsible cultivation of relationship with God.[27] In Levinasian parlance, the interruption to reason afforded by a consideration of the suffering Other is necessary for the ethical redemption of reason. The theological commitment of Catholic faith thereby includes a commitment to understand reason within the context of ethical interruption. In this sense, the "optics" of Catholic faith necessarily includes the ethical call.

---

23. Elsewhere a colleague and I have explored how Dietrich Bonhoeffer mounted a similar critique within the context of Christian theology, see Fleming and Lovat "Self-other or Other-self-other?"

24. As expressed in Guttierez, *A Theology of Liberation*; see especially 190–208. It is not the purpose of this particular study to analyse other precedents, and I do not claim here that liberation theology is the only one in Christian history. It is deployed here as a well-known approach which can highlight features of the argument developed throughout this chapter.

25. Guttierez, *A Theology of Liberation*, 12.

26. Guttierez, *A Theology of Liberation*, 276–77; see also 190–208.

27. Fleming, "Primordial Moral Awareness," 611.

To clarify the position further, it is helpful to introduce Søren Kierkegaard's "teleological suspension of the ethical" in favor of an absolute duty to God.[28] At first glance, this would seem to contradict what the perspective advanced above regarding the centrality of ethics. However, when understood along the lines that Westphal suggests, the matter becomes more clear:

> The object of a teleological suspension is negated in its claim to autonomy, to self-sufficiency and completeness; but it is affirmed in relation to that which is higher, that which draws it into a larger whole of which it is not the first principle. The highest card in its suit will take many tricks, but it can always be trumped.[29]

One must therefore attend to the method of Kierkegaard carefully here: the "ethical" he suspended in his work is a perspective informed by the dominant rationality of his time, namely that of the post-Enlightenment Danish bourgeoisie. To suspend as much is to stand outside this rationality in favor of an absolute duty to God, which rests not on metaphysical premises but on faith commitment. It is, in this sense, a teleological suspension of a dominant rationality. This is the origin of the famous Kierkegaardian "leap"—an intentional step outside of the foundations held in a system of reason in favor of faith, which may, from an analysis within the system of reason, appear as irrational.[30] To align with the perspective advanced above, faith on the Levinasian view is inseparable from an ethics that is at one and the same time a theosis, and it is radically beyond the operations of reason. Hence, it differs from the understanding of ethics that Kierkegaard wished to suspend. For both approaches, the activities of reason are held to account in relation to "that which is higher."[31] With this argument in place, it is now possible to look to a current example of such a method.

3. Cornel West and Racism in Modern Reason

The African-American philosopher Cornel West provides an example of how a method aligned with the argument above applies in theological and

---

28. Kierkegaard, *Fear and Trembling*, 83–95. On the study of Levinas and Kierkegaard alongside each other, see Simmons and Wood, eds., *Kierkegaard and Levinas*. In this volume, of especial relevance for the current study are Dudiak, "The Greatest Commandment?" and Minister, "Works of Justice, Works of Love."

29. Westphal, "Levinas's Teleological Suspension of the Religious," 153.

30. Kierkegaard, *Fear and Trembling*, 96–108.

31. Westphal, "Levinas's Teleological Suspension of the Religious," 153.

philosophical discourse, and also in social criticism.[32] Importantly, his work demonstrates that a *preference* for the interruption to reason put into effect from a position of faith and responsibility *does not* collapse into some form of fideism. Instead, it provides a method of checks, balances and challenges to reason's normal operations on a basis that takes the ethical call of Christianity as its starting point, without trying to ground this in the operations of reason. This is congruent with what Westphal says of approaches informed by Levinas and Kierkegaard: they do not seek to eliminate reason—they relativize it, placing it in some broader context within which it can be understood and held to account.[33]

West locates his thought within the Christian tradition which, in his words, is "a religion especially fitted to the oppressed. It looks at the world from the perspective of those below."[34] As such, his method follows "the biblical injunction to look at the world through the eyes of its victims, and the Christocentric perspective that requires that one see the world through the lens of the Cross–and thereby see our relative victimizing and relative victimization."[35] In encountering the world through this perspective, Christian faith, for West, acts as a form of encounter with the Other, which has the effect of interrupting our normal way of reasoning about the world. He describes this experience of interruption as being "unsettled, unnerved and unhoused. This experience of dialogue—the I-Thou relation with the uncontrolled other—may result in a dizziness, vertigo, or shudder that unhinges us from our moorings or yanks us from our anchors."[36] The position has its foundation in a deep concern for the vulnerable Other which commits to a form of sacrificial love that does not have its foundation in metaphysical certainties. Instead, it is "a leap that we make in our short lives that gives it so much meaning and infuses it with so much significance. It is a dangling experience. You take a tremendous risk, you become tremendously vulnerable, but there is no metaphysical ground. No security, nothing guaranteed, no surety whatsoever."[37] Note here the alignment with Levinas and Kierkegaard highlighted above: this perspective does not rest

---

32. I note here that West does not operate from a Levinasian basis (though he acknowledges the value of Levinas' work), nor out of the Catholic tradition, however his work is sympathetic to that tradition and openly draws from the liberation theology movement. The example is illustrative of what a method which aligns with the argument above may present when applied to a specific case.

33. Westphal, "Levinas's Teleological Suspension," 153.

34. West, *The Cornel West Reader*, 62.

35. West, *The Cornel West Reader*, 370.

36. West, *The Cornel West Reader*, xviii.

37. West, *The Cornel West Reader*, 228.

on reasonable argument, but rather grounds rationality in commitments that shape its function. As such, the search for truth takes on an ethical character which is answerable to the call of the vulnerable Other (and of conscience, cf. above). Consider the following from West: "The quest for truth, the quest for the good, the quest for the beautiful all require us to let suffering speak, let victims be visible and let social misery be put on the agenda of those with power."[38] Without the interruption of this "view from below," reason will simply be bound to do as Levinas suggested: exalt its freedom at the expense of the Other.

West's work has famously been focused on the issue of race, and how it is that racism has found its way into discourse that has been held as the product of reason, such as in the sciences. His approach aligns with what was described above, namely that by seeing the world through the eyes of the oppressed one will come to notice how it is that what is passed off as reason is actually protecting the freedom of some dominant power at the expense of some other. In particular, he highlights what he refers to as the logic of white supremacy, which "is manifest in the way in which the controlling metaphors, notions, and categories of modern discourse produce and prohibit, develop and delimit specific conceptions of truth and knowledge, beauty and character, so that certain ideas are rendered incomprehensible and unintelligible."[39] West proffers that scientific rationality—the dominant discourse since the Enlightenment—has implicitly (and explicitly in some cases) favoured a vision of the human person which supports the idea of white supremacy. What is particularly pernicious is that these discourses have been underpinned by the entire structure of modern discourse which, argues West, has hidden its underside: it is possible to experience and express such discourse without noticing the problematic foundations on which it is in part based.[40]

The outcome of this is precisely as Levinas described it: reason can justify violence against a vulnerable Other. Perhaps more frighteningly still, it does so in a manner that eventually presents as neutral. Obvious examples include the history of racism in West's own country, the United States, which continues to this day. However, West argues that we must look deeper than such issues to discover their root cause—lest we treat a symptom of a deeper issue without dealing with what has led to it. He suggests, in a manner of speaking, that there is a genealogy of racism which can be traced with careful analysis. To do this, West turns his attention to the modern

38. West, *The Cornel West Reader*, 2.
39. West, *The Cornel West Reader*, 70.
40. West, *The Cornel West Reader*, 71.

philosophical discourse on which scientific logic rests, and especially its conceptions of truth and knowledge. The following quote is lengthy, but clearly summarizes West's method of critique in this area:

> The scientific logic rests upon a modern philosophical discourse guided by Greek ocular metaphors (e.g., Eye of the Mind) and is undergirded by Cartesian notions of the primacy of the subject (ego, self) and the preeminence of representation. These notions of the self are buttressed by Bacaonian ideas of observation, evidence, and confirmation which promote the activities of observing, comparing, measuring and ordering physical characteristics of human bodies: given the renewed appreciation and appropriation of classical antiquity in the eighteenth century, these "scientific" activities of observation were regulated by classical aesthetic and cultural norms (Greek lips, noses, etc.). Within this logic, notions of black ugliness, cultural deficiency, and intellectual inferiority are legitimated by the value-laden yet prestigious authority of "science," especially in the eighteenth and nineteenth centuries. The purposeful distortion of "scientific" procedures to further racist hegemony has an important history of its own. The persistent use of pseudoscientific "research" to buttress racist ideology, even when the intellectual integrity of the "scientific" position has been severely eroded, illustrates how racist ideology can incorporate and use/abuse science.[41]

Following on from this, the dominant discourse of our time is "governed by an ideal value-free subject engaged in observing, comparing, ordering and measuring in order to arrive at evidence sufficient to make valid inferences, confirm speculative hypotheses, deduce error-proof conclusions and verify true representations of reality."[42] As indicated above, West is able to demonstrate that, at an implicit and unacknowledged level, such discourse is founded on classical conceptions of truth and beauty. These privilege the normative gaze held by (usually) white males, who preferred white bodies and perspectives as the norm by which all others should be measured. And, what careful analysis reveals here is that such conceptions *"provided an acceptable authority for the idea of white supremacy, an acceptable authority that was closely linked with the major authority on truth and knowledge in the modern world, namely, the institution of science."*[43] As a paradigm case, West looks to the rise of the discipline of natural history, which developed in the modern period and aims "to observe, compare,

---

41. West, *Prophetic Fragment*, 102.
42. West, *The Cornel West Reader*, 75.
43. West, *The Cornel West Reader*, 76.

measure and order animals and human bodies (or classes of animals and human bodies) *based on visible, especially physical, characteristics.*[44] The set of values used to compare and measure are linked in to the Greek cultural and aesthetic norms, hence holding some bodies as the norm by which others are measured, and establishing criteria for determining what is beautiful and what is not. This manner of thinking continues to exert influence on the way in which humans understand themselves today. West argues that the

> initial basis for the idea of white supremacy is to be found in the classificatory categories and the descriptive, representational, order-imposing aims of natural history. The captivity of natural history to what I have called the "normative gaze" signifies the first stage of the emergence of the idea of white supremacy as an object of modern discourse. More specifically . . . the genealogy of racism in the modern West is inseparable from the appearance of the classificatory category of race in natural history.[45]

In short, what is meant here is that a superiority of white races as against black races was built into the discipline of natural history from its outset, based on the suppositions of modern reason noted above. Over time, this way of reasoning gained an intellectual legitimacy and momentum, which for West "can be illustrated by the extent to which racism permeated the writings of the major figures of the Enlightenment. It is important to note that the idea of white supremacy not only was accepted by these figures, but more important, it was accepted by them *without their having to put forward their own arguments to justify* it."[46] Hence, we have here an operation of reason which presents itself as internally consistent but which—as we know from the sorry history of white supremacy in West's own American context and elsewhere—manifests in violence towards those who are outside of its logic:

> New World Africans enter European modernity cast as disposable pieces of property, as commodifiable bits of chattel slavery subject to arbitrary acts of violent punishment and vicious put-down. In short, legalized terror and institutionalised hatred, in the name of white supremacy and Western progress, rendered black peoples economically exploited, politically oppressed and culturally degraded.[47]

---

44. West, *The Cornel West Reader*, 76 (italics in original).
45. West, *The Cornel West Reader*, 77.
46. West, *The Cornel West Reader*, 82 (italics in original).
47. West, *The Cornel West Reader*, 52.

Significantly, this is not simply a case of a certain group of people claiming that whites are better than blacks: the more sophisticated analysis West is making is that the white supremacist ideology is *built into modern rationality* in such a way that it becomes unrecognizable; unless, of course, it is interrupted.

What is most important in this analysis is that the problematic nature of modern discourse, and specifically natural history, can be most readily discovered by taking the view of those who end up victims of its violence. To use the argument developed above, it is only when the vulnerable Other is able to interrupt the smooth flowing of reason here that some ethical redemption can take place. This is because the dominant "rationality" has no internal motivation for interrupting itself—its vested interest is in maintaining its freedom, and hence in working to support the created, dominant, discourse. In order for such interruption to occur there must be an anchor point outside of reason. This returns us to the argument advanced above, in which it was suggested that Catholic faith encourages a position which intentionally takes on the perspective of the vulnerable Other in holding reason to account.[48] When such a teleological suspension takes place, what emerges is a potentially transformative engagement with reason that may overcome its violent tendencies by relativizing its primacy in favor of situating it within the context of ethical responsibility.[49]

Conclusion

To conclude, I return to the question animating this contribution, namely "what happens when faith interrupts reason?" Based on the argument developed above, there are cases wherein the interruption of reason is necessitated by faith, especially if that faith involves the "optics" of ethics, in Levinasian language, or viewing reality from the foot of the cross, as West would put it. The chapter began with St John Paul II's elegant metaphor of faith and reason being "like two wings on which the human spirit rises to the contemplation of truth."[50] That analogy has an important function, as

---

48. As should be clear, it is of course *not* the case that the Catholic tradition provides the only place from which such a critique may be made, however that is the focus of this article. The same kinds of critique are exemplified in other Christian traditions (as will be shown below) and in other world religions, too.

49. Cf. West, *Prophetic Fragments*, 103–4; Westphal, "Levinas's Teleological Suspension," 153. In West's more recent work, he highlights concrete instances of this approach from within the black community, including Martin Luther King, Jr., Ella Baker, Malcolm X. and Ida B. Wells. See West, *Black Prophetic Fire*.

50. John Paul II, *Fides et ratio*, 1.

demonstrated throughout the encyclical and through other contributions to this volume. My hope is that this contribution has helped to extend the analogy and highlight one of its less-recognized subtleties. The wings of a bird do not always flap in perfect synchronicity. At times, where direction needs to be corrected, one wing may move in a different direction to the other for the good of some higher goal.

8

BELIEF, ACCEPTANCE, AND DIVINE HIDDENNESS

—Emma Wood

Introduction

The argument from divine hiddenness poses the following question to the theist: if God existed, wouldn't we expect all reasonable people to believe in him? Isn't the existence of reasonable nonbelief incompatible with the existence of God? This argument was made famous by John Schellenberg and can be summarized most simply as follows:[1]

1. If a perfectly loving God exists, reasonable non-belief does not occur.
2. Reasonable non-belief occurs.
3. No perfectly loving God exists.

In this chapter, I will argue against premise 1. I will grant, in agreement with Schellenberg, that a perfectly loving God must make it possible for human beings to voluntarily enter a *relationship* with him. However, I will argue that the mental state of acceptance of God's existence (along with other propositions about him), rather than the mental state of belief, is what is required for humans to have such a relationship. Acceptance, unlike belief, is voluntary. So long as acceptance of God's existence is rationally permissible, which, I shall argue, it is, it is at any point in time possible for human beings to enter into a relationship with God and have many of the benefits from such a relationship that Schellenberg believes obligates

---

1. Schellenberg, *Divine Hiddenness and Human Reason*.

a perfectly loving God to make possible. I will concede that there may be some benefits in this life mentioned by Schellenberg that "theistic accepters" miss out on, which only strong theistic *belief* can provide. However, I shall argue that such benefits are equally hard to come by through some weaker of belief that Schellenberg allows.

In section 2 of this chapter, I will unpack Schellenberg's argument more thoroughly, and in particular will outline some reasons he gives for premise 1. In section 3, I will outline the distinction between belief and acceptance as I understand it. In section 4, I will discuss the idea that a relationship with God requires acceptance rather than belief. Specifically, I will discuss what relationship with the Christian God requires. (It is this God Schellenberg seems to have in mind, given the philosophers he makes reference to.) Finally, in section 5, I will discuss the extent to which acceptance of God's existence is possible for different human beings, and will suggest that acceptance is at least rationally permissible.

1. Schellenberg's Argument

Schellenberg describes a relationship between a human being and God as one in which God provides divine guidance, support, forgiveness, and in which a human provides trust, obedience, and worship.[2] Schellenberg recognizes many benefits to human beings of such a relationship. Firstly, Schellenberg thinks, there are ethical benefits of human relationship with God which are obvious.[3] The experience of God's grace and forgiveness toward oneself, and the conviction that all humans (even the most uncongenial) are creatures loved by him provide powerful sources of moral motivation. Though Schellenberg does not discuss this, I would add that the Christian belief in God's restoration of creation provides yet another resource for moral motivation. When doing the morally right thing becomes costly, and fighting moral causes becomes tiring through the course of life, the thought that one lives in an impersonal universe that ultimately does not care about one's efforts can be disheartening. The Christian belief in a loving God who will one day renew creation and make sure justice wins is, by contrast, a great encouragement: good causes are all the more easy to fight if one believes that victory is in sight. So I am happy to grant, with Schellenberg, that a perfectly loving God would seek relationship with all humans even if only for these ethical benefits. If God loves humanity, then he wills our wellbeing, and the wellbeing of humanity is frustrated by humans acting unethically

2. Schellenberg, *Divine Hiddenness and Human Reason*, 18.
3. Schellenberg, *Divine Hiddenness*, 19–20.

toward each other. So, given that relationship with God is likely to enable humans to act more ethically, I think it can be granted that a perfectly loving God would desire relationship with all humans.

Secondly, Schellenberg claims that relationship with God directly contributes to human wellbeing in and of itself. Schellenberg calls this second class of benefits the "experiential" benefits, and they too are wide ranging:[4]

> Consider, for example, the peace or sense of security mentioned by Adams, the joy that may come from the conviction that one is rightly related to what is ultimately real, the self-enrichment experienced in worship, the experience of God's loving presence.[5]

Once again, I will grant that such benefits provide good reasons for a perfectly loving God to desire relationship with human beings. Importantly, Schellenberg thinks, the experiential and ethical benefits of relationship with God are benefits that a perfectly loving God would desire for humans not simply at some point (for instance, after death in a post-mortem existence), but at *all points* in their life.[6] From this it follows that a perfectly loving God will seek to enable a relationship with all human beings at all points in their life.

Two qualifications of Schellenberg's need mentioning at this point. Although God may desire to enable a relationship with all human beings at every point in their life, Schellenberg acknowledges that this does not mean, necessarily, that such a relationship is assured by a loving God's existence: that there are human beings not in a relationship with God is consistent with God's existing and God's desiring such relationships. Schellenberg follows a number of other religious thinkers in claiming that God's perfect love requires that God respects human freedom—even the freedom to reject a relationship with him, which many humans choose.[7] Although a perfectly loving God will *enable* human beings to believe in him, humans may nevertheless put in a less than reasonable effort to expose themselves to evidence for his existence. I would add to this that even if God did not merely provide evidence of his existence but strongly *compelled* a human to believe (through, for instance, providing a human with the kind of strong "seeming" experience that would render a belief in him non-inferentially justified), that human would still be free to decline a relationship with God.

---

4. Schellenberg, *Divine Hiddenness*, 20.
5. Schellenberg, *Divine Hiddenness*, 20–21.
6. Or, at least all points at which human beings are capable of having thoughts about God. It would be uncharitable to assume Schellenberg believes infants are owed such benefits in exactly the same way, given their cognitive capacities.
7. Schellenberg, *Divine Hiddenness*, 27.

For a human may believe that God exists yet still decline a relationship with him, given that a relationship with God requires more than mere belief in his existence: as Schellenberg himself notes, it requires trust, obedience, and worship. So, though a loving God will desire relationship with human beings and will seek to *enable* such relationship by enabling belief in his existence, this does not necessarily entail that such relationships will eventuate: God's enabling belief is a necessary, but not sufficient condition for relationship between him and a human being.

The second qualification to Schellenberg's claim (that the experiential and ethical benefits available to humans provide reason to think that a loving God would desire a relationship with all humans at all times) is that Schellenberg is careful to claim that he is not "asking for the beatific vision in this life."[8] The benefits of a relationship with God—particularly, perhaps, the experiential ones—do not have to be experienced in this life to the extent that they will be experienced in the post-mortem state anticipated by the Christian tradition. So although a loving God would desire relationship with human beings at all points in their life, Schellenberg denies that such love involves the desire that humans experience the benefits of such a relationship to their *maximal extent* at all points in their life.

To sum up the first step in my more detailed look at Schellenberg's argument: Schellenberg claims that a loving God would make it possible for humans, if they so choose, to enter into relationship with him, at any point in their life. Such a desire of God's is entailed by his being all-loving, as theists have traditionally claimed he is.

According to Schellenberg, a human's belief in God is a precondition for a human's relationship with God. In order to have the attitudes of gratefulness, trust, dependence, worship or submission characteristic of a relationship with God, one must believe that he exists: "It is not as though someone who cannot be grateful to God or praise God because she does not believe there is a God could do so if only she *tried* a little harder. Such attitudes and actions are not just contingently difficult but *logically impossible* for one who does not believe that God exists."[9] Given this, and given the arguments in favor of the claim that a loving God would want to make human relationships with him possible, it follows that a loving God will do what it takes to enable belief. That God must play such a part in such enabling is important, since belief is involuntary. Beliefs about certain propositions are formed either when we encounter evidence that compels us to infer that they are true, or they may be formed non-inferentially, through direct

---

8. Schellenberg, *Divine Hiddenness*, 28.
9. Schellenberg, *Divine Hiddenness*, 30.

experience. It follows, then, that God must provide the degree of evidence that compels receptive humans[10] to believe, or must provide them with a strong sense of his presence, or some kind of other religious experience that might generate belief.

Since Schellenberg sees no barrier to an omnipotent God doing such things, Schellenberg sees the existence of those who earnestly seek but do not find God to entail his non-existence. According to Schellenberg, there exist many people who desire to believe in God, and who expose themselves to theistic evidence and arguments to the best of their ability, but for whom such endeavours do not result in belief in God.[11] Obviously, there may be many non-believers who are culpable for their non-belief. Some may seek evidence for God's existence but do so half-heartedly, failing to apply the same rigor to the investigation into God's existence as they do to other important areas of life. Others may take attitudes toward God that are so antagonistic that they culpably "blind" themselves and are unable to reason clear-headedly about God's existence. Still others may not search at all. But still, Schellenberg thinks, it is unreasonable to insist that *all* non-believers fall into these categories. There are non-believers who have done the searching that could reasonably be expected of them with their given abilities, and who have failed to find God.

Although human beings can take certain voluntary actions that make belief in God possible, such as searching for and exposing oneself to evidence in favour of God's existence, the formation of belief itself is

---

10. I say "receptive humans," as this qualification is important to Schellenberg. In his discussion of the human freedom to reject relationship with God, he concedes that God may even allow human beings to culpably close their minds off to him such that they are not receptive to evidence for his existence in a way that is commensurate with their general intellectual capabilities (Schellenberg, *Divine Hiddenness*, 27–28). But if humans have sufficient integrity about the question of the existence of God, and are appropriately receptive, such evidence should, when encountered, generate belief.

11. If one is tempted to object at this point that this may be because humans, however earnest in their efforts, may make cognitive mistakes in searching for evidence, or may lack the ability to evaluate arguments at the intellectual level required to gain belief in God, we should reply that this does not lessen the force of Schellenberg's argument in *Divine Hiddenness*. Schellenberg perhaps anticipates such an objection when he discusses different types of rationality, some of which humans are culpable for and some of which they are not (ibid., 61–64). Two relevant types of rationality to be contrasted here are 1) the application of epistemic reasoning to a situation in which one undertakes all the practices one regards as normally relevant for discovering the truth of things, and 2) the doing so to the extent required to know the objective truth of a matter. I think Schellenberg argues correctly that individuals can only be culpable for 1), since 2) may be beyond the ability of many. If a loving God desired to be in a relationship with a particular human, I think we should grant that he would not require a process of investigation or reasoning that is beyond an individual's cognitive abilities.

involuntary: when the evidence we have exposed ourselves to finally causes us to feel convinced that God exists, this effect of evidence on our mental state is not something we have control over. But if we do not have control over this mental state, and yet this mental state is required for God to have a relationship with us, then it follows that if God desires a relationship with all human beings, he must enable this mental state to arise after any honest search for him is undertaken. Should some honest human beings lack the cognitive ability to search for evidence at all, God must endow them with non-inferentially justified belief; a strong "seeming" experience.

But reasonable, non-resistant non-belief does occur. Therefore, Schellenberg concludes, a perfectly loving God does not exist.

2. Belief and Acceptance

As we have seen, much of Schellenberg's argument hangs on the fact that belief is *involuntary*. It is, in an important sense, *not up to humans* whether they believe in God. So, the absence of theistic belief in earnest seekers suggests a failing on God's part and not on theirs. Such a failing is incompatible with the existence of a God who is perfectly omnipotent and loving.[12]

But what if what was required for relationship with God was not *belief* proper, but something voluntary, such as the closely related epistemic state of acceptance? If acceptance, rather than belief, is what is required for relationship with God, this re-opens the avenue of human responsibility and once again makes human failure the likely explanation for the many humans, even the seemingly reasonable ones, who are not in relationship with God. Since this important distinction between belief and acceptance is largely overlooked by Schellenberg, it will help to summarize it for the remainder of this section.

An example of a belief I hold is that human-induced climate change is real. Due to the consensus in the scientific community on the matter, and due to the fact that I am usually disposed to trust the scientific community on their areas of expertise, I have a high degree of confidence that the planet is warming due to carbon dioxide emissions. This belief of mine affects my actions in various ways, and shows itself through various dispositions. For example, if someone asks me whether human-induced climate change is real, I am disposed to reply "yes." Given my desire that future generations experience a safe and beautiful environment, my belief in human-induced

---

12. It may be commented here that this failing is incompatible with the existence of a God who is both perfectly loving *and* omnipotent. I shall treat Schellenberg's argument in *Divine Hiddenness* as if this is assumed.

climate change spurs me on to take various actions, such as protesting the opening of new coal mines, powering my home with 100% renewable electricity, and making sure no money of mine is invested in the fossil fuel industry. Another disposition this belief of mine gives rise to is the disposition to be *surprised* were I to find out that it is false.

Imagine the following scenario in which I do not *believe* a proposition, but merely *accept* it. I am collecting philosophy assignments, and a student complains that she could not turn her assignment in due to computer failure. As I listen to her story, I do not experience the same overwhelming conviction that she is innocent. There is a decent chance that she is not culpable, but there is also a decent chance that she is: some details of her story do not add up, and her behavior throughout the course suggests that she isn't the most dedicated student. But despite my lack of confidence either way about whether she is culpable, I have to make an assumption about the matter, because I need to decide how I will treat her. I need to decide whether to assume she is telling the truth and therefore refrain from penalizing her, or assume she is telling less than the truth and penalise her. Suppose I choose to accept the former—to act on the assumption that she is telling the truth. I do not penalise her.

The above examples of belief and acceptance illustrate a number of important similarities and differences between the two epistemic states. A belief about a proposition is a mental state involving a high degree of confidence that it is true. Acceptance of a proposition, on the other hand, occurs when one is not confident in the truth of the proposition to such a high degree, but when one nevertheless acts on, or reasons from, the assumption that it is true. There are two major areas of difference between belief and acceptance, and one major area of similarity. They are different attitudes toward propositions, they are similar in that they are expressed by dispositions, and they are different in that one is involuntary and the other is voluntary. I will comment briefly on these features now.

Belief about a proposition involves the mental state of *taking it to be true* (and therefore its denial to be false), and doing so with a great deal of surety about its truth. Though some philosophers prefer to define belief as consisting in degrees from "weak" to "strong" belief, where weak belief about the truth of a proposition involves merely taking it to be more likely true than false, and strong belief involving the ascription of a very high credence, I prefer not to think of belief this way and to classify what is often called "weak belief" as a mental state better associated with acceptance.[13] It is often said about belief that it is something that disposes one to be surprised if one

---

13. As can be seen by Schellenberg himself, *Divine Hiddenness*, 32.

were to find out its falsity.[14] But this statement about belief would make little sense if belief included the state of merely thinking a proposition to be more likely true than false. If I assign a credence of, say, 0.7 to the proposition that Joe Biden will have a second term as U.S. President, I am hardly going to be *surprised* if she is not. Belief about a proposition must involve a degree of confidence about its truth such that one would be surprised if one found out that it was false. I propose, then, that the weakest belief could be while still counting as belief would involve an assignment of credence around 0.9 (though I concede it would be difficult to argue for a precise "cut-off point" at which surprise at falsity occurs). When one accepts a proposition, on the other hand, one may not be inclined to be so confident about its truth, even if one may regard it as more likely to be true than not.

I would go further and allow also that one can also accept a proposition while being *uncertain* as to whether it is more likely to be true than not. For my purposes, I will say that acceptance of a proposition must involve at least the belief that there is a reasonable chance that it is true, such that one would not be surprised if one had it confirmed. Whatever minimum credence fits this description (perhaps anything above 0.1) can be thought of as the lower limit that one's uncertainty about what credence to assign ranges from. Acceptance of a proposition can occur even while we are uncertain about what credence above this minimum we should assign. Such a mental state describes well the one involved in my accepting my suspect student's story. I think there is a significant chance she is telling the truth (0.1 or higher, perhaps), but I am uncertain as to just how great that chance is.

A similarity that belief and acceptance share is that they are expressed dispositionally: in conjunction with our given desires, the attitudes of belief and acceptance toward propositions have effects on our actions. It is necessary to define belief and acceptance in partly dispositional terms, as it would be difficult to make sense of what it means to believe or accept a proposition when we are not consciously thinking about it. We hardly want to say that, if I happen at a given moment not to be thinking about the fact that climate change is occurring, I cease to possess that belief. As Alston puts it, it makes more sense to affirm that beliefs are both conscious and latent. And the best way, it seems, to make sense of what it means for a belief to be present but latent is to speak of the dispositions it gives rise to. To take my belief about climate change as our example: even when I am not consciously thinking about climate change, it is nevertheless a fact about me that I am disposed to answer "yes" to the question, "is human-induced climate change real?" and that I am disposed to use the proposition that climate change is real as

---

14. See for instance Alston, "Belief, Acceptance, and Religious Faith," 4.

a premise in ethical arguments when the occasion arises. As has been said already, both belief and acceptance of a proposition give rise to a number of other dispositions and actions that have the potential to shape one's life: the belief in climate change, coupled with a desire to care for the future of humankind, gives rise to my being involved in rallies, switching my electricity plan, and divesting from fossil fuels. And acceptance of similarly important propositions will have these sorts of life-shaping effects also: particularly, as I will argue, acceptance of certain propositions about God.

Another thing worth saying about acceptance of a given proposition is that it, just as much as belief in a proposition, will dispose us to reason in certain ways for more theoretical purposes. If I am a scientist who believes in climate change, and I observe, over time, movement of many animal species away from the equator and toward the poles, my belief in climate change will likely lead me to reason that climate change is a cause of this. But acceptance of a proposition can figure in our reasoning and theory-building in the same way. Suppose, as a philosopher, I have considered the merits of libertarianism and compatibilism as competing views about the nature of free will. Suppose that, though I fall short of believing in libertarian free will, given the controversy of the topic, I decide to accept libertarianism because I think the arguments for it are stronger than its rivals. Having accepted the libertarian account of free will, I then proceed to use it in a premise as part of a free will defence when confronted by the problem of evil where, if I accepted compatibilism, I could not.

The final and most important difference to mention between belief and acceptance is the involuntary nature of the former and the voluntary nature of the latter. Though, as has already been said, one can take a number of voluntary actions that are more likely to give rise to the formation of beliefs, such as exposing oneself to evidence, the effect of exposure to evidence on one's mind—the "feeling something to be true" as a result of such exposure—is involuntary. This fact is all the more apparent when we reflect that occasionally, when we form beliefs that we wish we did not have, it is not under our voluntary control to rid ourselves of them or get them out of our head. Despite the fact that I sometimes wish I could be blissfully ignorant of climate change, I cannot rid myself of my belief in it, having exposed myself to the evidence in favor of it.

Of course, the mental states about a proposition's truth that are involved in acceptance—a "weak belief" that a proposition is more likely true than not, or an uncertainty about the credence within a certain range—are just as involuntary as belief. Just as exposure to strong evidence in favor of a proposition's truth causes us to believe it is highly likely to be true, exposure to weaker evidence for a proposition (or mixed evidence) causes us to have the mental states associated with acceptance of a proposition in this involuntary way. Nevertheless, the decision to act on, or reason from, the assumption that a proposition is true is voluntary. And this voluntary element of acceptance, I will argue, causes great problems for Schellenberg's arguments.

3. Acceptance as Sufficient for Relationship with God

Relationship with the Christian God involves some sort of intellectual commitment to core Christian doctrines: the existence of God, the reality of sin and our need for God's forgiveness, the divinity of Jesus, the saving work of his death on the cross, the need to repent in order to benefit from this and receive forgiveness, and the hope of God's coming kingdom for the saved as evidenced by Jesus' resurrection. Must commitment to such doctrines involve belief, in the technical sense just defined, or will *acceptance* of these doctrines suffice, in order for a human relationship with the Christian God to be possible?

I think there is a sound theological case to be made that acceptance of core doctrines about God, ourselves, Jesus and his death on the cross, the goodness of following him, and the need for repentance, is needed for human relationship with God. Although, in English Bibles, the term "belief" is spoken of as being required for salvation, this is of course no argument in favor of the idea that belief in our technical sense is being spoken of. For one thing, speakers of the English language frequently use the term "belief" in colloquial settings to refer to *either* belief or acceptance—the two concepts are often conflated under the term *belief*. Secondly, when scrutinising the meaning of words in Scripture at this level, we must take into account the meaning of words in their original language. As Alston argues, the words translated to "belief" are sometimes taken from the original Greek *pisteuo*, a word arguably closer to "acceptance" in our technical sense, than belief. The fact that this Greek word is translated to "belief" owes, once again, to the commonplace conflation between belief and acceptance on the part of English translators.

There are further reasons to suppose that acceptance of core Christian doctrines, rather than belief, is sufficient for Christian faith. Frequently in Scripture, God asks people to respond, as if this were under their voluntary control, to his call. In light of this it makes sense to think that God is asking for acceptance of the things he tells us, rather than belief. Furthermore, when one reflects on all the things the response to God's call involves: repentance, acknowledgement of Jesus' divinity and lordship, the obeying of

Jesus in keeping with this, the acknowledgement of one's unrighteousness before a righteous God, the viewing of others as creatures of God and the loving of them in keeping with this, the prayer and seeking of God's guidance, and the worship of God, one can see that all these things can be done through acceptance of this gospel, as well as through belief. Even if one is uncertain about God's existence or that the evidence for the resurrection is as compelling as apologists say, one can still choose to resolve to take seriously the chance that Christianity is true, repent on this basis, and ask God for forgiveness. Even if one is unsure to what extent one ought to be convinced by the evidence for Jesus' divinity, one can still fairly easily accept that, *if* he is divine, he is entitled to worship and obedience, which one can choose to live out in one's life. If one is convinced that there is a significant enough chance that Jesus is in fact divine, even if one is not overwhelmingly convinced, one can still resolve to act and live on this assumption of Jesus' divinity rather than on the opposite assumption. Even if, when one prays, one does not have a sense that anyone is listening (an experience that many devout Christians have), one can still utter words of prayer having decided that one is going to proceed with life on the basis that there is a God who is listening, with a desire to be guided by him, whatever this might mean, if this is the case. And even when one experiences doubts about the existence of the Christian God, one can still choose to follow the commands of the Christian God to love one's neighbor as oneself.

When Jesus asks us if we are for him or against him, I believe both Scripture and common sense points to the idea that it is a normative commitment that he is primarily after. Those who lack the high degree of confidence in his words may still say to him, like the man from Mark 9:24 "I believe! Help me with my unbelief!" and be heard by God. What does such a statement mean if not "I want to believe! (I am normatively committed to following and trusting you, thus I accept!) Help me with my unbelief!" That someone would ask Jesus to help him with his unbelief already indicates that he has accepted Jesus' lordship, despite wavering confidence of conviction. What is striking about this story of acceptance from Scripture is the outcome: Jesus accepts the man's prayer for his demon-possessed son, despite his lack of belief, and cures him. This seems to me to constitute Scriptural warrant for the idea that God may find a person's acceptance of him as a reason for mercy and thus the basis of a relationship, rather than full-blooded belief.

One might respond at this point that I have merely shown that Christian acceptance is good enough for relationship with God *according to Christian theology*. But, it might be objected, Christian theology might simply be mistaken, having not taken seriously enough Schellenberg's claim that one cannot love God, worship God, trust God, or do anything else a relationship with God requires, unless one believes in God. This, Schellenberg says, is logically impossible.

But Schellenberg overstates his case. It may be logically impossible to love X if one does not possess the *concept* of X: I cannot say that I love pasta, horses, or God if I do not possess these concepts. If I do not possess the concepts of pasta, horses, or God, I cannot direct any love toward them. But there is no logical impossibility involved in possessing the concept of God, being unsure about his existence, and directing love and devotion toward him nevertheless. The following argument might help us to see how this is possible. Suppose there are many people in my life whom I love: friends, family, colleagues, and the like. Suppose one day I come to doubt the existence of other minds after delving into some skeptical arguments. Though I continue to care for, listen to, and help the people in my life, I am constantly plagued by doubts that these people really exist, have minds, or benefit from receiving my love, in a very similar way to the way in which a doubting Christian might wonder if there is anyone on the receiving end of her prayers. Suppose that, despite my doubts, I resolve to accept the fact that the other minds of the people in my life are real. I commit, despite my doubts, to act and treat people as though they do have minds, are not zombies, and can be benefitted by my love. I think we can see that it would be implausible to claim that it is not logically possible that I love these people. After all, if these people do exist, as I have accepted they do, they will certainly have been on the receiving end of my love and will therefore have *been loved*. In the very same way, if God does exist, he will have been on the receiving end of every hopeful prayer uttered even by doubters who wonder if he hears them. God will have received trust from people who base important life decisions on his revealed wisdom and commands, even if they experience doubts as to whether he exists. God will have been on the receiving end of every worshipper who has resolved to worship in a similar manner. Love, worship, trust, and anything else involved in human relationship with God is certainly logically possible under acceptance, and does not need to involve belief.

But perhaps there are other possible grounds for objection, even if the points just made are conceded. Schellenberg's argument that God would want to make relationship with himself possible for all people is based, after all, on the claim there are human benefits to be had by his doing so. But, it may be argued, such benefits are only experienced in relationships with God in which a human *believes*. Mere acceptance of God's existence (and other core Christian doctrines) will not provide the ethical and experiential benefits that give a loving God reason to enable human relationship in the first place. If this is the case, then proving that acceptance makes a relationship with God possible achieves a fatally hollow victory: because it does not make the *kind* of relationship possible that Schellenberg thinks a perfectly loving God has reason to enable. For the remainder of this section, I turn to such an objection.

I think it is clear that the ethical benefits Schellenberg discusses can be had from acceptance of Christian doctrines as well as from belief. Indeed, the endeavor to ethically improve one's life makes up much of what Christian acceptance amounts to. The ethical improvements to one's life that Schellenberg speaks of reflect the taking on of certain normative commitments as a result of faith. And Christian acceptance involves, precisely, the taking on of normative commitments: repentance for one's flaws, seeking of God's guidance, and trusting that God's commands are for one's own good and for the good of others.

Perhaps it could be argued that the experiential benefits discussed by Schellenberg are harder to come by in a relationship with God that merely involves acceptance. For instance, the comfort and joy one experiences from knowing God is there and has promised salvation from one's own suffering, and from the suffering of the world, would be somewhat mitigated if one is plagued by doubts about the very existence of this God, as one can be if one merely accepts, but does not believe, in his existence. I think it can be granted that Christian believers, as opposed to Christian accepters, can have easier access to these experiential benefits. But Schellenberg's own statements about belief would prevent him from concluding on this basis that a perfectly loving God must enable everyone to believe. For it isn't clear that all forms of belief, as Schellenberg defines belief, would lend itself to the discussed experiential benefits to a great extent either. Schellenberg grants that "belief" may include "weak belief" or believing God's existence to be more likely true than not—such a mental state is one I have said can be involved in instances of acceptance.[15] Such weak belief is certainly compatible with many doubts about God's existence: the very kind of doubts that could compromise one's comfort and joy in believing, but it nevertheless counts as belief according to Schellenberg. The diminished experiential benefit that one gains from "weak belief," I suggest, would be quite similar to the diminished experiential benefit one gains even from mere acceptance in which one is uncertain as to whether God's existence is more likely than not. It follows that if it is sufficient for a loving God to enable only weak belief—if the experiential benefits of weak belief are *good enough* for a God

---

15. Schellenberg, *Divine Hiddenness*, 32–33.

who enables it to count as loving—then it is sufficient for a loving God to enable acceptance, rather than belief, as a basis of relationship.

I would say also that it is not just the distinction between weak and strong belief that prevents, by Schellenberg's own lights, an objection that acceptance is not an experientially good enough state for relationship with God. The distinction between inferentially formed and non-inferentially formed belief may create a problem also. While some people have formed strong beliefs in the existence of God on the basis of what they take to be good evidence, others do not need such evidence, and believe in God simply as a result of a very active *sensus divinitatus* or strong "seeming" experience of God's presence. Now, for the class of people who do not "feel" it to be true that God exists, but who believe he does on the basis of evidence, it is arguable that they might lack some experiential benefits when compared to theists who have formed beliefs on the basis of "seeming" experiences. Particularly, an "evidentialist" may feel less *comfort* from God's existence than those who can simply sense God's presence, especially in troubling times of life. After all, when one receives comfort from other human beings in times of trouble, this is not because we have convinced ourselves, through painstaking evidence and argument, that our comforter really does have a mind and really is directing comfort toward us. The comfort we feel consists in the very fact that we simply have the overwhelming *sense* that another empathetic mind is sharing in our troubles. In the very same way, a believer who simply *senses* God's comforting presence may feel a lot more comfort from their belief in God than a believer who feels no such thing but whose belief - even strong belief - is based strictly on argument and evidence. And yet, despite these experiential disadvantages, Schellenberg seems to accept provision of such evidentialists' beliefs as befitting of a perfectly loving God.

I ought to add one qualification to what has been said above. In my attempt to argue that acceptance is experientially good enough a state for a loving God to be obligated to enable for humans, I have argued that some forms of belief, as Schellenberg has defined them, are the same as or similar to the very mental states involved in acceptance. But it is also worth saying that "mere acceptance" may turn out to not be so experientially poor after all. Anecdotes suggest that the very decision to accept God's existence can indeed result in stronger belief than one had before, and even of a very non-inferential, "feeling" sort. Many believers have reported the experience of being quite doubtful about God's existence, but deciding to accept his existence anyway, and pray a first prayer of repentance. On praying such a prayer, many have experienced being struck by a strong sense of God's presence. We know that voluntary actions, such as the seeking of evidence, may lead to the involuntary experience of gaining a belief about a certain proposition. Accepting a proposition itself might be just another voluntary belief-producing action itself.

The upshot of all this discussion is that acceptance provides a means for relationship with God that is just as experientially beneficial as many instances of belief: in particular, of weak belief and evidence-based belief. If one wants to deny that acceptance provides human beings an "experientially good enough" relationship with God, and that God is less than perfectly loving for not enabling some people to do more than just accept his existence, one would have to modify Schellenberg's entire argument. One would have to claim not just that reasonable lack of *belief* is incompatible with the existence of a perfectly loving God, but would have to claim that reasonable lack of *strong, non-inferentially formed* belief is incompatible with the existence of a perfectly loving God. And such a modified premise, it seems to me, is quite dubious. There could be many conceivable long-term human benefits if some humans were not granted the ability to believe as strongly as others, or some the ability to believe only on the basis of evidence. Those who must settle for acceptance may develop moral virtues that untroubled believers may not, for instance. Furthermore, if a good argument from divine hiddenness ought not rely on the supposition that a loving God must provide everyone "the beatific vision in this life," then a good argument from divine hiddenness probably ought not to have a problem either with the idea that some people in this life—believers—might be experientially closer to the beatific vision than others—accepters.

Let me now summarize the arguments of this section, and tie them back into my response to Schellenberg's argument from divine hiddenness. I have argued, in this section, that human beings do not need to *believe* that the Christian God exists (or believe the other core doctrines) in order to have a relationship with the Christian God: human beings can choose to accept the existence of the Christian God (and the other core doctrines) in order to have such a relationship. More importantly, acceptance can provide human beings the kind of ethical and experiential benefits to be from such a relationship as many kinds of belief can.

The fact that voluntary acceptance provides a viable route to relationship with God undermines Schellenberg's argument from divine hiddenness. The reason, Schellenberg claims, that a loving God would need to enable belief for all humans is because belief is both required for relationship with God and is *involuntary*. If belief is necessary for human beings to form a relationship with God, and if some humans, no matter how many earnest voluntary actions they undertake to generate a belief in God, cannot do so, then it appears that there is no loving God doing the enabling of belief. But suppose acceptance is all that is needed for a human being to form a relationship with God. If this is true, then God cannot be "blamed" for failing to enable people's acceptance, for acceptance is completely voluntary and up to *humans*. I put it to the reader that the fact that many people are not in relationship with God is due primarily to a failure to voluntarily accept, rather than a failure to involuntarily believe, and such a voluntary failure on the part of humans is not in the least inconsistent with the existence of a perfectly loving God.

I would be so bold as to suggest that involuntary lack of belief might be frequently used as an excuse not to enter in a relationship with God, and if I am right about this, such a fact would further undermine the hypothesis that there are people who sincerely want to be in a relationship with God but who are not. The claim "but I simply cannot bring myself to believe!" while true in many cases, may be being used as something of an excuse to avoid what is really necessary for relationship with God: acceptance. Indeed, if such people sincerely do want to believe so badly in God for whatever experiential or ethical benefits they may gain, one must wonder why these same people do not make any attempt to accept, and see whether such benefits can be had nonetheless. The existence of earnest seekers who "want to believe" in God but refuse to accept him throws serious doubt on the claim that they really want to believe so badly after all.

4. Final Objections and Responses: Acceptance as Rationally Permissible and Easily Available

I have argued that since acceptance of truths about the Christian God is voluntary, a relationship with the Christian God is something that anybody can voluntarily enter into. Given that anybody can voluntarily enter into relationship with God via acceptance, it represents no failure on the part of a loving God that he has not enabled everybody to believe.

There are two major objections that can be put to the statement that anybody can enter into relationship with the Christian God through acceptance of his existence and certain other propositions about him. Firstly, one might object that Christian acceptance is irrational in some way, and therefore that sufficiently rational people are involuntarily prevented from Christian acceptance in the very same way that others are prevented from belief. A second objection is that many core Christian doctrines cannot be accepted by many people, since, due mainly to geographical location, many people do not have access to Christian concepts central to these doctrines.

Keeping our definition of acceptance in mind, the first objection must state that the mental states associated with acceptance are irrational, not rationally permissible. Recall the two mental states involved in Christian acceptance—either thinking Christianity to be more likely true than not, or thinking that Christianity could be assigned a range of credences above a certain minimum, while being unsure exactly which one. Thus sufficiently rational people, the objection goes, will involuntarily be *unable* to be Christian accepters if it is rationally impermissible to believe there is a decent chance that Christianity is true. We are left with our original problem: the fact that God does not enable everyone to enter into relationship with him, and that this is inconsistent with perfect love. This objection, I believe, can be answered rather simply: the mental states associated with Christian acceptance are not rationally impermissible. Conclusively defending this claim is beyond the scope of this chapter, given that several other papers could be written on this topic.

However, I hope I can say enough to at least give the reader optimism that this statement could be defended by subsequent discussion, and this objection addressed.

Christian apologetics, and an abundance of arguments in Christianity's favor, are as old as the faith. Before criticizing the merits of such arguments, would-be detractors must recall that one need not even believe Christianity to be more likely true than not in order to accept it. Above I said that one merely needs to take there to be a reasonable chance that it is true—a big enough chance such that one should not be surprised were one to find out it was true, such as a 10 percent chance. It is one thing to claim that, all arguments considered, Christianity is more likely to be false than true though for my part, I disagree. It is quite another claim—I dare say a very difficult one to defend—that Christianity deserves an assignment of credence less than 0.1. The work of Richard Swinburne, among others, deserves particular attention when considering this point. Though, Swinburne argues, deductive arguments for the existence of the Christian God may have failed, there is a good inductive case that could be made for it.[16] If one takes observations about the world on which cosmological, teleological, miracle, and resurrection arguments rest, considers that each observation raises the probability of the Christian worldview, it starts to appear as though the atheist has a lot of data to explain away. According to Swinburne, such observations, even when placed alongside atheological observations such as the existence of evil, raise the probability of the truth of Christianity to well over 50 percent.[17] While I cannot discuss Swinburne's arguments in enough detail to answer our objection, his work has made a considerable

---

16. Swinburne, *The Resurrection of God Incarnate*.
17. Swinburne, *The Resurrection of God Incarnate*.

impact on philosophy of religion: that he and countless others, have made such a case for Christianity shows that there is a real conversation to be had about the possibility that Christianity is more likely to be true than not, and that the contrary assumption no longer enjoys default status. It may well be the case that Christianity is more likely true than not—so for one to argue that it is not rationally permissible to even think there to be at least a significant *chance* that it is true would be a difficult task indeed. Given the abundance of Christian apologetic work available, any atheist who simply believes, without much investigation into the matter, that it is not rationally permissible to believe there to be such a chance, could easily be accused of wilful blindness. There is reason to believe that, for anyone who puts an honest effort into investigating its merits, the belief that it is rationally permissible to think Christianity to have at least that 10 percent chance of being true, will not be hard to come by. This claim, as I said, cannot be conclusively defended in the space left in this chapter. But there is reason to think its defence a hopeful and worthwhile enterprise for subsequent discussion. And such discussion, in conjunction with the other arguments made in this chapter, would spell defeat for Schellenberg's argument in the absence of further objections.

Also worthy of mention is the fact that the rational permissibility of theism has been well defended on non-evidentialist grounds as well. Certain theistic beliefs may be properly basic in the way that many other rationally permissible beliefs not based on evidence or argument are. One who is unaware of evidentialist apologetics (or perhaps intellectually incapable of appreciating them) may still be acting within the bounds of rational permissibility by following the lead of their *sensus divinitatus*. Whether Christianity is true or false, or more likely to be true than false, are still considered by many to be live and controversial questions. But an argument that Christian philosophers have perhaps "won" is that Christian belief is *rationally permissible*—one is not irrational for having it. So much more rationally permissible, then, is Christian acceptance.

I shall now move onto the second question raised at the beginning of this section. The Christian faith and its core doctrines involve concepts and ideas—a creator God, our own sinfulness, Jesus of Nazareth, his crucifixion, his atoning sacrifice, his resurrection, and the new creation—which are simply not accessible to people who are sufficiently geographically or culturally isolated from them. One cannot accept propositions that involve concepts that one does not possess. Does the existence of people, past and present, who happen to not possess concepts involved in core Christian doctrines, entail that there are people who are, once again, involuntarily unable to enter relationship with the Christian God?

This question steps into another grand question within theology and religious philosophy: the question about the extent to which knowledge of religious truths is necessary for an individual's salvation. While a considerable number of theologians have not been bothered by the idea that individuals might be condemned to eternal suffering due partly to a lacking of information they were simply unable to acquire, many others have concluded that such a situation is incompatible with God's love. Those on this latter side of the debate have often proposed that, for those to whom more specific Christian concepts are unavailable, a more "basic," more intuitively or naturally accessible set of truths need to be acknowledged and lived out.[18]

I am quite sympathetic to this idea, and I happen to believe two such concepts within the Christian faith may be universally accessible. Firstly, the concept of a supreme creator God is arguably a concept that is possessed by all humans. While not all humans in the world may *believe* in God, it is possible that everybody understands the concept of a personal being who is both a powerful creator and a moral authority, and that a disposition to believe in him arises at a very early age.[19] Secondly, the concept of "sin"—the idea that human beings have a tendency to regard ourselves as of utmost importance, that we do not live as we ought, and that if there is a loving creator, we will not have treated ourselves and others as he intended—is a rather intuitive one. Even the most ardent humanists, if they are honest, believe there is such a thing as the dark side of human nature. And most humanists would probably be willing to agree that, *if* there were such a thing as a perfectly good God, he would be displeased with this side of us.

Given that the concepts of both God and sin are intuitive, I would think that it would be possible for any human to accept in some sense, their flawed nature and their need for the mercy of God. If such an attitude of the heart is really all that is necessary for salvation and relationship with God, then such a thing is certainly possible for anybody, even those lacking awareness of more specific Christian concepts, to enter into. When I said above that Christian acceptance involves the acceptance of all the core Christian doctrines, this can be read as applying to people who have *access* to the concepts involved in such doctrines. One may still take a generous theological view about the fate of "the unreached," and that the doctrinal requirements for a reconciled relationship with God are commensurate with one's epistemic resources. On this understanding, the definition of a "core Christian doctrine" is a doctrine which disqualifies one from counting

---

18. Osburn, E. "Those Who Have Never Heard: Have They No Hope?"; Rahner, *Theological Investigations*.

19. Richardson. *Eternity in their Hearts*; Petrovich, "Japanese Children's Explanations of the Origins of Natural Objects," 304.

as Christian if one *consciously rejects* it, rather than if one happens to not possess it due to ignorance.

Conclusion: Our Response to God is on Us

In this chapter, I have looked at Schellenberg's argument from divine hiddenness, and have argued that the distinction between belief and acceptance gives us good reasons to doubt the success of his argument. If a perfectly loving God exists, one would not expect reasonable, non-resistant nonbelief to exist. This is because belief in God is involuntary, so a perfectly loving God, who would want a relationship with all human beings, would have to enable it.

I have argued that relationships with God do not require beliefs about him, but rather, *acceptance* of certain propositions about him. Acceptance is voluntary, so lack of it points to no lack of love on God's part (much as human resistance to belief, as Schellenberg concedes, shows no lack of love) either. The existence of a perfectly loving God is compatible even with widespread lack of human relationships with him. While it is believable that there may be many people who sincerely wish to believe in God but cannot, it is far less believable that there are people who sincerely wish to accept but do not. If acceptance, unlike belief, is voluntary, one's sincere desire to accept should result in one's acceptance.

I have considered the objection that Christian acceptance may not be irrational, such that it too is beyond the voluntary reach of sincere and rational people who would desire a relationship with God, and I have given reasons to think that such an objection could be met. I also considered the objection that some propositions might be beyond the epistemic reach of people culturally or geographically isolated from Christianity, and argued that in such cases, there are more accessible propositions that may be accepted and may provide basis for relationship with God. If my responses to these objections are sound, the distinction between belief and acceptance provides good grounds for rejecting Schellenberg's argument from divine hiddenness.

9

THE EUCHARISTIC HORIZON OF REASON

—Nigel Zimmermann

Introduction

The towering figure of St John Paul II (1920–2005) held an abiding interest in the beautiful friendship between faith and reason.[1] John Paul II had endured the atheistic totalitarianism of the Nazis in his native Poland and the long years of Soviet imperialism. For the young Karol Wojtyla, watching as his beloved homeland bled under the foot of an ideology that hated faith, it is intriguing that his burgeoning intellectual interests weaved together a blend of both faith (including prayer, piety, liturgy, social activity, and public religion) and reason (including science, philosophical rigour, intellectual debate, and the search for truth and meaning), without belittling either. As Bishop of Rome preparing the global Catholic community to enter its third millennium of growth and exploration, John Paul talked of faith and reason being like two wings taking us to greater heights. He looked to the great thinkers of the past and reminds us that many of the most important ones were both philosophers and theologians, arguing:

> One thing is certain: attention to the spiritual journey of these masters can only give greater momentum to both the search for truth and the effort to apply the results of that search to the service of humanity.[2]

---

1. See especially John Paul II, *Fides et Ratio*.
2. John Paul II, *Fides et Ratio*, 74.

Here, the soaring together of faith and reason is no whimsical flight of fancy, nor an escape from the world, but an expansion of human reflection in service to the human family. John Paul II is not only one of the most prolific writers to occupy the See of St Peter, he is also a spiritual guide in the most "catholic" sense of that term; a writer who wished to broaden the imagination of his listeners, challenge the narrow-mindedness of readers, and invite all kinds, including the mystics and the scientists, to work together in the "service of humanity." It is simplistic to try and corner John Paul II into a limiting category in the faith/reason debate, simply because as a Catholic he firmly resists the kinds of entrapment contemporary argument generally descends into, by which one is labelled a liberal or a conservative, or a "religious" or "reasoned" person. As a theologian, he was keen to show that a logical and thoughtful limit on one's actions for sound moral reasons does not mean a limit on one's imagination or hopes for humanity. Nevertheless for many readers of the Polish pope, it can be difficult to read his theology without thinking about the broader issues facing the Catholic Church during his time. When doing theology with St John Paul II, David Albert Jones' suggestion is helpful:

> In order to appreciate John Paul II as a theologian (without either excessive deference or excessive defensiveness) it seems better to try to forget that he was also Pope.[3]

This may not really be possible, but nevertheless in what follows John Paul II will be viewed as a particularly helpful guide who challenges us with both the possibilities and the limits of faith and reason. This chapter considers the Eucharistic horizon, so rigorously defended by St John Paul II, and how reason operates within this realm of the good, the beautiful and the true. Such a reflection discerns the shape of the vistas and horizons the present volume has been exploring, with special regard for reason and the Eucharistic mystery, the Eucharistic face of Christ, and finally the Eucharist and Mary.

1. Reason and the Eucharistic Mystery

The Eucharistic mystery, in which the incarnate Lord, the Creator of the Universe paradoxically present in the limitations of flesh and blood, so gives that same corporeal presence to his disciples in perpetuity, is the high point of Christian worship and a defining element of any Christian sacramentality. In it the risen Lord is not just manifest but proximate in the Christian

3. Jones, "John Paul II and Moral Theology," 103.

assembly, and by a sharing among the faithful enters their midst as a personal source of renewal. The Eucharistic sacrifice describes the "source and summit" of the Christian life, what the everyday Catholic will call "Mass."[4] The Eucharist is spiritual but it is also material in that the elements of bread and wine are believed to be transformed, thus extending the life of the incarnation across generations in radical resistance to the temptation to see ourselves as having a complete power over the parts and the elements of our time. Something beyond time and generations enters time, and gives itself for the sake of an almost unknowable love. Our own time happens to be one of secularization, rampant individualism, and moral relativism. To resist and overcome these things, while exercising fully the faculties of reason, we can return to the resources of Scripture and the oldest and ongoing sense of what John Henry Newman called the "sacramental principle."[5] For Newman this principle sums up what is characteristic of a distinctively Catholic world-view. In the words of John Thornhill:

> Tradition has seen this sacramental theology—which presents the life of the believing community as a sharing in the realization of God's hidden purpose in the Christ-event—as coming to its climax in John's solemn reference to the blood and water flowing from the pierced side of Christ.[6]

The pouring out of the life of Christ in his life and death symbolized for the early Church Fathers a permanent commitment of Christ to give his abundant life for his people in every situation, not limited to a single story in first century Galilee. Through the waters of baptism and the real presence of his body and blood, the person of Jesus transcends time and space, forgiving and renewing his people in their own local circumstances and contexts. The image is poetic and troubling for us, because it is rich in mercy and yet shows the palpable cost of what Christ gave: a life of suffering and a journey of sweat and blood culminating in a torturous public death. The richness of mercy is contrast and informed by the cost of the sacrifice.

In *Veritatis Splendor*, John Paul II presents a moral vision informed by the giving of mercy. In a section on the role of moral theologians, he writes how faith makes an appeal to reason through the calling of the theologian in the mission of the Church:

---

4. John Paul II, *Ecclesia De Eucharistia*.

5. The principle is worked out in a number of homilies but developed especially in Newman, *An Essay on the Development of Christian Doctrine*.

6. Thornhill SM, *Christian Mystery in the Secular Age*, 208.

> By its nature, faith appeals to reason because it reveals to man the truth of his destiny and the way to attain it. Revealed truth, to be sure, surpasses our telling. All our concepts fall short of its ultimately unfathomable grandeur (cf. *Eph* 3:19). Nonetheless, revealed truth beckons reason—God's gift fashioned for the assimilation of truth—to enter into its light and thereby come to understand in a certain measure what it has believed.[7]

The Eucharist gives us the experiential context in which we encounter that "ultimately unfathomable grandeur," even, as I would suggest, in the most meagre, self-indulgently horizontal expression of the liturgical rites. In other words, the Eucharist is the beautiful event that bequeaths mercy, even overcoming the worst examples of its own abuse, be it by the disobedient priest or the poorly behaved congregant. By its nature the Eucharist is a form of giving that is rich in mercy.

While the connections between the Eucharist and John Paul's vision of the human person are numerous, it is difficult to pithily phrase the profound connections between his sacramental theology and his anthropology. Here I will summarize these connections as John Paul II's "Eucharistic anthropology of the gift." The relationship between his philosophical anthropology and the Eucharist has been largely overlooked in secondary literature, although intimations of it abound. There are studies on Karol Wojtyla's understanding of the human person, of the Trinity, of freedom, phenomenology, of the Church. Yet, in the Eucharist, we find probably his most regularly practiced ritual event, the defining feature of his every day routine and, if you like, his common *habitus* in the Christian life. For John Paul II, celebrating Mass was more aptly described as his "home" than any earthly address. Some of his most innovative thought, for example his catechesis on human and divine love otherwise known as his "theology of the body," was written on his knees before the Blessed Sacrament before or after Mass. While it is common amongst Wojtyla scholars to remark upon his developed notion of God who gives himself as gift, and who gifts the human person to him or herself by way of responsible action, little has been said on the relationship between the Eucharist and the mystery of the person in his logic of the gift. John Paul II's first papal encyclical, *Redemptor hominis*, was on Christ who redeems the human person and it was a remarkable theological anthropology. His final was *Ecclesia de Eucharistia*, on the relationship between the Church and the Eucharist, both of which we refer to as Christ's body. These two bookends to the John Paul II papacy also encapsulate all his thought between two complementary poles: the human person and the Eucharist.

---

7. John Paul II, *Veritatis Splendor*, 109.

In his last encyclical, we find an expression of the notion in *Veritatis Splendor* that the turn to Christ is an orientation towards the truth in its fullness and such an action is an expression of human reason. As such, the context of Eucharistic worship is not an empty ritual but a context of learning and discovery, a *school* of human relationships, in which we draw near to that which is properly human, and learn from it how to be human ourselves. This is put beautifully by Ernest Lussier SSS:

> Christ bodily, and if you will, bloodily present in the Eucharist is not merely a human being. He is *the* human being, the model, the standard, the blueprint, the die that determines what authentic humanity is, from the first human being to the last. He stands both as the initial and as the ultimate man, the exemplar of human virtue in its most eminent perfection and the one whose irrefragable integrity stands as the judgment upon all our lapses from genuine humanity. Not the least of his virtues is the unselfishness which he exhibits in the act which the Eucharist primarily makes present again, his sacrificial death on the cross for our benefit, the climax and epitome of his redemptive work, of his unswerving obedience to his heavenly father.[8]

For Lussier, and for John Paul, the Eucharistic environment, its action and its symbolism, is the facilitation of encounter with Jesus Christ in his passion, death, and resurrection. Because it is an encounter with Jesus, it is an encounter with perfect humanity that invites us, calls us, ushers us to aspire to its own form and content. The form and content of the Christ includes and does not discard his faculty of reason, his inherent sense of rationality and openness to new discovery.

It starts to become evident why, in his twilight, John Paul II turned to the common sacramental practice of the Eucharist for his final encyclical, which came to bookend *Redemptor hominis*. In section 11, he explicitly states that of all gifts, the Eucharist is not just one of many, but serves as the gift *par excellence*. And while he uses this encyclical to clarify the Church's teaching and canons in areas where it had been neglected there seems a more fundamental anthropological orientation going on; one which, in relation to Mary, Christ and the cross, alters our anthropological perception. That is to say, the Eucharist is not simply the gift, and does not only take up the human person within the logic of the self-gift of the Incarnate Logos, but effects a re-shaping of our imagination regarding the human person. We do not merely receive them as gift in a kind of passivity, but we perceive

---

8. Lussier SSS, *Living the Eucharistic Mystery*, 141.

them as also caught up in a non-cyclical, yet eternal, divine self-offering that causes us to realize our own inherent dynamism.

The Eucharist is a place of learning how to be human, causing us to see the humanity of the risen Christ as something to aspire to, and opens our hearts to the bonds of human friendship. We are not merely human; we are humans together.

2. The Eucharistic Face of Christ

Veritatis Splendor—the splendor of truth—hardly mentions the Eucharist. It does so explicitly only twice. First in section 21:

> Having become one with Christ, the Christian *becomes a member of his Body, which is the Church* (cf. 1 Cor 12:13, 27). By the work of the Spirit, Baptism radically configures the faithful to Christ in the Paschal Mystery of death and resurrection; it "clothes him" in Christ (cf. *Gal* 3:27): "Let us rejoice and give thanks," exclaims Saint Augustine speaking to the baptized, "for we have become not only Christians, but Christ (. . .). Marvel and rejoice: we have become Christ! ." Having died to sin, those who are baptized receive new life (cf. *Rom* 6:3–11): alive for God in Christ Jesus, they are called to walk by the Spirit and to manifest the Spirit's fruits in their lives (cf. *Gal* 5:16–25). Sharing in the *Eucharist*, the sacrament of the New Covenant (cf. *1 Cor* 11:23–29), is the culmination of our assimilation to Christ, the source of "eternal life" (cf. *Jn* 6:51–58), the source and power of that complete gift of self, which Jesus—according to the testimony handed on by Paul—commands us to commemorate in liturgy and in life: "As often as you eat this bread and drink the cup, you proclaim the Lord's death until he comes" (*1 Cor* 11:26).[9]

Also in section 109:

> The life of holiness thus brings to full expression and effectiveness the threefold and unitary *munus propheticum, sacerdotale et regale* which every Christian receives as a gift by being born again "of water and the Spirit" (*Jn* 3:5) in Baptism. His moral life has the value of a "spiritual worship" (*Rom* 12:1; cf. *Phil* 3:3), flowing from and nourished by that inexhaustible source of holiness and glorification of God which is found in the sacraments, especially in the Eucharist: by sharing in the sacrifice of

---

9. John Paul II, *Veritatis Splendor*, 21.

the Cross, the Christian partakes of Christ's self-giving love and is equipped and committed to live this same charity in all his thoughts and deeds.[10]

This latter reference regards the relationship between moral life and the New Evangelisation, both of which are lived derivations of the work of the Holy Spirit. In fact, for John Paul II the work of evangelization meets a particular challenge because in the new context of individualism and relativism we witness the "obscuring of the moral sense." The Eucharist is a powerful remedy for moral relativism because it is a sharing in the passion of the Christ, whose putting to death is the opportunity also for every sin and clouded judgment to be crucified. It tells us that some objects, even when immersed in symbol and tradition, have an irreducible value that are not there to carry the imprint of just any meaning with which we wish to invest them. The experience of Jesus' death, so powerfully told in the liturgies of the Triduum carries an incarnate drama that also points towards the absolute nature of some moral truths. In words we might find unsettling Tad Guzie SJ writes:

> The death of that man, without becoming anything other than what it empirically is, says life. And the bread and wine, without becoming empty shells into which another content needs to be poured, are our way of sinking our teeth into the mystery of the cross.[11]

Again and again liturgical theology and spirituality of every hue bring Christian faith back into a concrete encounter with the real; with the hard truths of an incarnate existence alongside one another. This kind of world view brings Christians into conflict with cultures that attempt a marginalization of spirituality for the sake of some myopic vision of rational life. Some would even argue in contemporary Western culture that we live in an age of reason, or an age of science. And yet, apart from the world, in the mysterious and often mundane liturgical action of the Eucharist in any given church, Christians believe they are in fact sinking their teeth into the "real." Not only that, but on any number of political and social issues it is the promise of Christ in the Eucharist that shapes and inspires those Christians to act humanly and mercifully to their brothers and sisters. None of them protests ill-treatment of refugees, or fight for reconciliation with First Peoples experiencing discrimination, or struggle against war or racism or domestic violence because of "science" or of a bare rationality devoid of

---

10. John Paul II, *Veritatis Splendor*, 109.
11. Guzie SJ, *Jesus and the Eucharist*, 102.

affectation. Christians who act on these and any other number of social problems do so because they are motivated by faith. They find in the face of Christ one who weeps for the widow and the orphan, and who is reflected in their faces when we find them on the unloved fringes of our culture.

In *Ecclesia de Eucharistia*, John Paul II referred to the "Eucharistic face" of Christ. He said that from it: "The Church draws her life."[12] In his papal writings he endorses Henri de Lubac's announcement that "The Eucharist makes the Church and the Church makes the Eucharist."[13] The ongoing theme of John Paul's intellectual project however, is the inviolable dignity of the human person. As a young philosopher, his ethical understanding of human life was shaped profoundly by a critical reading of Max Scheler, in whose work personhood is radically open to sociality and the transcendent. John Paul's early phenomenological interests served his poetic and dramatic explorations of what it meant to live as a person—and to live well. That is to say, to live authentically and to live truthfully. For him, the Eucharist is a radical disclosure of the meaning of human life, precisely in the form of the God-man Jesus, who gives himself as the person-for-others. Because of the Christ of Eucharistic presence, the phenomenon of human personhood can never be understood apart from a) its proximate embodied context and b) the lived communities in which it is situated. These themes become particularly clear when reading *Ecclesia de Eucharistia* in light of earlier works such as *The Acting Person*, the Lublin lectures (collected in English as *Person and Community*) and his central anthropological text *Redemptor Hominis*.

We cannot forget the teaching of the second Vatican Council in *Gaudium et spes*:

> The Church, by reason of her role and competence, is not identified in any way with the political community nor bound to any political system. She is at once a sign and a safeguard of the transcendent character of the human person. (GS 26.)

The Church, confected by the Eucharist, is a sign and safeguard; not just of the human person in his and her concrete vulnerability, but in transcendent character, and carries an inherent anthropological commitment of openness to alterity.

---

12. John Paul II, *Ecclesia De Eucharistia*, 7.
13. John Paul II, *Ecclesia De Eucharistia*, 26.

3. The Eucharist and Mary

In a message to the 1996 International Marian Congress in Poland, Wojtyla explicitly enjoined the Eucharist and Mary by way of Christ's passion. The Congress's theme was "Mary and the Eucharist," and he prayed that Mary would lead disciples to the Eucharist. He remarked:

> Every Holy Mass makes present in an unbloody manner that unique and perfect sacrifice, offered by Christ on the Cross, in which Mary participated, joined in spirit with her suffering Son, lovingly consenting to his sacrifice and offering her own sorrow to the Father. (cf. *Lumen gentium*, n. 58).[14]

This reflection, given on the Feast of the Assumption, highlights the Christological centrality in John Paul II's thought that makes possible the continual thematic connection between Mary and the Eucharist. Mary is spoken of devotionally and personally in such works as *Crossing the Threshold of Hope*, but his chief Marian documents are his Wednesday catechesis on the Virgin Mary (1995–97), *Redemptoris Mater* (1987), and *Rosarium Virginis Mariae* (2002).[15] In the first, he produced a sustained meditative study of the role of Mary in the life of faith, placing it foundationally within the saving work of Christ in history.[16] In the last, he added specific scriptural narratives to the formal prayers of the Rosary, named the "luminous mysteries," and explained the focus of its prayers as the contemplation of the face of Jesus, via the "School of Mary."[17] Similarly, the Eucharist is a continual theme in his work, but the only two full-length documents devoted entirely to its meaning are his early letter, *Dominicae Cenae* (1980) and his final encyclical, *Ecclesia de Eucharistia* (2003).[18]

Other writings with significant Eucharistic themes include *Dies Domine* (1998), the final section of his Trinitarian catechesis (*The Trinity's Embrace*, 2000–2001), and of course he called the year of the Eucharist for 2004–5 in which he produced the apostolic letter *Mane Nobiscum Domine* (2004).[19]

In his Lenten sermons in the presence of Pope Paul VI (1976), Wojtyla makes reference to the "fundamental subject" of priestly prayer—liturgical

---

14. John Paul II, "Mary Leads Us to Eucharist."

15. John Paul II, *Crossing the Threshold of Hope; Redemptoris Mater;* and *Rosarium Virginis Mariae:*

16. John Paul II, *Redemptoris Mater*, 1.

17. John Paul II, *Rosarium Virginis Mariae*, 1, 3, 9, 10, 15, 18, 21, 23, 25, 40, 43.

18. John Paul II, *Ecclesia De Eucharistia.*

19. John Paul II, *Dies Domine; The Trinity's Embrace;* and *Mane Nobiscum Domine.*

prayer—as well as non-liturgical prayer.[20] In liturgical prayer, it is primarily the Eucharist he writes of. The Eucharist is such a constant presence in the life and ministry of Wojtyla, it might be difficult to pinpoint its critical role in his broader theology, but a brief outline of its significance is important, along with the Marian arc under which his thought always operates.

The Eucharist is the key liturgical rite within catholic worship, called by the Catechism the "source and summit" of the Christian life.[21] Its liturgy is both the thanksgiving offered by the ecclesial community, but also participation in that thanksgiving offered by Christ to the Father; that is to say, the full self-offering of Christ, profoundly in relation to the cross. The community offers its worship therefore by way of participation in the "presence" of the divine and the role of the priest is an irreducible element of the celebration. Wojtyla remarks in his Trinitarian catechesis:

> It is the divine presence, then, which "sanctifies" the community of believers "in the truth" (Jn 17:17, 19). The loftiest sign of this presence is constituted by the liturgy, which is the epiphany of the consecration of God's people.[22]

By "consecration," Wojtyla is referring to the sustained (re)commitment of the people of God to the path of holiness. The process of sanctification requires a free agency in each human subject, by which the subjugation of the self's desires to God's will is made possible through a free response to God's initiative. The centrality of the Eucharist contains many facets and the Trinitarian catechesis concludes with a section titled "The Eucharist and the Kingdom." Those facets include the Eucharist as "celebration," "memorial," "sacrifice of praise," "banquet of communion," "taste of eternity in time," and "sacrament of the Church's unity."[23] The baptized Christian finds in the Eucharist a uniquely repeatable participation in the one unrepeatable historical event of Christ's passion and a share in his resurrected life. This is possible in spite of the historical trajectories of "war, violence, oppression, injustice and moral decay," which call to mind the apocalyptic visions of the Book of Revelation (cf. 6:1–8).[24]

Again, we see here how for John Paul II, the Eucharist enlivens our imagination not just for beauty and the enticement of mystery, but helps to re-configure our understanding of evil and the shadows that fall upon

---

20. John Paul II, *Sign of Contradiction*, 134.

21. CCC 1324.

22. John Paul II, *The Trinity's Embrace*, 350.

23. John Paul II, *The Trinity's Embrace*, 387–90, 391–94, 395–98, 399–402, 403–6, 407–10.

24. John Paul II, *The Trinity's Embrace*, 435.

our lived experience. We find here not a life-less sanitization of harm, but a powerful cleansing of sin and a revealing of its ultimate powerlessness before goodness and light, much like in the icons of St Michael's battle with Satan—the latter is present but underfoot and imposed upon by a greater force.

On Wojtyla's account, Eucharistic worship gives way to an anthropological route, a hopeful embodiment of the future life pledged in the Eucharistic feast, in which evil and sin are ultimately destroyed. In other words, the Eucharist is a central point of convergence for the life of persons in *communio*:

> For Christians in general, the concept of *communio* itself has a primarily *religious and sacral meaning, one connected with the Eucharist, which is a sacramentum communionis* between Christ and his disciples—between God and human beings.[25]

The sacral meaning of *communio*—especially as expressed in the Marian typology of the Church, cannot be separated from the Eucharistic encounter with the risen Christ. The "sacramentum communionis," the sacred, or Holy Communion, is a cosmic social moment, embracing the human person in their totality while feeding them with the redemptive person of Christ. There is a sense in which Wojtyla's explanation of the Church's doctrine concerning Christ and his work is, at times, more catechetical than dogmatic. That is to say, he is offering the content of dogma in a pastoral and teaching mode of delivery. Avery Dulles calls this Wojtyla's "method of correlation," emphasising the correspondence between the questions of human existence and the divine answers that arrive in the person of Christ.[26] In fact, both the Eucharistic and the Marian aspects of Wojtyla's thought are always in relation to an appreciation of the existential anxiety that is wrought in the human condition.

The human person exits between multiple plains of meaning, desire, temptation, and only finds the fullness of life in the paradoxical relinquishment of the self in God; this is made concrete in the Eucharist.

The Eucharistic encounter with Christ is also the affirmation of the Marian arc, in which the Lord's Mother acts as the type *par excellence* of the Church. The typology of Mary also speaks of her as a living disciple in the life of the Church, one who is an object of devotion for John Paul II. His Episcopal Coat of Arms carried the Latin words *"Totus tuus"* (Totally yours), which comes from the mystical Marian writings of St Louis-Marie

---

25. John Paul II, *Person and Community*, 320.
26. Dulles, *The Splendor of Faith*, 33.

Grignion de Montfort in his treatise on Marian devotion: "*Totus tuus ego sum, et omnia mea tua sunt.*"[27] That is to say, to be given totally over for the sake of the other, and specifically within the matrix of Trinity-Christ-Mary. To think of one, is for Wojtyla, to act in concert with the others.

In the Apostolic Letter, *Redemptoris Mater*, Mary is presented as central to the gospel mission in the Church's life.[28] From the beginning, it is Wojtyla's Christo-centrism that defines the terms in which Mary is treated. She is the human factor in the Holy Spirit's cooperative work of the incarnation, by which the Word takes flesh.[29] In one sense, she is the fleshly hinge upon which the Holy Spirit's action turns. She is the human person whose faithful obedience in the "fullness of time" precedes the conception, birth and work of Christ, whose gift of her own flesh made possible the incarnation.[30] In the hidden-ness of Mary's embodied interiority, the Church's own pilgrim journey locates its beginning, for she is both *Theotókos* and Mother of the Church.[31] As the Mother, Mary plays a continually active role in the life of the Church, so she cannot be relegated simply to historical, typological, or theological significance. In fact, in each of these three categories, her significance continues, for she intercedes as an active agent of grace fully obedient to the Son. In our own circumstances, the contemporaneous confrontation with sin and evil—that ancient "enmity"—is given impetus and encouragement by the prayerful involvement of Mary.[32] Her involvement is maternal, but always directed towards the same end: Jesus Christ, just as it was at the beginning of his public ministry in Cana.[33]

John Paul develops the teaching of Vatican II and St Paul VI on Mary, with a lively emphasis on the presence of Mary as a kind of arc to the entire Christian life, one that is holy, spotless, maternal and faithful; again he says: "Mary guides the faithful to the Eucharist."[34] It is clear that for Wojtyla, the possibility for each of these roles in Mary is her vocation as a person in history who was characterized as the particular mother of a particular person,

27. 'I am all yours, and all that I have is yours.' See his prayers in de Montfort, *A Treatise on the True Devotion to the Blessed Virgin*.

28. John Paul II, *Redemptoris Mater*.

29. John Paul II, *Redemptoris Mater*, 1.

30. The term "fulness of time" (*pleroma tou chronou*) is crucial to Mary's role in history. Wojtyla (John Paul II) included in footnote two of *Redemptoris Mater* an explanation of its use in Scripture, especially Gen 29:21; 1 Sam 7:12; Tob 14:5; Mark 1:15; Luke 21:24; John 7:8; Eph 1:10; and Gal 4:4 Ibid., 49.

31. John Paul II, *Redemptoris Mater*, 1–2.

32. John Paul II, *Redemptoris Mater*, 11.

33. John Paul II, *Redemptoris Mater*, 21–22.

34. John Paul II, *Redemptoris Mater*, 42–47.

the Son of God. Without the peculiarly local aspect of her vocation at a fixed point in history (the "fullness of time"), Mary's over-arching vocation in regards to the *ecclesia* and to every individual believer would be a transcendent impossibility. A mother is a mother of *someone*. A person is a person *somewhere* and at *some time*. The Marian arc only makes sense in Wojtyla's theological structure because of its shared vocational context in the dark complexities of history. "She [the Church] sees Mary deeply rooted in humanity's history, in man's eternal vocation according to the providential plan which God has made for him from eternity."[35] The maternal vocation then is central in Wojtyla's theology, but precisely because of the historical particularities of the person of Mary.

In light of all these themes, *Ecclesia de Eucharistia*, is a sustained reflection on the relationship between the liturgical rite of the Mass and the lived practices of the Church.[36] The supernatural change of the Eucharistic elements constitutes for Wojtyla both the constant presence of Christ in his earthly body and the sacred marking of time in history.[37] In both, the Eucharist acts as that intersection between the Trinity and creation that is manifest most clearly amongst Christian disciples. The emphases in his Trinitarian encyclicals of the dramatic relationship between the human person and the Triune God are made concrete in the Eucharist. As Tracey Rowland describes, "the most dramatic intersection of all three relationships is to be found in the Eucharistic Mystery."[38]

While John Paul had said the Church's beginnings are found in the grace-filled life of Mary in *Redemptoris Mater*, in *Ecclesia de Eucharistia* he says the Church is "born" of the Paschal mystery.[39] In the Paschal Triduum, the foundation and wellspring of the Church is "gathered up, foreshadowed and 'concentrated' forever in the gift of the Eucharist."[40] The presence that is observed in this liturgical and communal offering is that of the *person* of Christ. By way of the Trinitarian involvement with the entire rite, John Paul describes the showing forth of the "Eucharistic face of Christ," made tangible by our education in the "school of Mary."[41] The mother directs our gaze to Christ's face.

---

35. John Paul II, *Redemptoris Mater*, 52.
36. John Paul II, *Ecclesia De Eucharistia*.
37. John Paul II, *Ecclesia De Eucharistia*, 1.
38. Tracey Rowland, "In Search of Real Freedom."
39. John Paul II, *Ecclesia De Eucharistia*, 3.
40. John Paul II, *Ecclesia De Eucharistia*, 5.
41. John Paul II, *Ecclesia De Eucharistia*, 7.

Furthermore, the Eucharistic contemplation of Christ's face within the context of the school of Mary is laid before the Church as John Paul II's program for the third millennium.[42]

It is in *Dominicae Cenae* that Wojtyla outlines the dually-constituting relationship of Eucharist and the Church in his logic of the gift. He writes: "The Church 'makes the Eucharist' and 'the Eucharist builds up' the Church" (echoing section 11 of *Lumen Gentium*).[43] Foundational elements of the apostolic ministry and its successive priestly and episcopal forms are built into the establishment of the Eucharist in the Last Supper; and so just as priestly sacrifice is given to the Church in union with her Lord, so too is the priesthood to offer it. The Marian arc, of open obedience to the Lord and the gradual contemplation of his face, acts as the constant reference point by which Eucharistic devotion finds its orientation.

Mary is considered in close approximation to Wojtyla's concern to emphasize the Eucharist. Indeed, he concludes his final section (on the Eucharist) in his Trinitarian catechesis with a reflection titled "Mary, Eschatological Icon of the Church."[44] In it, he brings to a close a four-year catechetical program by emphasizing the typological interpretation of Our Lady as the People of God. He takes his point of departure as the account in the Book of Revelation of the woman with child, giving birth while the dragon rages against her (Rev 12:1–6).[45] Of course, the interpretation of this woman as both the mother of Christ and as a type of the Church is not unusual within the patristic traditions of the Church.[46]

For John Paul II, the human person is a participant in the same historical drama of good versus evil, acting in a free agency which is fundamentally open to the divine Other. Life, lived according to its sacred meaning, is the radical openness to the gift given Eucharistically. This same divine Other—the blessed Trinity—bestows upon the lowly, poor, refugee, prayerful virgin a powerful intercessory role. In her vocation as the teacher and orientation of Eucharistic understanding, Mary, for Wojtyla, is "woman of the Eucharist."[47]

That role is crucial to John Paul II's theology, as is the notion that the Eucharist confects a change in our anthropological vision. It is a vision not

---

42. John Paul II, *Ecclesia De Eucharistia*, 6.

43. John Paul II, *Dominicae Cenae*, 5; Second Vatican Council, *Lumen Gentium*.

44. John Paul II, *The Trinity's Embrace*, 450–53.

45. John Paul II, *The Trinity's Embrace*, 450.

46. See for example, Ambrose, *Exposition of the Holy Gospel According to Saint Luke*, II, 7.

47. John Paul II, *Ecclesia De Eucharistia*, 53–58.

just of the giftedness in which the human person—the other—may be seen, but of the work that is to be done on their behalf. John Paul links these two facets of what the Eucharist opens up simply, but profoundly. He says:

> A significant consequence of the eschatological tension inherent in the Eucharist is also the fact that it spurs us on our journey through history and plants a seed of living hope in our daily commitment to the work before us. Certainly the Christian vision leads to the expectation of "new heavens" and "a new earth" (*Rev* 21:1), but this increases, rather than lessens, *our sense of responsibility for the world today*.[48]

In the Eucharist, truth is manifest, reason is strengthened, our human nature is blessed and redeemed, and the splendor of Christ expands the horizon of imagination for what is possible in light of that which is true. Such things could only be possible in the face of Christ. Reason has a capacity much greater than what we give it credit for, and it becomes all the more expansive, curious and intrigued by the transcendent within the horizon of the Eucharist.

We find that in the Eucharist, reason is both lifted up and it reaches its limits. As St John Paul II observes towards the close of *Ecclesia de Eucharistia*:

> In the humble signs of bread and wine, changed into his body and blood, Christ walks beside us as our strength and our food for the journey, and he enables us to become, for everyone, witnesses of hope. If, in the presence of this mystery, reason experiences its limits, the heart, enlightened by the grace of the Holy Spirit, clearly sees the response that is demanded, and bows low in adoration and unbounded love.[49]

---

48. John Paul II, *Ecclesia De Eucharistia*, 20.
49. John Paul II, *Ecclesia De Eucharistia*, 62.

BIBLIOGRAPHY

Allen, Prudence. "Person and Complementarity in Fides et ratio." In *The Two Wings of Catholic Thought*, edited by David R Foster and Joseph W Koterski, 36–68. Washington, DC: The Catholic University of America Press, 2003.

Alston, W. "Belief, Acceptance, and Religious Faith." In *Faith, Freedom and Rationality: Philosophy of Religion Today*, edited by J. Jordan and D Howard-Snyder, 3–27. Lanham, MD: Rowman & Littlefield, 1996.

Ambrose. *Exposition of the Holy Gospel According to Saint Luke: With Fragments on the Prophecy of Isaia*. Translated by Theodosia Tomkinson. Etna, CA: Center for Traditionalist Orthodox Studies, 1998.

Amia, Srinivasan. "The Aptness of Anger." *The Journal of Political Philosophy* 26.2 (2018) 123–44. Online: https://onlinelibrary.wiley.com/doi/abs/10.1111/jopp.12130.

Aquinas, Thomas. *The Disputed Questions on Truth*, Vol. 1. Translated by Robert William Mulligan S.J. Chicago: Regnery, 1952.

———. *Summa Contra Gentiles*, Book 1. Translated by Anton C. Pegis FRSC, 1955. London: University of Notre Dame Press, 2009.

———. *Summa Theologica*. Translated by Fathers of the English Dominican Province, 1911–25. New York: Cosimo, 2007.

Aristotle. *Metaphysics*. In *Complete Works of Aristotle: The Revised Oxford Translation*, edited by Julian Barnes, Vol. 2, 1552–1728. Bollingen Series LXXI, 2. Princeton, NJ: Princeton University Press, 1984.

———. *The Politics*. Translated by T. A. Sinclair. Rev. ed. London: Penguin, 1981.

Augé, Matias. *Liturgia*. Milano: San Paolo, 1992.

Augustine. *De Trinitate*. Translated by Edmond Hill, OP. New York: New City, 2015.

———. *Of True Religion*. Translated by J. H. S. Burleigh. London: Regnery, 1991.

Australian Catholic Bishops Conference. *Become One Body, One Spirit in Christ*. DVD produced by Fraynework Digital Storytelling, Melbourne, 2010.

Australian Health Practitioner Regulation Agency. *Code of Conduct for Nurses*. Nursing and Midwifery Board: https://www.nursingmidwiferyboard.gov.au/Codes-Guidelines-Statements/FAQ/Fact-sheet-Code-of-conduct-for-nurses-and-Code-of-conduct-for-midwives.aspx. The Australia Health Practitioner Regulation Agency (Aphra), 2020.

Batson, Daniel C. *Altruism in Humans*. Oxford: Oxford University Press, 2011.

Bauerschmidt, Frederick Christian. "Shouting in the Land of the Hard of Hearing: On Being a Hillbilly Thomist." *Modern Theology* 20.1 (2004) 163–83.

Bibliography

Benedict XV. *Fausto Appetente Die*. Encyclical Letter. Vatican Website. June 29, 1921. https://www.vatican.va/content/benedict-xv/en/encyclicals/documents/hf_ben-xv_enc_29061921_fausto-appetente-die.html.

Benedict XVI. *Address at the University of Regensburg*. Vatican Website. September 12, 2006. https://www.vatican.va/content/benedict-xvi/en/speeches/2006/september/documents/hf_ben-xvi_spe_20060912_university-regensburg.html.

———. *Caritas in Veritate: Encyclical on Integral Human Development in Charity and Truth*. Vatican Website. June 29, 2009. https://www.vatican.va/content/benedict-xvi/en/encyclicals/documents/hf_ben-xvi_enc_20090629_caritas-in-veritate.html.

———. *Deus Caritas Est: Encyclical Letter on Christian Love*. Vatican Website. December 25, 2005. https://www.vatican.va/content/benedict-xvi/en/encyclicals/documents/hf_ben-xvi_enc_20051225_deus-caritas-est.html.

———. *General Audience*. Vatican Website. May 21, 2008. https://www.vatican.va/content/benedict-xvi/en/audiences/2008/documents/hf_ben-xvi_aud_20080521.html.

———. [then Joseph Ratzinger, Dean of the College of Cardinals]. *Homily at the Mass for the Election of the Pope*. Vatican Website. April 18, 2005. https://www.vatican.va/gpII/documents/homily-pro-eligendo-pontifice_20050418_en.html.

———. *Spe Salvi. Encyclical Letter on Hope*. Vatican Website. November 30, 2007. https://www.vatican.va/content/benedict-xvi/en/encyclicals/documents/hf_ben-xvi_enc_20071130_spe-salvi.html.

Bernasconi, Robert. "What Is the Question to Which 'Substitution' is the Answer?" In *The Cambridge Companion to Levinas*, edited by S. Critchley and R. Bernasconi, 234–51. Cambridge: Cambridge University Press, 2002.

Breslin, John B. "'The Open-Ended Mystery of Matter': The Allusive Presence of God in Catholic Fiction." In *Examining the Catholic Intellectual Tradition*, edited by Anthony J. Cernera and Oliver J. Morgan, 58–69. Fairfield, CT: Sacred Heart University Press, (2000).

Burggraeve, Roger. "Violence and the Vulnerable Face of the Other: The Vision of Emmanuel Levinas on Moral Evil and Our Responsibility." *Journal of Social Philosophy* 30.1 (1999) 30–31.

Campanini, Massimo. *An Introduction to Islamic Philosophy*. Translated by Caroline Higgitt. Edinburgh: Edinburgh University Press, 2008.

Campbell, Stanislaus. "Pastoral Issues in the Translations of Liturgical Text." In *The Voice of the Church: A Forum on Liturgical Translation*, edited by Gilbert Ostdiek, Jeremy Driscoll OSB, Stanislaus Campbell FSC, Joseph A. Fiorenza, and Jerome G. Hanus, 97–141. Washington, DC: USCCB, 2001.

Carbone, Vincenzo. "Vatican Council II: Light for The Church and for The Modern World, 1 May, 1997." http://www.vatican.va/jubilee_2000/magazine/documents/ju_mag_01051997_p-21_en.html.

Catechism of the Catholic Church: With Modifications from the Editio Typica. 2nd ed. New York: Doubleday, 2003.

Cavanaugh, William T. "The Invention of Fanaticism." In *Faith, Rationality and the Passions*, edited by Sarah Coakley, 29–40. Malden, MA: Wiley-Blackwell, 2012.

Cicero, Marcus Tullios. *On Duties*. Translated by Benjamin Patrick Newton. Ithaca, NY: Cornell University Press, 2016.

Clark, Patrick. "Is Martyrdom Virtuous? An Occasion for Rethinking the Relation of Christ and Virtue in Aquinas." *Journal of the Society of Christian Ethics* 30.1 (2010) 141–59.
Coakley, Sarah. *Faith, Rationality and the Passions*. Oxford: Wiley Blackwell, 2012.
Congregation for Divine Worship and the Discipline of the Sacraments. "Fifth Instruction for the Right Implementation of the Constitution on the Sacred Liturgy of the Second Vatican Council, *Liturgiam authenticam: On the Use of Vernacular Languages in the Publication of the Books of the Roman Liturgy*, 25 April 2001." http://www.vatican.va/roman_curia/congregations/ccdds/index.htm.
Congregation for the Doctrine of the Faith. "Instruction on the Ecclesial Vocation of the Theologian, *Donum Veritatis*, 24 May, 1990, 7–8: AAS 82 (1990)." http://www.vatican.va/roman_curia/congregations/cfaith/documents/rc_con_cfaith_doc_19900524_theologian-vocation_en.html.
Contino, Paul J. "Fiction and Catholic Themes." In *Teaching the Tradition: Catholic Themes in Academic Disciplines*, edited by John J. Pederit, SJ and Melanie M. Morey, 151–70. Oxford: Oxford University Press, 2012.
Cooperman, Alan. "The Big 20: The Changing Religious Landscape in the Last 20 Years". Interview by Andrew West, *Religion and Ethics Report*. ABC, November, 25, 2020. Audio, 11:46. https://www.abc.net.au/radionational/programs/religionandethicsreport/the-big-20-the-changing-religious-landscape-in-the-last-20-years/12916468.
Critchley, Simon. "Introduction." In *The Cambridge Companion to Levinas*, edited by S. Critchley and R. Bernasconi, 1–32. Cambridge: Cambridge University Press, 2002.
de Montfort, Louis Marie Grignon. *Treatise on the True Devotion to the Blessed Virgin*. Edited by Frederick William Faber and Mary Faber. London: Faber, 1863.
DeYoung, Rebecca Konyndyk. "Power Made Perfect in Weakness: Aquinas's Transformation of the Virtue of Courage." *Medieval Philosophy and Theology* 11 (2003) 147–80.
Dixon, Thomas. *From Passions to Emotions: The Creation of a Secular Psychological Category*. Cambridge: Cambridge University Press, 2003.
Dudiak, Jeffrey. "The Greatest Commandment? Religion and/or Ethics in Kierkegaard and Levinas." In *Kierkegaard and Levinas: Ethics, Politics, and Religion*, edited by Aaron J. Simmons and David Wood, 99–124. Bloomington, IN: Indiana University Press, 2008.
Dulles, Avery Robert. *The Splendor of Faith: The Theological Vision of Pope John Paul II*. New York: Crossroad, 1999.
Duns Scotus, John. *Philosophical Writings: A Selection*. Translated by Allan Wolter OFM. Cambridge: Hackett, 1987.
Elie, Paul. *The Life You Save May Be Your Own: An American Pilgrimage*. New York: Farrar, Straus & Giroux, 2004.
Emery OP, Gilles. "The Doctrine of the Trinity in St. Thomas Aquinas." In *Aquinas on Doctrine: A Critical Introduction*, edited by Thomas G. Weinandy, Daniel A. Keating, and John P. Yocum, 45–66. London: T. & T. Clarke, 2004.
———. *The Trinitarian Theology of St. Thomas Aquinas*. Oxford: Oxford University Press, 2007.
———. *The Trinity: An Introduction to Catholic Doctrine*. Washington, DC: Catholic University of America Press, 2011.

Fagerberg, David W. *Theologia Prima: What Is Liturgical Theology?* Chicago: Hillenbrand, 2004.
Fisher, Anthony, and Hayden Ramsay, eds. *Faith and Reason: Friends or Foes in the New Millennium.* Adelaide: ATF, 2004.
Fitzgerald, Robert H. "Flannery O'Connor's 'Everything That Rises Must Converge': The Teilhardian Dimension." *Notre Dame English Journal* 2.2 (1967) 36–50.
Fleming, Daniel. "The Enduring Contribution of Religious Education to Reason's Good Functioning: The Case of Moral Excellence." In *Value Learning Trajectories: Theory, Method, Context*, edited by Liam Gearon and Arniika Kuusisto, 31–42. Munster: Waxmann, 2017.
———. "Primoridal Moral Awareness: Levinas, Conscience and the Unavoidable Call to Responsibility." *The Heythrop Journal* 56.4 (2015) 604–18.
Fleming, Daniel, and Terence Lovat. "Self-Other or Other-Self-Other? A Conversation between Bonhoeffer and Levinas on Vulnerability." *The Bonhoeffer Legacy: Australasian Journal of Bonhoeffer Studies* 1.1 (2013) 133–49.
Forrester, Katrina. *In the Shadow of Justice: Postwar Liberalism and the Remaking of Political Philosophy.* Princeton, NJ: Princeton University Press, 2019.
Francis. *Fratelli Tutti. Encyclical Letter on Fraternity and Social Friendship.* Vatican Website. October 3, 2020. https://www.vatican.va/content/francesco/en/encyclicals/documents/papa-francesco_20201003_enciclica-fratelli-tutti.html.
———. *Laudato 'Si: Encyclical on Care for our Common Home.* Vatican Website. May 24, 2015. https://www.vatican.va/content/francesco/en/encyclicals/documents/papa-francesco_20150524_enciclica-laudato-si.html.
———. *Magnum Principium. Apostolic Letter.* September 9, 2017. https://press.vatican.va/content/salastampa/en/bollettino/pubblico/2017/09/09/170909a.html.
Freddoso, Alfred. J. "Editor's Note." In *Pope John Paul II's Fides et Ratio.* Study notes with excerpts, edited by Alfred J. Freddoso. University of Notre Dame, Notre Dame, IN, USA, September 14, 1998. https://www3.nd.edu/~afreddos/papers/fides-et-ratio-notes.htm.
Gardner, Margaret. "A Higher Purpose: Universities, Civic Transformation and the Public Good." *Speech to the National Press Club of Australia*, 27 February 2019. https://www.universitiesaustralia.edu.au/media-item/a-higher-purpose-universities-civic-transformation-and-the-public-good/.
Gentile, Mary C. *Giving Voice to Values: How to Speak Your Mind When You Know What's Right.* New Haven, CT: Yale University Press, 2010.
Gopnik, Alison. "When Truth and Reason Are No Longer Enough." Review of *Enlightenment Now*, by Steven Pinker. *The Atlantic*, April 2018: https://www.theatlantic.com/magazine/archive/2018/04/steven-pinker-enlightenment-now/554054/.
Guttierez, Gustavo. *A Theology of Liberation.* Maryknoll NY: Orbis, 1971.
Guzie SJ, Tad W. *Jesus and the Eucharist.* New York: Paulist, 1974.
Haddox, Thomas F. "'Something Haphazard and Botched': Flannery O'Connor's Critique of the Visual in 'Parker's Back.'" *Mississippi Quarterly* 57.3 (2004) 407–21.
Haldane, John. *Faithful Reason: Essays Catholic and Philosophical.* London: Routledge, 2004.
———. *Practical Philosophy: Ethics, Society and Culture.* St Andrews Studies in Philosophy and Public Affairs (series). Charlottesville, NC: Imprint Academic, 2009.

Harris, Sam. *The End of Faith: Religion, Terror, and the Future of Reason*. New York: Norton, 2004.
Heidegger, Martin. "On the Essence of Ground." In *Pathmarks*, edited and translated by William McNeill, 97–135. Cambridge: Cambridge University Press, 1998.
———. *The Principle of Reason*. Translated by Reginald Lilly. Bloomington IN: Indiana University Press, 1996.
Herdt, Jennifer A. "Aquinas's Aristotelian Defense of Martyr Courage." In *Aquinas and the Nichomachean Ethics*, edited by Tobias Hoffman et. al., 110–28. Cambridge: Cambridge University Press, 2013.
———. *Religion and Faction*. Cambridge: Cambridge University Press, 1997.
Honderich, Ted, ed. *The Oxford Companion to Philosophy*. 2nd ed. Oxford: Oxford University Press, 2005.
Hume, David. *A Treatise of Human Nature*. Edited by L. A. Selby-Bigge. 2nd ed., revised by P. H. Nidditch. Oxford: Oxford University Press, 1978.
Hursthouse, Rosalind. *On Virtue Ethics*. Oxford: Oxford University Press, 2000.
Inglehart, Ronald F. "Giving Up on God: The Global Decline of Religion." *Foreign Affairs* 99.5, (Sept/Oct 2020). https://www.foreignaffairs.com/articles/world/2020-08-11/religion-giving-god.
International Theological Commission. *Theology Today: Perspectives, Principles and Criteria*. 29 November, 2011. http://www.vatican.va/roman_curia/congregations/cfaith/cti_documents/rc_cti_doc_20111129_teologia-oggi_en.html.
John Paul II. *Address to the Participants in the Eighth International Thomistic Congress*. Vatican Website. September 13, 1980. https://www.vatican.va/content/john-paul-ii/en/speeches/2003/september/documents/hf_jp-ii_spe_20030929_congresso-tomista.html.
———. *Crossing the Threshold of Hope*. Translated by Vittorio Messori. London: Cape, 1994.
———. *Dies Domine: Apostolic Letter on Keeping the Lord's Day Holy*. Vatican City: Catholic Truth Society, 1998.
———. *Dominicae Cenae: Apostolic Letter on the Mystery and Worship of the Eucharist*. Boston: St. Paul Editions, 1980.
———. *Ecclesia De Eucharistia: Encyclical Letter on the Eucharist in Its Relationship to the Church*. London: Catholic Truth Society, 2003.
———. *Ex Corde Ecclesiae*. Encyclical Letter. Vatican Website. August 15, 1990. http://www.vatican.va/content/john-paul-ii/en/apost_constitutions/documents/hf_jp-ii_apc_15081990_ex-corde-ecclesiae.html.
———. *Fides et Ratio*. Encyclical Letter. Vatican Website. September 14, 1998. http://www.vatican.va/content/john-paul-ii/en/encyclicals/documents/hf_jp-ii_enc_14091998_fides-et-ratio.html.
———. *Mane Nobiscum Domine: Apostolic Letter for the Year of the Eucharist October 2004–October 2005*. Dublin: Veritas, 2004.
———. "Mary Leads Us to Eucharist: Message to 19th International Marian Congress Czestochowa, Poland." Castel Gandolfo, August 15, 1996. https://www.ewtn.com/catholicism/library/mary-leads-us-to-eucharist-8755.
———. *Message to the Catholic University of the Sacred Heart*. Vatican Website. April 13, 2000. https://www.vatican.va/content/john-paul-ii/en/speeches/2000/apr-jun/documents/hf_jp-ii_spe_20000413_univ-catt-sacro-cuore.html.

———. *Message to the Sixth National Meeting of Catholic University Professors.* Vatican Website. October 4, 2001. https://www.vatican.va/content/john-paul-ii/en/messages/pont_messages/2001/documents/hf_jp-ii_mes_20011005_docenti-cattolici.html.

———. *Novo Millennio Iunente: Apostolic Letter at the close of the Great Jubilee of the Year 2000.* London: Catholic Truth Society, 2001. http://www.vatican.va/content/john-paul-ii/en/apost_letters/2001/documents/hf_jp-ii_apl_20010106_novo-millennio-ineunte.html.

———. *Person and Community: Selected Essays. Catholic Thought from Lublin Series,* Vol. 4. New York: Lang, 1993.

———. *Redemptoris Mater: On the Blessed Vigin Mary in the Life of the Pilgrim Church.* London: Catholic Truth Society, 2003.

———. *Rosarium Virginis Mariae: Apostolic Letter on the Most Holy Rosary.* London: Catholic Truth Society, 2002.

———. *Sign of Contradiction.* Translated by Mary Smith. London: Chapman, 1979.

———. *The Trinity's Embrace, God's Saving Plan: A Catechesis on Salvation History.* Boston: Pauline, 2002.

———. *Veritatis Splendor: Encyclical on Fundamental Questions of Moral Theology.* Vatican Website. August 6, 1993. https://www.vatican.va/content/john-paul-ii/en/encyclicals/documents/hf_jp-ii_enc_06081993_veritatis-splendor.html.

Jones, David Albert. "John Paul II and Moral Theology." In *The Legacy of John Paul II,* edited by Michael Hayes and Gerald O'Collins, 79–109. London: Continuum, 2008.

Kant, Immanuel. *Critique of Pure Reason.* Translated by Norman Kemp Smith. London: Palgrave Macmillan, 1990.

———. *Religion within the Boundaries of Mere Reason: and Other Writings.* Translated by Allen Wood and George di Giovanni. Cambridge: Cambridge University Press, 1998.

Kavanagh, Aidan. *On Liturgical Theology.* New York: Pueblo, 1984.

Kierkegaard, Søren. *Concluding Unscientific Postscript to the Philosophical Crumbs.* Translated and edited by Alistair Hannay. Cambridge: Cambridge University Press, 1968.

———. *Fear and Trembling.* Translated by Alistair Hannay. London: Penguin, 1985.

Kilby, Karen. "Perichoresis and Projection: Problems with Social Doctrines of the Trinity." *New Blackfriars* 81.957 (2000) 432–45.

Kinney, Arthur F. "Flannery O'Connor and the Fiction of Grace." *The Massachusetts Review* 27.1 (1986) 71–96.

Kisiel, Theodore. "Heidegger (1920–21) on becoming a Christian." In *Reading Heidegger from the Start: Essays in His Earliest Thought,* edited by Theodore Kisiel and John van Buren, 175–92. New York: State University of New York Press, 1994.

Lee, Jacob C., Deborah L. Hall, and Wendy Wood. "Experiential or Material Purchases? Social Class Determines Purchase Happiness." *Psychological Science* 29.7 (2018) 1031–39. https://doi.org/10.1177/0956797617736386.

Leo XIII. *Æterni Patris.* Encyclical Letter. Vatican Website. August 4, 1879. https://www.vatican.va/content/leo-xiii/en/encyclicals/documents/hf_l-xiii_enc_04081879_aeterni-patris.html.

Leigh SJ, Davis J. "Suffering and the Sacred in Flannery O'Connor's Short Stories." Special Issue: Flannery O'Connor. *Renascence* 65.5 (2013) 365–79.

Lemay, Blue. "God's Back: Tattoos, Theology, and the Postmodern Pantocrator in 'Parker's Back." *Literature Interpretation Theory* 25.1 (2014) 41–56.

Levering, Matthew. *Scripture and Metaphysics: Aquinas and the Renewal of Trinitarian Theology*. Oxford: Blackwell, 2004.

Levinas, Emmanuel. "Ethics as First Philosophy." In *The Levinas Reader*, edited by S. Hand, 75–87. Oxford: Blackwell, 1989.

———. *Otherwise Than Being or Beyond Essence*. Translated by Alphonso Lingis. Pittsburgh: Duquesne University Press, 1998.

———. "Philosophy, Justice, and Love." In *Is It Righteous to Be? Interviews with Emmanuel Levinas*, edited by Jill Robbins, 165–81. Stanford: Stanford University Press, 2001.

———. *Totality and Infinity: An Essay on Exteriority*. Translated by A. Lingis. Pittsburgh: Duquesne University Press, 1969.

———. "Useless Suffering." In *The Provocation of Levinas*, edited by Robert Bernasconi and David Wood, 156–67. London: Routledge, 1988.

Lombardo, Nicholas. *The Logic of Desire: Aquinas on Emotion*. Washington, DC: Catholic University of America Press, 2012.

Lussier SSS, Ernest. *Living the Eucharistic Mystery*. New York: Alba House, 1976.

MacIntyre, Alasdair. *Dependent Rational Animals: Why Human Beings Need the Virtues*. Chicago: Open Court, 2009.

———. *God, Philosophy, Universities: A Selective History of the Catholic Philosophical Tradition*. London: Rowan and Littlefield, 2009.

Malka, Saloman. *Emmanuel Levinas: His Life and Legacy*. Translated by M. Kigel and S. Embree. Pittsburgh: Duquesne University Press, 2006.

Maritain, Jacques, and Ralph M. McInerny. *Degrees of Knowledge: Collected Works Jacques Maritain*, Vol. 7. South Bend, IN: University of Notre Dame Press, 1995.

Marshall, Bruce. "The Unity of the Triune God." *The Thomist* 74 (2010) 1–32.

McManus, Dennis. "Translation Theory in *Liturgiam authenticam*." In *Benedict XVI and the Sacred Liturgy*, edited by Neil J. Roy and Janet E. Rutherford, 116–31. Dublin: Four Courts, 2011.

Miller, Christian. "Improving Our Characters with Divine Assistance." In *The Character Gap: How Good Are We?* 219–54. Oxford: Oxford University Press, 2018.

Minister, Stephen. "Works of Justice, Works of Love: Kierkegaard, Levinas, and an Ethics beyond Difference". In *Kierkegaard and Levinas: Ethics, Politics, and Religion*, edited by Aaron J. Simmons and David Wood, 229–43. Bloomington, IN: Indiana University Press, 2008.

Monbiot, George. "Why We Fight for the Living World: It's about Love, and It's Time We Said So." *The Guardian*, June, 17, 2015. https://www.theguardian.com/commentisfree/2015/jun/16/pope-encyclical-value-of-living-world.

Murray, John Courtney. *We Hold These Truths: Catholic Reflections on the American Proposition*. Kansas City, MO: Sheed and Ward, 1960.

Newman, John Henry. *The Idea of a University*. Edited by Frank M. Turner. New Haven, CT: Yale University Press, 1996.

Norris, Pippa, and Ronald Inglehart. *Sacred and Secular: Religion and Politics Worldwide*. Cambridge: Cambridge University Press, 2004.

Nussbaum, Martha C. *The Monarchy of Fear: A Philosopher Looks at Our Political Crisis*. New York: Simon & Schuster, 2018.

———. *Political Emotions: Why Love Matters for Justice.* Cambridge, MA: Harvard University Press, 2013.

———. *The Therapy of Desire: Theory and Practice in Hellenistic Ethics.* Princeton, NJ: Princeton University Press, 1994.

———. *Upheavals of Thought: The Intelligence of the Emotions.* Cambridge: Cambridge University Press, 2001.

O'Connor, Flannery. "Everything That Rises Must Converge." In *Everything That Rises Must Converge.* In *Three By Flannery O'Connor*, 425–42. London: Signet, 1986.

———. "The Fiction Writer and His Country." In *Mystery and Manners: Occasional Prose*, edited by Sally and Robert Fitzgerald, 23–35. New York: Farrar, Straus & Giroux, 1969.

———. *The Habit of Being: Letters of Flannery O'Connor.* Edited by Sally Fitzgerald. New York: Farrar, Straus & Giroux, 1979.

———. "On Her Own Work" In *Mystery and Manners: Occasional Prose*, edited by Sally and Robert Fitzgerald, 107–20. New York: Farrar, Straus & Giroux, 1969.

———. "Parker's Back." In *Everything That Rises Must Converge.* In *Three by Flannery O'Connor*, 425–42. London: Signet, 1986.

———. *The Violent Bear It Away.* In *Three By Flannery O'Connor*, 121–268. London: Signet, 1986.

———. *Wise Blood.* In *Three by Flannery O'Connor*, 1–120. London: Signet, 1986.

———. "Writing Short Stories." In *Mystery and Manners: Occasional Prose*, edited by Sally and Robert Fitzgerald, 87–106. New York: Farrar, Straus & Giroux, 1969.

O'Neill, Colman E., and Romanus Cessario. *Meeting Christ in the Sacraments.* Rev. ed. New York: Alba House, 1991.

Osburn, E. "Those Who Have Never Heard: Have They No Hope?" *Journal of the Evangelical Theological Society* 32.3, (1989) 367–72.

Paul VI. *Lumen Ecclesiæ.* November 20, 1974. Vatican Website. https://www.vatican.va/content/paul-vi/la/letters/1974/documents/hf_p-vi_let_19741120_lumen-ecclesiae.html.

Petrovich, O. "Japanese Children's Explanations of the Origins of Natural Objects: Some Comparisons with UK Children." *International Journal of Psychology* 35.3–4 (2000) 304.

Pierdziwol, Annette. "Cultivating Empathic Concern and Altruistic Motivation: Insights from Hume and Batson." In *Hume's Moral Philosophy and Contemporary Psychology*, edited by Rico Vitz and Phil Reed, 142–69. London: Routledge, 2018.

Pinckaers, Servais. "Virtue Is Not a Habit." *Cross Currents* 12.1 (1962) 65–81.

Pius XI. *Studiorum Ducem.* Encyclical Letter. Vatican Website. June 29, 1923. https://www.papalencyclicals.net/pius11/p11studi.htm.

Pius XII. *Humani Generis.* Encyclical Letter. Vatican Website. August 12, 1950. https://www.vatican.va/content/pius-xii/en/encyclicals/documents/hf_p-xii_enc_12081950_humani-generis.html.

Pontifical Council for Justice and Peace. *Compendium of the Social Doctrine of the Church.* Vatican Website. April, 2005. http://www.vatican.va/roman_curia/pontifical_councils/justpeace/documents/rc_pc_justpeace_doc_20060526_compendio-dott-soc_en.html.

Purcell, Michael. *Levinas and Theology.* Cambridge: Cambridge University Press, 2006.

Putnam, Hilary. *Jewish Philosophy as a Guide to Life: Rosenzweig, Buber, Lévinas, Wittgenstein.* Bloomington, IN: Indiana University Press, 2008.

Rahner, Karl. *Theological Investigations*, Vol. 16. Baltimore: Helicon, 1979.
———. *The Trinity*. New York: Herder and Herder, 1970.
Ratzinger, Joseph Cardinal. "Liturgy and Sacred Music." *Communio* 13.4 (1986) 377–90.
———. *A New Song for the Lord*. Translated by M. M. Matesich. New York: Crossroad, 1996.
Rawls, John. *Political Liberalism*. New York: Columbia University Press, 1993.
———. "The Sense of Justice." *Philosophical Review* 72.3 (1963) 281–305.
Richardson, D. *Eternity in their Hearts*. Bloomington, MN: Bethany House, 1981.
Roman Missal. London: Catholic Truth Society, 2010.
Rowland, Tracey. "In Search of Real Freedom." *The Tablet*, April 30, 2011, 6–7.
Sacred Congregation for Catholic Education. *Ratio Fundamentalis Institutionis Sacerdotalis*. January 6, 1970. AAS 62, 321–84.
Sacred Congregation of Divine Worship. *Notification: Instructione de Constitutione*, 14 June 1971. Congregation for Divine Worship. Notification Instructione de Constitutione. 14 June, 1971. AAS 63, 712–15.
Schellenberg, J. *Divine Hiddenness and Human Reason*. Ithaca, NY: Cornell University Press, 1993.
Second Vatican Council. "*Apostolicam Actuositatem: Decree on the Apostolate of the Laity*, 18 November, 1965." http://www.vatican.va/archive/hist_councils/ii_vatican_council/documents/vat-ii_decree_19651118_apostolicam-actuositatem_en.html.
———. "*Lumen Gentium: Dogmatic Constitution on the Church*, 21 November, 1964." https://www.vatican.va/archive/hist_councils/ii_vatican_council/documents/vat-ii_const_19641121_lumen-gentium_en.html.
———. "*Gaudium et Spes: Pastoral Constitution on the Church in the Modern World*, 7 December, 1965." http://www.vatican.va/archive/hist_councils/ii_vatican_council/documents/vat-ii_cons_19651207_gaudium-et-spes_en.html.
———. *Gravissimum Educationis: Declaration on Christian Education*. Vatican Website. October 28, 1965. https://www.vatican.va/archive/hist_councils/ii_vatican_council/documents/vat-ii_decl_19651028_gravissimum-educationis_en.html.
———. *Optatam Totius: Decree on Priestly Training*. Vatican City: Vatican Website. October 28, 1965. https://www.vatican.va/archive/hist_councils/ii_vatican_council/documents/vat-ii_decree_19651028_optatam-totius_en.html.
———. "*Sacrosanctum Concilium: Constitution on the Sacred Liturgy*, 4 December, 1963." http://www.vatican.va/archive/hist_councils/ii_vatican_council/documents/vat-ii_const_19631204_ sacrosanctum-concilium_en.html.
Simmons, Aaron J., and David Wood, eds. *Kierkegaard and Levinas: Ethics, Politics, and Religion*. Bloomington, IN: Indiana University Press, 2008.
Stein, Edith. *Knowledge and Faith*. Translated by Walter Redmond. Washington, DC: ICS Publications, Institute of Carmelite Studies, 2000.
Stiglitz, Joseph. "Progressive Reform in a Populist Era." *Address to the National Press Club of Australia*, 14 November 2018. The Australia Institute Transcript. https://www.tai.org.au/content/joseph-stiglitz-national-press-club-address-transcript.
Swinburne, Richard. *The Existence of God*. 2nd ed. Oxford: Oxford University Press, 2004.
———. *The Resurrection of God Incarnate*. Oxford: Oxford University Press, 2003.

Taft, Robert. "Mass without the Consecration." Paper given at 5th Annual Conference in Honor of Father Paul Wattson and Mother Lurana White. Rome, 20 March 2003. https://www.americancatholicpress.org/Father_Taft_Mass_Without_the_Consecration.html.

Tamir, Christine, Adrian Connaughton, and Ariana M. Salazar. "The Global Divide: People's Thoughts on Whether Belief in God Is Necessary to be Moral Vary by Economic Development, Education and Age." The Pew Research Centre, Washington, DC, July 20, 2020. https://www.pewresearch.org/global/2020/07/20/the-global-god-divide/.

The Bible. New Revised Standard Version. Oxford: Oxford University Press, 1990.

Thornhill SM, John. *Christian Mystery in the Secular Age: The Foundation and Task of Theology*. Westminster, MD: Christian Classics, 1991.

Torrell, Jean. *Saint Thomas Aquinas, Volume 2: Spiritual Master*. Translated by Robert Royal. Washington, DC: The Catholic University of America Press, 2003.

Turner, Frank M. "Reading the Idea of a University." In *The Idea of a University*, edited by Frank M. Turner, et al., xiv–xxv. New Haven, CT: Yale University Press, 1996.

Turner, Paul. *Understanding the Revised Mass Texts*. 2nd ed. Chicago: Liturgy Training, 2010.

United States Conference of Catholic Bishops. "And with Your Spirit". No pages. Online: https://www.usccb.org/prayer-and-worship/the-mass/order-of-mass/and-with-your-spirit.

Van Buren, John. "Martin Heidegger, Martin Luther." In *Reading Heidegger from the Start: Essays in His Earliest Thought*, edited by Theodore Kisiel and John van Buren, 159–74. New York: State University of New York Press, 1994.

Waugh, Evelyn. *Brideshead Revisited: The Sacred and Profane Memories of Captain Charles Ryder*. 1945/46. Reprint, Harmondsworth, UK: Penguin, 2020.

West, Cornel. *Black Prophetic Fire*. Boston: Beacon, 2014.

———. *The Cornel West Reader*. New York: Basic Civitas, 1999.

———. *Prophetic Fragments: Illuminations of the Crisis in American Religion & Culture*. Grand Rapids: Eerdmans, 1988.

Westphal, Merold. "Levinas's Teleological Suspension of the Religious." In *Ethics as First Philosophy: The Significance of Emmanuel Levinas for Philosophy, Literature and Religion*, edited by Adriaan T. Peperzak, 151–60. London: Routledge, 1995.

White, Richard. "Levinas, the Philosophy of Suffering, and the Ethics of Compassion." *The Heythrop Journal* 53.1 (2012) 111–23.

Zubeck, Jacqueline A. "Alpha & Omega: 'Parker's Back' and O'Connor's Farewell to Satire". *Renascence* 65.5 (2013) 381–98.

INDEX

Abelard, Peter, 39
Abraham, 109
Acceptance, 120, 126–37, 139
Actuosa, 55
Alston, William, 127–29
Altruism, 96–98, 101–3
Anselm, of Canterbury, 39
Anthony, the Great, 56
Anthropology, 39, 45, 53, 143–44, 147, 153
Apologetics, 136–37
Aporia, 70
Aquinas, Thomas, 2, 21–28, 30, 32–37, 39–48, 54, 57, 61, 67, 77, 80–82
Arius, 42
Aristotle, 23, 69, 75, 77, 80, 93, 98
Artistic representation, 21–23, 25, 29, 31–32, 34, 36–37
Ascension, 54
Assumption, 148
Atheism, 136–37, 140
Auffassen, 108
Augustine of Hippo, Saint, 39–40, 47, 145
Averroes, 77, 80
Avicenna, 81

Balthasar, Hans Urs von, 39
Baptism, 35, 56–57, 62, 65, 142, 145, 149
Barth, Karl, 39
Batson, C. Daniel, 96–97, 99, 104
Beauty, 21, 23, 31–34, 73, 115–17

Belief, 8, 11, 22, 25, 29, 53, 62, 86–87, 120, 122–30, 132–35, 137–39
Benedict XVI, Pope, 62–63
Bonaventure, 39

Carbon emissions, 87, 125
Catechesis, 52, 58, 65, 143, 148–49, 153
Catholic education, 2–6, 8–18, 67, 81–83
Cavanaugh, William, 89–90, 105
Chaplaincy, 13, 51, 58, 62, 65
Chardin, Teilhard de, 27
Children, 73, 96
Climate Change, 125–28
Comfort, 132–33
Common good, 13–15
Compassion, 95–101, 103–4
Compatibilism, 128
Concomitance, 65
Confirmation, 57
Congregation of Worship and the Discipline of the Sacraments, 59
Conscience, 7, 100, 107, 111, 115
Consensus, 2, 14, 18, 125
Conservatism, 141
Convergence, 27–28
Cosmology, 136
Council of Nicaea, 59
Courage, 23–24, 26, 37
Cross, 31, 54, 112, 114, 129, 144, 146, 149

Death, 25–26, 30, 54, 67, 142, 144–46
Democracy, 3, 84, 87 90–91, 100

Index

Derrida, Jacques, 70
Descartes, René, 109
DeYoung, Rebecca Konyndyk, 26
Disagreement, 7–8, 84, 88–90
Discrimination, 87
Discussion, 7–9, 12, 18, 88,
Disunity, 86–87
Diversity, 84, 87, 99
Divine hiddenness, 120, 134, 139
Divinity, 40–41, 48, 129–30
Dixon, Thomas, 94
Domestic violence, 146
Dualism, 80–81
Dulles, Avery, 150
Duns Scotus, 81

Ecumenism, 52
Education Staff, 6–10, 13–18, 71, 126
Ekstasis, 38
Elie, Paul, 21
Emotion, 11, 85, 92–104
Empathy, 95, 97, 104
Empiricism, 69, 75–78, 80, 90, 95–96
Enlightenment, 85, 87, 89, 113, 115, 117
Environmentalism, 102, 125–26
Epistemology, 10, 74–75, 85–87, 112, 126, 139
Eschatology, 65, 153
Estevez, Cardinal Medina, 64
Ethics, 8, 14–16, 106, 108–9, 111–13, 115, 118, 121–22, 128, 131–32, 135
Eucharist, 51, 54, 57, 60–61, 63–65, 141–54
Eudaimonia, 95, 97–99, 101–2
Evangelisation, 52, 146
Evidentialism, 122–25, 128–30, 133–34, 137
Evil, 6, 75, 79, 110, 128, 136, 149, 151, 153
Existentialism, 69
Exitus, 45
Extremism, 88

Faith, 1–7, 9–12, 16, 21–28, 30–38, 40, 42, 48–52, 54–68, 71–83, 85–88, 90, 95, 104–7, 110–14, 118, 129, 132, 136–38, 140–43, 146–48, 151
Fanaticism, 89
Fascism, 100
Fassen, 108
Fideism, 79–80, 114
First cause, 70–71, 73–74, 76–78, 80–81
First Peoples, 146
First principles, 68–72, 74, 80–81
Fitzgerald, Robert H., 27
Flaubert, Gustave, 21
Forgiveness, 121, 129, 138
Francis, Pope, 102
Freddoso, Alfred, 10
Freedom, 7, 15, 70, 79, 106–8, 115, 118, 120, 122–23, 125–26, 128–29, 133–35, 139, 143, 149, 153
Fundamentalism, 10, 78, 80,

Gardner, Margaret, 3
Globalisation, 99
Gopnik, Alison, 90, 103
Grace, 47–48, 121, 151
Guzie, Tad, 146

Haldane, John, 88–90
Harbert, Monsignor Bruce, 60
Hegel, Georg Wilhelm Friedrich, 69
Heidegger, Martin, 70, 77, 81
Herdt, Jennifer, 86, 88
Heresy, 21, 23, 26, 34, 37
Hermeneutics, 76
Hineni, 109
Hitler, Adolf, 100
Holiness, 53–55, 149
Holocaust, 106–7, 109–10
Holy Spirit, 39–41, 44–48, 57–58, 146, 151, 154
Hope, 24, 92, 101
Humanism, 138
Human nature, 82, 96, 105, 125, 154
Hursthouse, Rosalind, 17
Hymns, 63

Icons, 20, 25, 31–37
Idealism, 6, 75, 80

Identity, 2, 6, 70, 76–78
Imagination, 11, 99, 102, 105, 144, 154
Imago Dei, 45, 48
Imperialism, 140
Individualism, 142, 146
Induction, 14
Injustice, 87
International Commission on English in the Liturgy (ICEL), 60
Irrationality, 88–89, 113, 135, 139
Islam, 82

Jesus Christ, 14–15, 20–25, 27–29, 31–39, 46, 49–51, 54, 59, 61, 63–66, 111, 114, 129–30, 137, 141–54
John Paul II, Pope, 2, 6, 9–10, 12, 106, 118, 140–44, 146–54
John, the Apostle, 61
John, the Baptist, 25
Jones, David Albert, 141
Judaism, 82
Justice, 15, 63, 75, 92, 94, 100, 103, 105

Kant, Immanuel, 75, 79
Kavanagh, Aidan, 56
Kenosis, 38
Kierkegaard, Søren, 78, 113–14
King Jr., Martin Luther, 102

Latin, 52, 54, 58, 61, 150
Law, 53, 92, 95
Levinas, Emmanuel, 106–15, 118
Lex orandi, lex credendi, 50, 53, 56, 58, 62–64
Liberal education, 4
Liberalism, 91–93, 95, 100, 103, 105, 141
Liberation theology, 112
Libertarianism, 128
Literalism, 79
Liturgical Reform, 52
Liturgy, 49–66, 140, 143, 146, 148–49
Logos, 40, 42, 48, 72, 144
Lombardo, Nicholas, 23

Love, 24–27, 29–32, 34, 37–38, 40–41, 43–45, 47–48, 50, 85, 89, 93, 96, 98, 100–105, 114, 120–21, 123, 125, 130–36, 138–39, 142, 146, 148, 154
Lubac, Henri de, 147
Lussier, Ernest, 144

MacIntyre, Alasdair, 1–3, 5–7, 11–12
Maimonides, 70, 77
Marianism, 149–53
Maritain, Jacques, 22
Marriage, 65, 90
Martyrdom, 21, 23–36, 47
Mary, mother of Jesus, 141, 144, 148, 150–53
Mass, 49–50, 58–59, 61–63, 66, 142–43
Materialism, 27
Matthew, the Apostle, 56, 111
Mengzi, 103
Metaphysics, 39, 41, 48, 67–70, 72–78, 80–83, 114
Michael, Saint, 150
Miracle, 47, 136
Moderate realism, 75–78
Modernism, 22–23
Moltmann, Jürgen, 39
Monbiot, George, 102
Montfort, Saint Louis-Marie Grignion de, 150–51
Morals, 3, 6, 10, 13–15, 18, 85, 87, 91, 94, 104, 138, 142, 146
Moses, 31
Murray, John Courtney, 2

Nazism, 107, 110, 140
Newman, Saint John Henry, 4–5, 11, 142
Normative, 131–32
Nussbaum, Martha, 85, 91–98, 100–105

Obedience, 122–23, 129, 144, 151, 153
O'Connor, Flannery, 20–34, 37
Ontology, 57
Opus dei, 63

Order, 74, 76, 78, 81–82
Other 108, 110–12, 114–15

Parmenides, 74
Paschal, 54–55, 57, 63, 66, 145 152
Pastoral, 51, 58, 150
Patriotism, 100–101
Patrology, 58, 153
Paul, the Apostle, 27, 145
Paul VI, Pope, 148, 151
Penance, 57
Pentecost, 46
Pessimism 80, 92
Phenomenology, 77, 143, 147
Philosophy, 4–7, 9–13, 18, 23, 26,
　40–41, 67–73, 76–78, 80–82,
　85, 87–88, 90–91, 94–95, 102,
　104–5, 107–8, 110, 114, 116, 126,
　128, 137–38, 140, 143
　analytic, 67, 69
　Cartesian, 116
　Catholic, 5–7, 9–10, 12, 82
　medieval, 69
　post-Cartesian, 70
　pre-Enlightenment, 77
Physicalism, 77–78, 80
Pisteuo, 129
Pius X, Pope, 54
Plato, 39, 69, 74, 80, 93, 98, 103
Plotinus, 69
Pluralism, 2–3, 73, 84–85, 87–91, 95, 105
Politics, 85–102, 104–5, 146
Positivism, 6
Prayer, 52–53, 57–59, 62, 130, 133, 140, 148–49
Procession, 41–46
Prophecy, 47
Pseudo-Dionysius, the Areopagite, 70
Psychology, 94–96
Pythagoras, 74

Racism, 115–17, 146
Rahner, Karl, 39
Rationalism, 74–80
Rationality, 11, 22, 27, 35, 45, 66, 74, 79, 85–89, 109, 113, 115, 118–19, 136–37, 144

Rawls, John, 84, 88, 91–94, 102–3
Realism, 41 48 75 80
Reality, 71–72, 74–76, 78–79, 81–83, 107, 115, 146
Reason, 1, 3–6, 8–12, 16, 20–24, 26, 31–33, 35–41, 43, 50–52, 54, 56–58, 62–72, 74–83, 85–90, 104, 106–15, 117–18, 124, 126, 128–29, 140–42, 144, 146, 154
Redemption, 34–35, 54, 144
Reditus, 45
Reductionism, 79
Refugees, 146
Relativism, 6, 118, 142, 146
Resurrection, 54, 129–30, 136–37, 144–45, 149
Revelation, 38–41, 65, 107
Richard of Saint Victor, 39
Rights, 95
Ritual, 53
Rowland, Tracey, 152
Rousseau, Jean-Jacques, 94

Sabellius, 42
Sacrament, 51–52, 56–57, 65, 141–43, 149
Sacred Congregation for Divine Worship, 58
Sacrifice, 13, 26–27, 35, 48, 102, 114, 137, 142, 145, 148–49
Sacrosanctum Concilium, 51–54
Salvation, 41, 55, 129, 138
Satan, 150
Scheler, Max, 147
Schellenberg, John, 120–25, 129–34, 137, 139
Science, 3, 5, 11, 41, 69, 71, 79, 115–16, 125, 140, 146
Scientism, 80
Scripture, 55, 60, 107–9, 111, 129–30, 142
Sebastian, Saint, 28, 30
Second World War, 107, 110
Secularism, 2–3, 5, 8, 10, 17–18, 89, 142
Self-awareness, 13
Self-control, 13
Self-reflection, 25, 33

Self-reflexivity, 13
Sensus divinitatus, 133, 137
Sensus fidei, 64
Sin, 129, 137–38, 145, 150
Skepticism, 131
Slavery, 87
Smith, Adam, 94
Social stability, 84, 87, 89–90, 92, 94, 96, 103, 105
Solidarity, 13, 15
Soul, 45, 47, 75, 79
Soviet Union, 140
Spinoza, Baruch, 69
Stiglitz, Joseph, 3
Stoicism, 69
Students, 7–9, 14, 16, 126
Suffering, 96–99, 101, 110, 112, 115, 132, 148
Swinburne, Richard, 136
Sympathy, 96

Tate, Caroline Gordon, 21
Teleology, 113, 118, 136
Theism, 120–21, 123–24, 133, 137
Theodicy, 107, 110
Theology, 4–6, 9, 11–13, 18, 35, 39, 40–41, 45, 48–49, 53, 55–56, 59, 65–67, 72, 86, 107, 110–13, 129–30, 138, 140–43, 149, 151
Theosis, 38, 111, 113
Theotókos, 151
Thornhill, John, 142

Totalitarianism, 140
Triduum, 146, 152
Trinitarianism, 39–41, 45–46, 48, 149, 152
Trinity, 38–40, 45–48, 56–57, 64–65, 143, 151–53
Trust, 73–74, 76, 80, 123, 126, 131–32
Truth, 3–5, 8, 10–11, 15, 34, 39–41, 50–51, 54, 60, 70–74, 78–80, 82, 85–86, 115–16, 121, 126–28, 136–38, 140, 144, 146–47, 154
Turner, Frank, 4

Unity, 74–76, 78, 81–82, 87, 91
University, 2–18, 51, 67, 81–83

West, Cornel, 107, 113–18
Western civilisation, 39–40, 48, 85, 89, 107, 117, 146
Westphal, Merold, 113–14
Will, 43–44, 79, 128, 137
White, Richard, 110
White supremacy, 115–18
Worship, 52–54, 57–58, 121, 123, 130–31, 144–45, 149

Vatican Council II, 51–52, 57, 147, 151
Violence, 89–90, 106, 108–9, 112, 115, 117–18, 149
Virtue, 8, 16–17, 23–26, 35, 57, 144

www.ingramcontent.com/pod-product-compliance
Lightning Source LLC
Chambersburg PA
CBHW051745230426
43670CB00012B/2162